Trapped in Mediocrity

Trapped in Mediocrity

Why Our Schools Aren't World-Class and What We Can Do About It

KATHERINE BAIRD

ROWMAN & LITTLEFIELD PUBLISHERS, INC.
Lanham • Boulder • New York • Toronto • Plymouth, UK

KH

Published by Rowman & Littlefield Publishers, Inc.
A wholly owned subsidiary of The Rowman & Littlefield Publishing Group, Inc.
4501 Forbes Boulevard, Suite 200, Lanham, Maryland 20706
www.rowman.com

10 Thornbury Road, Plymouth PL6 7PP, United Kingdom

British Library Cataloguing in Publication Information Available

Library of Congress Cataloging-in-Publication Data
Baird, Katherine, 1958-
  Trapped in mediocrity : why our schools aren't world-class and what we can do about it
/ Katherine Baird.
      p. cm.
  Includes bibliographical references and index.
  ISBN 978-1-4422-1547-4 (cloth : alk. paper) — ISBN 978-1-4422-1549-8 (electronic)
  1. Public schools—United States. 2. Education—Standards—United States. 3.
Educational change—United States. I. Title.
  LA217.2.B33 2012
  370.973—dc23
                                                                    2012009975

∞™ The paper used in this publication meets the minimum requirements of
American National Standard for Information Sciences—Permanence of Paper for
Printed Library Materials, ANSI/NISO Z39.48-1992.

Printed in the United States of America

8/28/13

To
Mary Ann Knerr and Jim Baird
and the memory of Velma and Herbert Corbett

Contents

Part IV: The Way Forward

Acknowledgments

This book could not have been written without the advice, encouragement, and help of many friends, colleagues, and family members. The most important of these were Dave Corbett, Mary Hanneman, Turan Kayaoğlu, Jim Baird, Mary Ann Knerr, Andy Coons, Pete Knerr, Bob Costrell, Andrew Milton, and Joe Pitcavage, all of whom read drafts of the book or book chapters; Bilgehan Jansen, who did a superb job assembling the book's references, footnotes, and figures; and Pat O'Callahan and Cheryl Tucker of Tacoma's newspaper *The News Tribune*, who supported and developed my writing for a general audience. Patti Davis and her assistant Jin Yu at Roman & Littlefield deserve thanks, too, for their support in publishing this book.

A number of individuals made particularly valuable contributions to this project. Turan Kayaoğlu provided a steady flow of counsel and coffee when it was most needed, ensuring that I actually completed this book. Always willing to discuss anything, Mary Hanneman made insightful comments during a conversation some time ago that wound up forming the basis of chapter 9. Andy Coons shared details with me about school district politics, many of which I incorporated into these pages. Pat O'Callahan cast the keen eye of a professional writer and public commentator on each of the book's pages. If it reads well, Pat is to thank. My sons, Ben and James Corbett, studiously avoided reading anything I wrote—I still find pages of book drafts scattered around their rooms—but their perceptive dinnertime comments about both their schools and their education helped shaped some of my arguments.

I owe my husband, Dave Corbett, special thanks. Not only did he provide his usual ample supply of excellent suggestions, but he also gave me the time needed to write this book. I'm far behind on my household, parental, and dog-walking duties, and appreciate that Dave never once brought this to my attention.

I have dedicated this book to my parents and to the memory of my in-laws. Herb and Velma Corbett both devoted their careers to educating public school students. My mom, Mary Ann Knerr, also spent her career in the public schools, and she and my dad, Jim Baird, both did and continue to do superb jobs as parents.

Introduction

A recent government study of adult literacy estimates that 14 percent of adults in the United States have difficulty with tasks more complex than signing a form or filling out a bank deposit slip. More stunning is the estimate that almost half of these adults graduated from high school—that is, they've completed thirteen years of formal education. Even among recent graduates seeking to join the Army, almost one-quarter are disqualified for lack of academic preparation.[1]

Despite frequent reference to our "world class" system of higher education, it isn't immediately obvious that it is. One study found that fewer than four of every ten graduating college seniors are able to compare the viewpoints in two editorials, for example, or compute and compare the per-ounce cost of food items. Moreover, a high percentage of college graduates demonstrate only basic literacy levels, such as the capacity to use a guide to figure out the time a TV show airs.[2] There is evidence, too, that literacy levels among college graduates are declining.[3] Add to all of this growing proof that citizens' literacy and complex thinking abilities drive prosperity, and it's apparent we face a real problem.

This raises a crucial question: Why do American citizens not have stronger academic and cognitive skills?

For sure the causes of these academic shortcomings among Americans cannot all be laid at the feet of our school system. Many social, cultural, political, and economic factors beyond it make important contributions as well. These other causes might even be more important than those directly associated with formal education—there is tremendous debate over precisely this issue. Without doubt poverty and other socioeconomic characteristics of youth have an important, *direct* effect on their educational outcomes. But our public schools contribute to, rather than ameliorate, the inequalities that children experience in other aspects of their lives. Moreover, our schools are not well designed to develop the skills and abilities in all youth the way we expect them to—especially among those who already have fewer advantages than others.

The purpose of this book is to make this argument: that our school system's institutional environment doesn't offer the right incentives or provide the support needed to establish and sustain high academic standards for all students. Rather, the policymaking environment in which decisions are made and budgets determined, and in which teachers teach and students learn, doesn't give rise to practices that ensure all kids have a fair shot at acquiring strong academic skills. In fact, design features in our K–12 system conspire to give us very mediocre schools. I'll start off the book by detailing exactly how low standards are in our schools, and then discuss a wide range of ways that these low expectations harm us.

My book's second objective is to explain why this is so. What it is about our educational system that causes such mediocrity to persist? Understanding which features lead to less effective schools enables us to identify the sorts of reforms that will change them. Too much discourse over educational reform—whether about merit pay, accountability, charter schools, unions, vouchers, or a multitude of other issues—occurs within a vacuum. Critics identify purported problems—teacher unions, ineffective teachers, little parental voice—without referencing the institutional detail, or the relevance of that detail, from which the problems arise. This matters because too often our policies address the symptoms of deeper ailments. Students don't have strong math skills? Require them to take more math classes. Schools vary in quality? Hold them accountable for their performance. But this approach fails to undo the essential reasons why students lack math skills, or why school quality varies. Until we get to the source of the problem, all of our interventions and policy initiatives will not accomplish much.

After detailing the causes and consequences of low expectations and subpar student performance, I'll identify the specific changes our school system needs in order to address the root causes of student underperformance. These changes fall into four different categories. Foremost, we must reform our educational system's governance structure; it's way too bureaucratic and pays too much attention to process as opposed to outcomes. We also must establish high national standards applicable to all students. Many schools also require much more support than they currently have; I detail the type of support and sorts of new resources our schools must have. Finally, our schools need a missing ingredient: strong student incentives for hard work. The pages ahead highlight why these shortcomings in our school system lead our children to underperform.

Collectively the reforms I single out would require a very different set of policies and institutional arrangements than we currently have. Yet it's worth noting that we are hardly alone in the range of concerns we have with our schools. Countries all over the world have been thinking hard about how to improve education and are as challenged as we are by a rapidly changing global economy that places a high premium on broad-based access to an excellent education. In response, many nations have managed to significantly and in some cases dramatically reform their K–12 systems, such as occurred several decades ago in Finland when that country increased school funding, developed a new approach to teaching and teacher training, reduced the central government's management of schools, and pushed back the tracking of students from age fourteen to age sixteen. More recently Poland, too, restructured its school system. To increase both quality and equity, it lengthened the time that all Polish students take a common academic curriculum by one year, introduced a common national course of study, gave schools increased autonomy and responsibility, and established a national system of testing.[4] England also has substantially restructured its school system. Among other changes, it extended access to quality preschools, introduced a national curriculum, gave schools much greater autonomy over budgets and school management, and increased the role of the central government in funding schools and determining their curricula. In all of these instances, the changes did or are paying off. And these are just a few examples of the way nations all over the globe are transforming education within their borders. While systematic change in our country will be difficult, these instances show it isn't impossible. It's time for us, too, to undertake the hard work of rethinking core features of our schools. But to do that successfully, we must first understand why our current system is unintentionally designed to prevent this from happening.

PERSPECTIVE OF THE BOOK

Many factors help explain why our schools underperform. But this book takes a rather singular focus. It argues that education's institutional environment—and the incentives that emerge from it—are not well aligned with what it takes to have a high-quality K–12 system. To be more precise, features of it undermine efforts to improve our educational system—the institutional context in which policy is made and actions are taken reinforce low standards. And such low standards lead to the wasteful, unfair, and aggravatingly slow-to-change academic system that America's children grow up in, and help to explain why we rank so poorly on things like basic literacy. I make this argument by describing in these pages education's governance structure as well as other institutional features of our public schools. I then argue that these help account for the persistence of low standards and the inadequate education that so many youth receive.

One concept I draw on is useful to develop at the outset: the Principal-Agent Problem (PAP). A well-known concept in economics and political science, the PAP concerns itself with the difficulty within organizations of "keeping people on task." The idea is that organizations (typically firms) are created with some intended purpose. Someone may start a pizza parlor with the purpose of making money, for instance. The "Principals" in the Principal-Agent Problem can be thought of as the people whose interests the organization is primarily intended to serve. In the case of the pizza parlor, the "Principal" would be the owner.*

In many organizations, Principals find themselves in search of others to carry out the work of the organization (they have to hire people). The interests of these "others"—whom we call "Agents"—may be quite distinct from those of the Principals. The Principal-Agent Problem (PAP) hence concerns itself with the problem of what organizations (Principals) do to make sure that Agents act on their behalf. In essence, how do bosses motivate workers to do what the boss wants done? The solution to the PAP that we see in the typical workplace is straightforward: Principals (the bosses) hire supervisors to monitor the Agents (employees) with the Principals themselves in turn monitoring

---

*A separate question, of course, is to what extent organizations that do a good job serving the interests of their Principal also serve broader social interests. Critics of Wall Street would say, at least in this instance, not well. Such questions about the social properties of markets versus governments form the heart of economic and political inquiry. While important, this topic is tangential to our focus here; and anyway in applying the PAP to education I will characterize the Principal as (broadly speaking) society. In that sense there is no conflict between the Principal's interests and those of society.

the supervisors. Agents face the prospect of losing their job if they slack off and are caught. When an organization hasn't solved the PAP—or at least not solved it very well—the organization is not likely to do a good job serving the interests of the Principal. In complex organizations, the Principal-Agent Problem potentially becomes a very problematic one to solve. Complex organizations thus run the risk of not serving their intended purpose very well.

Complicated organizations typically have a number of different characteristics. For example, consider an organization in which there are lots of different Principals who don't agree about institutional goals. That makes it hard to monitor Agents because it isn't clear what exactly you should monitor them for. Or consider an organization in which there are multiple levels of supervision. One agent supervises another, who supervises another, and so on. This too makes it less likely that the Principal's interests will be acted upon by the Agents, and it makes it harder to figure out where the fault lies when they don't. Note that the practice of outsourcing or contracting work to outsiders can be seen as one way that complex organizations can and do address the PAP. Finally, consider an organization in which what exactly is being produced is hard to see or measure. This is yet another factor that obscures whether the Agents are acting on behalf of the organization's interests or not: How would you know who's doing a good job when it's hard to distinguish between productive and unproductive Agents?

These are reasons why many large nonprofits often have a difficult time with the PAP. It also helps explain why so many people think that government is inept. More importantly, as we'll see, all three of the above factors that compromise the effectiveness of organizations flourish in the mega-organization called "Public Education."

There's good news, though: recognizing these problems—along with others that arise from education's institutional features—means that they *can* be addressed. Later in the book I'll draw attention to these problems, and in the conclusions I'll describe the changes needed so that our educational system more successfully addresses its Principal-Agent Problem.

HOW WE COMPARE

As background, let's start with some quick indicators of how our students compare internationally. In a 2009 international test of fifteen-year-olds' reading, math, and science skills and knowledge (the Programme for International

Student Assessment, called the PISA for short), American students rated average in science and reading, and below average in math when compared with thirty-four countries in the Organisation for Economic Co-operation and Development (OECD) (see table below). In math, about one in four fifteen-year-olds failed to demonstrate even a very low level of math proficiency—a more dismal showing than in most OECD countries and about twice the rate found in Canada. At the same time, noticeably fewer American students scored at the highest level of math proficiency. In fact students in Belgium, Korea, Japan, and Switzerland were over three times more likely than were ours to score in this highest range. OECD countries roughly correspond with the world's rich, democratic nations, and will often be the set of countries I rely on when making international comparisons.

Our poor performance on the PISA is particularly noteworthy because the PISA assesses fifteen-year-olds, whereas other international tests assess younger students. The PISA thus provides a snapshot of student skills and knowledge at a

Average PISA Literacy Scores of Fifteen-Year-Old Students in Select OECD Countries

Country	Reading Literacy	Country	Math Literacy	Country	Science Literacy
Korea	539	Korea	546	Finland	554
Finland	536	Switzerland	541	Korea	538
Canada	524	Japan	529	New Zealand	532
New Zealand	521	Canada	527	Canada	529
Japan	520	New Zealand	519	Australia	527
Australia	515	Australia	514	Netherlands	522
Poland	500	Germany	513	United Kingdom	514
United States	**500**	Slovenia	501	Slovenia	512
United Kingdom	494	Slovak Republic	497	**United States**	**502**
OECD Average	*493*	*OECD Average*	*496*	*OECD Average*	*501*
Portugal	489	Sweden	494	France	498
Slovenia	483	Hungary	490	Austria	494
Spain	481	Portugal	487	Slovak Republic	490
Czech Republic	478	**United States**	**487**	Spain	488
Austria	470	Italy	483	Greece	470
Chile	449	Turkey	445	Chile	447
Mexico	425	Mexico	419	Mexico	416

Source: National Center for Education Statistics, "Highlights From PISA 2009: Performance of U.S. 15-Year-Old Students in Reading, Mathematics, and Science Literacy in an International Context," U.S. Department of Education, NCES 2011-004, December 2010, http://nces.ed.gov/pubs2011/2011004.pdf, pp. 8, 18, 24.

more advanced stage of their education than is true of other international tests. The PISA also reveals that our students' performance relative to those in other countries gets worse the older the age at which we make this comparison. Most dismally, the PISA shows that fifteen-year-olds' skills are especially weak relative to students elsewhere when it comes to tasks involving more complex problem solving—that is, with the most challenging sorts of intellectual endeavors.

In addition to widespread underperformance among America's students, one-quarter of our high school freshmen do not complete high school; this is the highest dropout rate among OECD countries. And among black and Hispanic youth, more than one in three don't complete high school.[5]

A third shortcoming of our schools is that despite a very high rate of college-going among high school graduates, our college graduation rate is below the OECD average; not long ago it was the highest in the world. While a large majority of American youth attends college, more than one-half of those who enroll don't end up with a four-year degree. The main reason is that half of those who start college wind up dropping out (and college dropout rates are highest among African American and Hispanic students). Compare this with an average college dropout rate of 29 percent among all OECD countries—and only 9 percent in Japan—and it's obvious what an outlier we are on this score.[6]

Thus the problem with our educational system is twofold: students don't acquire the cognitive skills and knowledge we expect of them, *and* they don't persist with their studies. To be blunt, the problem is that our public schools provide neither the quality of education nor the quantity of educated citizens needed for successful participation in the twenty-first century.

Yet it isn't right to say our schools are in decline; rather they have long been quite mediocre. The difference is that in the past this mediocrity was still better than what most countries offered. As mentioned above, over the last couple of decades other countries have made great strides in improving their own systems. While parallel attempts have been made in the United States— and there are signs of modest progress—other nations have and are carrying out much more significant changes that have led their students to surpass ours in both achievement and educational attainment.

The figure below provides one indicator of this change in the relative success of our school system. It shows the percentage of the population in OECD countries with a high school degree in 2009. The figure compares citizens from

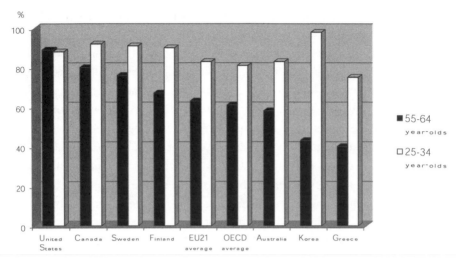

Percentage of Population with at Least a High School Degree (2009)

one generation (twenty-five- to thirty-four-year-olds) in 2009 with those from an older one (fifty-five- to sixty-four-year-olds) to show trends in graduation rates over the generations. As shown, about 88 percent of U.S. citizens in both generations have earned a high school degree.* While at 88 percent the United States once had the highest rate of high school completion, these rates have risen steadily over time in every country *but* ours. In fact, the average high school completion rate in OECD countries rose from 57 to above 80 percent over this thirty-year period. And graduation rates in ten countries are now above those in the United States, with many other countries close behind us. It is easy to imagine that shortly we will fall far behind other OECD countries in terms of the percentage of our students with a high school degree.

MEASURING STUDENT OUTCOMES

This book relies a lot on test scores—be it from the NAEP, TIMSS, PISA, ACT, or state tests—as indicators of students' cognitive abilities. I do this not intending to suggest that test scores are the essence of our schools' purposes. We primarily look to our educational system to provide kids with knowledge and cognitive skills—the ability to analyze and evaluate information, write

---

*This figure includes "high school equivalency degrees." In the U.S. context, this means it includes individuals with a General Educational Development (GED) degree.

with style and precision, read for comprehension, think analytically and creatively, be comfortable with abstractions, synthesize information and concepts, understand and apply core concepts in math and science, and so on. While test scores are imperfect measures of these capacities, most of the scores discussed in this book are correlated with outcomes that we care about such as high school graduation, college-going, income, health, poverty, voting, and at the national level, economic growth. While test scores are far from perfect, they are the best measures we have for the sorts of points I want to make in this book. They are best thought of as an imperfect but useful representation of what we *really* care about—well-educated and well-rounded youth.

Tests of students' cognitive abilities also fail to capture the noncognitive values we look to our schools to develop in children—to name several, empathy with others, leadership, a sense of social responsibility, honesty and integrity, a work ethic, curiosity, a moral code, civic engagement, adaptability and tolerance, and an ability to negotiate conflict. I can't think of a good reason why students who gain more cognitive skills will gain fewer of these noncognitive ones, nor am I aware of any evidence to this effect (just the contrary).[7] By focusing exclusively on cognitive skills in this book, I am not ignoring these noncognitive goals; I'm simply presuming that the development of students' cognitive abilities is not at odds with the development of their noncognitive ones as well. If this weren't true—if there were instead some tradeoff between the development of cognitive and noncognitive skills   then one would want to place less emphasis on the cognitive skills that are central to this book. But common sense tells you that developing students' ability to closely read and evaluate texts is not at odds with them also developing the characteristics of honesty and empathy with others. To date this is an underdeveloped area of inquiry. But it is worth pointing out that elite and private religious schools often do a very good job of developing both types of abilities in their students, and it's hard to see why public schools couldn't as well.

Test scores are controversial, so let me make one final note about their use here. One problem with individual test scores—a reason many people are outspoken in their opposition to relying on them as much as I do in this book—is that they are noisy. By this I mean that one individual's score may not be a good reflection of that student's *true* level of knowledge or cognitive ability. I hear this on occasion from my sons and to some extent from my students (unless of course the score at hand happens to be a good one!). So we say that the indicator (the test score) is noisy because it doesn't give a clear signal about the underlying "thing" (here, cognitive skills and knowledge) that it is supposed to be measuring. In statistical terms, to say a measure is noisy is to say that there is a large confidence interval around it. Indeed test scores are noisy—and perhaps even very noisy—measures of individuals' cognitive skills. But as long as they are just noisy and not biased (and some may say this is a big assumption to make), then there is no problem with using them as I do in this book. As long as you use the aggregated scores of many individuals, or you use scores to look for general population-wide tendencies, then the fact that a particular score may not match up all that well with what you want to know about a particular individual is not problematic. Noisy signals just mean you need to be careful about what information you can take from any one signal.

PLAN OF THE BOOK

To set the stage, chapter 1 presents an overview of the historical and institutional context in which educational policy has been formed, and compares education's institutional characteristics with those in other rich developed countries. Chapter 2 examines educational standards in the United States by first discussing various ways that one might define and measure "educational standards." It goes on to show that, however you define it, without a doubt academic expectations in the United States are significantly below those typically found in other developed countries.

Collectively, part II of the book argues that our mediocre school system imposes high costs on all of us. I single out four separate but also largely concealed ways that low expectations harm us. One of the most important of these is that low student effort and engagement follows (chapter 3). Chapter 4 argues that low standards compromise the mission of our colleges and universities: a large percentage of college students require pre-college classes before enrolling in credit-bearing classes; college classes often lack rigor; and poorly prepared students drop out at very high rates. A third problem taken up in chapter 5 is that underperformance leads to a less productive nation and greater wage inequality. Chapter 6 identifies a final way that low standards hurt us: we have an unfair school system that limits the opportunities of too many students—especially those who are already disadvantaged.

In part III I take up the central question this book considers: Why do low educational standards in the United States persist? The chapters in this section collectively argue that institutional features of our K–12 system reinforce low standards by yielding incentives that fail to prioritize educational quality. One reason is that the decentralized and bureaucratic nature of America's schools encourages, or reinforces, low standards (chapter 7). A second is that critics of low standards are quieted by a fragmented educational system that permits them to escape the worst of it (chapter 8). Finally, chapter 9 argues that the perceived payoffs from higher expectations in America are smaller than they are in other countries. At the same time, the perceived costs associated with them are also higher. This payoff structure to standards—high costs and low benefits—is particular to America and serves to squelch calls for expecting more out of all of our students. I thus argue in this set of chapters that institutional design features make achieving educational excellence an all but impossible goal.

By clarifying the many ways in which we are harmed by low expectations, and by identifying the core reasons why these persist, I hope in these pages to underscore why we must undertake dramatic reform of our K–12 system. The book's last chapter presents my view on what change must look like if we are to create an educational system designed to foster excellence rather than continue to trap our students in mediocrity.

I

SETTING THE STAGE

A Historical and Comparative Perspective on the United States' Educational System

What happens (or not) in schools is in good part a product of education's institutional setting. This environment shapes perceptions, expectations, and most of all the incentives and consequences for the choices that people make. To answer the question of why our educational system underperforms, we must first look to the institutions that help shape the choices policymakers pursue, the actions K–12 administrators take, the decisions of parents, the motivational level of students, and the use of class time by teachers. For that reason, in this book I focus primarily on the role that educational institutions play in explaining why students underperform in the United States.

I begin here with a very brief outline of the history of our educational system's organization and governance structure, because institutions take their shape over time. Understanding why and how our institutions came to be helps us figure out what changes are possible and desirable, and how these might come about. To bring further context, the second part of the chapter presents a broad view of how education's institutions and governance structures compare with those in other countries. It isn't very often that Americans look abroad to see how other countries run their school systems. But I'll argue throughout this book that we can learn important lessons by looking abroad. While all countries face common challenges and look to education to achieve similar purposes, we have also arrived at different solutions. Making this comparison also underscores how governance structures and institutions shape the performance of an educational system—that is, how well the Principal's (society's) interest is served by the Agents' (the educational bureaucracy and its schools) actions. This comparative perspective is important, and I will continue to develop it throughout the chapters ahead.

BRIEF HISTORY OF EDUCATIONAL GOVERNANCE AND POLICY IN AMERICA

Until the close of the 1800s, formal education in the United States remained mostly a local concern; for the most part it was organized, administered, and financed locally. Schools were largely governed by local school boards (where these existed) or less formally by school and community leaders. While legal authority for policymaking has always rested with state legislators and the governor, states played a very limited role until recently; they almost all left decision making and administrative responsibility up to school boards, school districts, and their schools. This practice reflected the presumption that education was a local good, and that local communities were better than distant political bodies at making the right decisions about how to best educate kids in their communities.

With time, as population density increased and schools came into closer proximity with one another, school districts formed; these were soon granted taxing and administrative authority by state governments. To this day, the local school boards of some fifteen thousand school districts have significant responsibility in terms of financing, setting policy, and administering education within their jurisdictions. Different districts commonly pursue differing policies and actions, depending on the resources available to them, the role the state government has delegated to them, their leaderships' agendas, and the populations they serve.

One hundred years ago, this local governance structure by and large determined each school's curriculum and standards—although for secondary schools, the curriculum was often driven by university requirements as those students were presumed to be headed to college. Secondary schooling at the end of the nineteenth century was also relatively rare. By 1900, in fact, only one in ten of the nation's fourteen- to seventeen-year-olds was enrolled in secondary school; moreover, one out of every four adults had spent less than five years in school. By 1919 only 13 percent of adults over the age of twenty-five had at least a high school degree.

While few attended school beyond the primary grades, high school during this era might best be characterized as educating the elite. High school's prevailing purpose was to establish mental discipline; to pass along Western tradition in the form of languages (Latin and Greek), history, and philosophy; and to prepare students for college-level work. As a consequence, secondary students typically took a fairly demanding course of college-preparatory classes. In 1901 the College Entrance Exam Board gave what became the first set of "college boards." Tests were given in chemistry, English, French, German, Greek, Latin, history, math, and physics, relying for their content on a recommended curriculum that high schools across the nation often followed (or soon came to follow). Taking these "boards," as they came to be called, became standard practice for those seeking entrance into college.

Around the turn of the century, though, the belief that high schools should prepare students for college through a fairly standardized and demanding curriculum became a contested one. This change can be attributed to interrelated developments. Industrialization, urbanization, and revolutions in transportation and communication made secondary education matter more for successful adult life: the rise in white collar and managerial jobs, and the continual demise of the agricultural sector, led to increased demand for a high school education. This transformation of the economy and the growing importance of school accompanying it contributed to steady increases in school enrollments. Between 1890 and 1910, the share of the population in high school more than doubled; by 1920 it doubled again. All told, over the brief forty-year span from 1890 to 1930, the share of fourteen- to seventeen-year-olds in high school increased from 6 percent to over 50 percent. One writer characterized this change as follows: "The American secondary school was transformed from an exclusive enclave of the best and brightest into an institution of the masses."[1]

As the characteristics and motives of high school students changed, so too did the way people thought about the purpose and philosophy of education. This rethinking was further spurred by a second development: new psychological theories of child development and intelligence called for a more "child-centered" approach to education. This movement led many to argue for fresh pedagogical approaches and expanded curricular offerings emphasizing the interests and choices of children.

These demographic, economic, and intellectual movements converged during the opening decades of the twentieth century to advance the argument that schools had to do a better job recognizing differences in students' abilities and life trajectories, and their need to be taught accordingly. The author of one influential 1909 study of school curriculum expressed dismay that the current curriculum was "fitted not to the slow child or to the average child but to the unusually bright one . . . the college preparatory curriculum needed to be replaced by a curriculum more attuned to the needs of a new population and a new industrial order."[2]

Such arguments that schools' curricula were outdated and unsuited to the entire range of students became increasingly commonplace. Edward Lee Thorndike of Columbia's Teachers College, an influential leader of this movement, wrote in 1906 that "no high school is successful which does not have in mind . . . the work in life its students will have to perform, and try to fit them for it. . . . [Most students are not] efficient at dealing with ideas, but . . . the manipulation of things, making them more suited for cooking than for writing compositions."[3] (One wonders how many young men he thought were better suited for cooking than for puzzling over ideas!)

Other pressures, too, contributed to demands that students be provided a variety of ways to complete high school. Many youth were not thrilled with spending more time in school, or with having increased academic demands placed on them. Growing support among parents, farmers, and labor groups contributed to pressure for radical reform in teaching practices and curricular offerings that met the needs of those less academically inclined. Indeed, advocates for curricular reform saw the "opening up of the curriculum" as key to society's commitment to equal educational opportunity and advancing the nation's dedication to a level playing field.

As reforms took place around the nation, they did so without any clear consensus over precisely what curricular change high schools needed. It was largely left to local communities and to some extent states to respond as they best saw fit to their growing numbers and the changing composition of students in their jurisdiction. But one thing is certain: the high school curriculum moved away from the classical model to one that offered vocational subjects such as bookkeeping, clerical studies, cooking, and machine work.

Not only did this more flexible model accommodate different students with diverse interests, objectives, and propensities, it also permitted the student-driven curricula that many were calling for. In this sense, school policy reflected a compromise among competing theories of how best to educate students by essentially providing some representation of every position. Indeed, you might say that accommodation of viewpoints rather than learning became the first priority of high schools as standards and requirements were significantly relaxed. Partly because of citizens' demand and partly because of the crucial role that education was seen to play in the economy and in individuals' life prospects, simply keeping students in school increasingly became a top priority.

That accommodation and retention became the new mantra of education is reflected in a 1933 study of high school; it reports that schools made "strenuous efforts" to avoid failing students, and even students who failed to show any sort of learning passed as long as they attended school.[4] One critic in 1949 wrote that more permissive and less demanding practices allowed educators to escape responsibility for failing to educate students. This philosophy "released the teacher from his responsibility . . . [and] implied that one need not adhere to any standards of knowledge but simply cater to individual interests."[5]

While accommodating a much more varied student body, high schools did continue to offer the old academic, classical curriculum. This was a response to vocal advocates who still thought that schools should prioritize this. Yet the "dead subjects" of Latin, Greek, and ancient history were increasingly replaced by the more "modern" ones of U.S. history, biology, and algebra.

As the new century progressed, high schools increasingly marginalized their academic tracks. Studies of secondary-school curricula as early as the 1920s reported that schools around the country often offered around fifteen different courses of study. The practice of social promotion also became common, so that progress through the educational system became based on time served rather than learning achieved. To maintain student interest and involvement, schools started the practice common today of offering a wide range of extracurricular activities such as sports teams, theater, band, and social clubs.

By 1930 high schools around the country had been thoroughly transformed. Perhaps only one-third of all secondary-school courses could now be considered academic as opposed to vocational in content.[6] This transformation was amplified by the Great Depression: enrollments grew as good jobs, especially for youth, became almost nonexistent. By 1940 a full two-thirds of eligible youth attended high school. And a separate process that began in

1926 was complete by 1942: the much easier SAT—a test not aligned to any particular curriculum and thus better suited to a nation where high school students did not take a common curriculum—replaced the old college boards as the nation's college entrance exam. This broke the once tight link between academic coursework and college admission, a break that remains to this day.

By the mid-twentieth century, a new model had been fully established whereby high schools provided opportunities and students chose which opportunity to take. Secondary schools had been turned into smorgasbords—or as others have termed it, they had become shopping malls and students the shoppers. No longer unified by the motive of intellectual development and mastery, the curricula became far more subject to the decisions and preferences of local educational bodies. In consequence, the decentralized educational system permitted the emergence of much greater variation in educational practices and content than had existed before.

Yet this variation—manifest as qualitative differences among schools—is what accounts for the next wave of educational reform. Starting shortly after the Second World War, education reformers increasingly argued that our educational system was both lax in terms of standards and unfair in the sorts of educational opportunity it offered different students. Much of the change in educational practices that occurred earlier in the twentieth century, in high schools in particular, had come under the banner of social justice. The hope was that a new mission for high schools (to educate everyone) and the new curricular model that accompanied it (something for everyone) would better meet the twentieth century's social and economic challenges.[7] By the second half of the century, however, this claim became almost impossible to make.

Two problems became evident. The first had to do with built-in inequities in the educational system. After World War II, the opening of the workforce to women led to huge teacher shortages across the nation as women left education for better jobs. This alone led to vast differences across districts in the characteristics of teachers that districts were able to hire, because the reliance on local funding meant that schools now differed greatly in their ability to attract and keep qualified teachers. As one indication, a 1947 study revealed that the nation's best-funded schools spent sixty times more than did the worst.[8]

This inequity helped usher in debate over how the educational system could best promote social justice. National commissions evaluated and made recommendations to improve the quality of the educational system, placing particular emphasis on ensuring that socioeconomic barriers did not limit educational attainment. The 1954 *Brown v. Board of Education* decision, along with new research findings, brought to the public's attention the fact that, despite rhetoric to the contrary, large gaps existed in the achievement levels of students from different racial and socioeconomic backgrounds.

By 1960 critics of America's educational system combined this with wider criticism of American society; schools were portrayed as part of a larger system that maintained and perpetuated economic and class relations. Such criticisms helped spur a period of unprecedented federal education initiatives; new federal programs and legislation gave special protection and resources to poor, minority, immigrant, and handicapped students. The largest accomplishment came in 1965 when President Johnson succeeded in bringing federal dollars to education with the Elementary and Secondary Educational Act (ESEA), which provided new dollars to those schools challenged by large numbers of poor children.

Soon thereafter, the federal government finally undertook the challenge of enforcing the integration of the nation's schools. In part due to desegregation and the resulting threat of "white flight" to the suburbs, many American school districts in the 1970s introduced newly enhanced practices of tracking. Tracking—which in fact dated to the turn of the century—had long been justified as a way to meet the needs of the academically inclined student as well as the nonacademic one. A stronger national commitment to meeting the needs of *every* child in the school system strengthened voices calling for even more varied curricula. And so the practice of providing a distinct curriculum to different "types" of students drew new levels of support and added justification. School systems responded by developing yet more sophisticated ways of separating their students into different curricular tracks.

In the last third of the twentieth century, a second problem came to the fore, this one having to do with the fundamental quality of education in the United States. After the Soviet Union's launch of Sputnik in 1957, the nation erupted in anxiety and debate. Americans were baffled at how the Soviets had bested us in technological and scientific prowess. Such concerns helped spur a movement that challenged the longstanding belief that most children needed only a basic and practical education.

This movement gained force over the 1970s and 1980s. In 1975 the College Board revealed that the SAT scores of college aspirants had been declining over the prior decade; it later attributed this to changes in schools' curriculum and the rigor of this curriculum.[9] Criticism of the American educational system came to a head after the release of the 1983 report *A Nation at Risk*, which blamed the system for contributing to losses in national and economic security and to America's declining position in the world. The report's second paragraph begins with the oft-repeated dire warning: "If an unfriendly foreign power had attempted to impose on America the mediocre educational performance that exists today, we might well have viewed it as an act of war."

A Nation at Risk helped launch in earnest a movement to improve the excellence of our educational system; one touchstone of this movement became the establishment of higher academic standards. Decades of active and ongoing—if not always fervent—educational reform followed the report, primarily involving state-level initiatives but at times accompanied by federal incentives.

The 1980s alone saw over three thousand school reform measures passed. And new dollars were generously allocated by state governments to pay for measures to improve educational quality in our schools. Over the decade of the 1980s, school spending on a per-student basis (adjusted for inflation) went up by almost one-third. Reform initiatives mostly took the form of state legislation prescribing more graduation requirements, a longer school year, tougher teacher qualifications with a more generous pay structure, or curricular reform placing greater focus on academics. Anticipating local opposition to its initiatives, legislatures also attempted to wrestle control of the curriculum and instruction away from teachers and principals. State policymakers often undertook initiatives without collaborating with school boards because these often reduced local education leaders' autonomy and hence would be met by their resistance.

Some of these reforms—along with the increased reliance on state dollars to fund schools—came after state governments lost legal battles that then forced them to take on a more expansive role in education. Other reforms simply reflected growing political will and public support for state action on the education front. On the whole, states' role in both funding and guiding public schools grew significantly after 1970. Starting around 1990, the charter school movement began, as did experiments in increased school autonomy. All of these succeeded in eroding the traditional role and power of school boards and districts. Yet districts remained loosely regulated and overseen by states, and ambiguity grew over the exact state versus local division of authority over schools and school policy.

As stated earlier, concerns over both educational excellence and equity led to a larger federal as well as state role. Around 1970 the federal government initiated a national test of select fourth, eighth, and eleventh graders called the National Assessment of Education Progress (NAEP). The NAEP's purpose was to provide national measures of students' skills at various points in the educational system, and to make possible comparisons of students' academic skills across states and across socioeconomic groups. Prior to the NAEP, no such accurate measure existed. The NAEP is the closest we have come to implementing national standards and national tests. Unlike other countries, though, NAEP scores are not generally released below the state level. Only a small random sample of students take the test, test takers never receive their individual scores, and the NAEP is administered only every couple of years.

Most recently, advocates for excellence and equity in our educational system have coalesced into the Standards Based Reform (SBR) movement. This movement is partially an outgrowth of the failure of prior efforts—those associated with bringing more dollars to education, creating a more demanding curriculum, and increasing teacher qualifications—to noticeably improve student outcomes. At its heart, SBR seeks to restructure public education by making systemic reforms to its governance structure and incentive system. It does this by establishing academic standards, measuring the extent to which students meet these standards, and instituting some form of accountability (whether at the administrative, school, or teacher level) when students fail to meet these standards. By and large, SBR advocates believe that the main problem with education in the United States is not one of money but is rather traceable to an educational system that lacks clarity of purpose or a sufficient focus on outcomes.

The standards-based movement originally succeeded in seeing a wave of policies enacted at the state level. Starting in the late 1980s, states individually set academic standards establishing what all students were expected to demonstrate in terms of skills and knowledge. Before then, states had specified only what courses students had to take in certain grades, how much time they had to spend in school, or what courses they needed to complete to graduate, without saying anything about what they should know or be able to demonstrate. In 1989 President George H. W. Bush brought federal clout to the movement by calling for "voluntary national standards" in core subjects—although his first actual proposal for such was soundly defeated by the Senate.

The federal government strengthened its commitment to the SBR movement in 1994; that year it passed legislation requiring (but leaving to states) the development and implementation of a system of standards with some measure of accountability. Due to slow and only partial compliance with this legislation, in 2001 the federal government took a more heavy-handed approach when President George W. Bush persuaded Congress to pass the No Child Left Behind Act (NCLB). This act required that states implement within a set time period a specific system of testing, measuring, reporting, and accountability for student performance.

NCLB gave the federal government an unprecedented and highly visible role in education. But because of deep-seated opposition (as well as legal limitations) to federal authority, states were made responsible for designing, implementing, and monitoring the policy. To comply with NCLB, states had to establish grade-level performance expectations for their students and measure the extent to which students in grades three through eight—plus grade ten—met these expectations. Schools and districts that repeatedly failed to show progress toward these goals were labeled as failing and would suffer both the stigma of the label as well as administrative and financial consequences. For many state governments, the deep involvement in student performance that NCLB dictated meant they were now playing a brand-new role in education.

Paradoxically, in some ways NCLB set back state efforts to strengthen educational standards and improve educational quality. To minimize sanctions under NCLB, some states set their performance bar low to make it easier for students to jump over it. As the next chapter shows, state assessment tests are exceptionally easy almost without exception; they are designed simply to identify those students who almost completely lack basic skills. Students who pass state tests and thus "meet their state's proficiency standard" (the NCLB goal) have been asked to jump over a very low bar.

To add to this problem, the increase in graduation requirements that states enacted over the last three decades has resulted in many districts offering an even more varied set of classes so that different students could meet the requirement of, for example, two years of high school math, by taking very different sets of math classes. Often too these requirements have not been accompanied by the dollars necessary to meet them, leaving districts scrambling to figure out how to comply without having the resources to do so.

To sum up, then, reforms in the last half of the twentieth century sig-nificantly expanded the state and federal roles in education at the expense of school districts. Most federal policy initiatives have also tended to strengthen the state role insofar as they typically require state departments of education to administer and provide regulatory oversight over them. A proliferation of regulations has also increased the administrative role of school boards while at the same time reducing their traditional role in policy formulation. In recent decades, experimentation with alternative forms of educational governance has reduced the role and authority of school boards further, often in ways that have left it unclear exactly what their role and authority is. Certainly, school boards today operate in a much more complicated institutional setting than they did several decades ago. These changes have been associated with even more variation in school- and district-level curricular offerings. And it is not obvious whether they have had any significant impact on the quality of educa-tion students receive.

In terms of the Principal-Agent Problem discussed in the introduction, the educational system in the United States is a highly complex one with an assortment of not-well-coordinated Agents. Moreover, policy lacks a clear consensus on what we want from our schools. This is reflected in unclear goals sought by the hierarchies of policymakers. In other words, the Principals disagree, and their collective purpose is ambiguous. The governance structure (Agents) have responded to this ambiguity in ways that have made the admin-istrative structure even more complex, with competing and sometimes con-flicting interests. Reforms have been piggybacked on existing obligations and roles without a fundamental reexamination of how the Agents interact with each other and what purpose they are intended to serve. Such complexity and ambiguity is the hallmark of our educational bureaucracy, and this feature has become especially pronounced over the last thirty years.

I'll return to say much more about education's governance structure in later chapters. For now let's turn to a brief comparison of our school system with those found abroad.

COMPARISON OF CONTEMPORARY EDUCATION POLICY IN THE UNITED STATES WITH OTHER COUNTRIES

Comparing the history of educational policy and its governance structure in America with those elsewhere is an undertaking meriting an entire book—or maybe three.[10] Indeed, there are as many types of "educational systems" as there are countries, because each one has some unique features. But I'll focus here on a few general tendencies. My intent is to provide an overview of how institutional arrangements in the United States differ from those in other nations, with an eye toward later analyzing and highlighting why and how such differences matter.

Centralization

One clear difference between America's educational governance structure and those in other nations is that most of them have a much more centralized administrative structure. A more centralized educational system is manifested in a number of ways. For one, local governments—which in the United States supply almost one of every two education dollars—provide few of the dollars that fund other countries' public (and often private) schools. In most other nations, at least three out of four education dollars come from regional (state) and national governments. In only a few countries—Canada being one—does the national government provide education with less of its funding than does the U.S. government.

The stronger role of national governments in other countries shows up in a second way: common national standards for all students until at least the eighth or tenth grade. That is, in many countries all students in the same grade are expected to meet certain common expectations in terms of knowledge and academic skills. In a large majority of nations, central education ministries set broad learning goals for students at different stages in their education. In China, for instance, nationwide mathematics standards call for students to learn ten different topics during the first through third grades concerning numbers and operations and geometry; similar standards exist for the fourth through sixth grades, and again for grades seven through nine. At each stage, the standards entail increasingly complex and sophisticated mathematical concepts.[11] These sorts of expectations made at the national level only make sense when they are accompanied by national dollars as it would be perverse to expect uniform practices from schools with unequal resources.

In many countries, national education ministries go beyond such broad goals by also making decisions about which courses will be offered for students of different ages, and perhaps what the course syllabi will cover. If course content is not set at the national level, it is typically set by the department or the school, but rarely (as is common in the United States) by the teacher. In quite a few countries, central education ministries set teacher salaries and hours of instruction, and may go so far as to make textbook decisions—although countries usually leave such details to the local level. Asian countries tend to have a more prescriptive central government that sets standards and then even aligns teacher preparation programs, professional development, and textbooks with those standards. In these nations, the role of teachers in terms of curriculum is left to planning lessons and carrying them out. This contrasts with the American deference to local authorities, schools, and teachers, who collectively exert enormous influence over expectations, goals, course offerings, course content, and assignments.[12] Very few countries rely on their local governments for such policy decisions to the extent that the United States does. Another way other countries exercise central control is through national exams at transitional times in a student's education. These tests measure student progress, sometimes they determine students' future placement, and they are used to assess the effectiveness of the overall educational system.

A final feature of the more centralized model found abroad is that the completion of high school (or what is at least recognized as equivalent to high school) often requires passing an exam, as opposed to completing a certain number and distribution of credits (as is common in America). In numerous countries, these or other exams are also used to determine who has access to state-subsidized public higher education. In fact, the United States is almost alone among OECD countries in not having a direct link between what students can show they learned in high school and their access to public colleges and universities. It's also noteworthy that, unlike the United States, in other countries students (as opposed to teachers, schools, and districts) are typically held accountable for how much they learned in school. This accountability occurs through students' access (or lack thereof) to college and career opportunities.

Because of its importance, coursework in other countries leading up to national exams is closely sequenced; at each step, students are given explicit expectations of what they should learn. Because of their immediate importance and the consequences to them if they fail, these courses command students' attention. Such direct linkages between the K–12 curriculum and college entrance examinations have no real counterpart in the United States. Here, colleges rarely if ever request that students include in their college application test results from state high school exams; instead, they request ACT or SAT scores. America's only close equivalents to foreign national exams are Advanced Placement tests, which are based on certain high school classes with an AP designation. While it is true that higher AP scores *can* help advance one's college application, AP classes—not to mention the AP tests themselves—are optional and not available at all of the nation's high schools.

In terms of local control, few countries permit students or schools to make significant decisions over curricular choices; instead school systems abroad rely on fairly uniform course sequencing, course offerings, or at least expectations of student performance. Often other nations have no counterpart to our school district structure, or if they do, the districts are much less important. Even where substantial regional autonomy exists, the central government may dictate grade-level coursework.

Over the last couple of decades, numerous OECD countries have moved in the direction of allowing schools greater autonomy over curriculum and course content, with the central government focusing more exclusively on monitoring and financing schools. Individual schools in Austria, Finland, and England, for example, have some degree of autonomy in both managing their budgets and choosing their curriculum, but curricular expectations are spelled out by the national government.

The American practice starting in middle school of allowing students in the same grade to pursue quite different coursework is not found in many other countries. At least through the middle school, most provide all students in the same school with the same curriculum. For instance, in school systems where algebra and geometry are introduced in middle school, this coursework is almost always expected of all students.

Vocational Education

Another common characteristic of educational systems abroad is the practice of offering different curricular tracks to students. In many nations, students at particular ages are sorted into what are typically different schools offering distinct curricular "tracks." The Germanic countries of Germany, Austria, and Switzerland have similar approaches that evolved from a very old system in which students learned trades by entering in apprenticeships. Contemporary policy has students being separated at an early age (typically around eleven) into one of three tracks—one being academic, one vocational, and one professional. Those aspiring to college attend the academic schools. At age sixteen, students take a test to determine if they can continue with (or switch to) the academic track. At the end of this period, students take a national exam (*Abitur* in Germany) that determines whether or not they gain access to college. But even in these school systems, there is curriculum that all of the tracks share, and within the track-segregated schools students have little choice over the courses they must take to complete their degree.

The Germanic countries are unusual in that they begin tracking students at such an early age. A more common practice, found in Finland, France, Japan, Norway, and Denmark, is to offer students a common curriculum until around age sixteen. At that age, students choose between an academic, vocational, and in some cases professional track. The decision of what track to go into is sometimes based on choice, but more usually on past performance or measures of ability. While some countries, such as England, have moved away from tracking, a more common trend is to push back the age (now commonly sixteen) at which students can abandon the academic track for one designed with a particular career in mind.

Organization

An important feature of the more centralized model is the greater ease with which curricular changes occur. Change is easier than in the United States, with its more complex governance structure and decentralized decision making over curriculum. Because of the important role that school districts and schools have in curricular decisions, policy around curriculum in the United States is strongly influenced by the preferences of local communities.

Moreover, centralized curriculum results in less variation in the content of courses, as centralized standards or a core national curriculum dictate common expectations across districts, schools, and classrooms. In the United States, more stakeholders weigh in and influence school-level decisions, leading to schools (and even teachers within schools) offering different coursework, using distinct instructional practices, and holding students to different standards.

While each nation's school system has unique features, it's probably fair to say that America's is the most unusual. The primary difference is that ours permits a wide range of local variation—be it in financing, curriculum, the content of different courses, teacher preparation, or decisions over tests and the use of these tests. Because of the way it has evolved, our educational system is extremely bureaucratic, prioritizing control over process rather than attention to outcomes.

This is an odd combination: we have both local control, which leads to wide variation across districts, along with a complex bureaucracy, which makes change difficult to come by. Generally, bureaucracy comes with more central control and less variation in decision making. But the nature of the American governance structure does not lend itself to uniform outcomes. This is due to the fact that our school system is marked by a complex set of relationships among the Agents, with some relationships conflicting with others. These Agents collectively exert little direct control over classroom instruction, which means that the effects of policy changes are far from uniform at the school or classroom level. Recent reforms have addressed this in competing ways: some have attempted to clamp down on schools by increasing bureaucratic control over what schools can do and how they operate, while others have increased school-level decision-making authority. We have a very complicated educational system, the end result being that, for good or bad, much is left to the discretion of districts, schools, and ultimately teachers (the most local of all the Agents). As I'll start to argue in the next chapter, there is good reason to think that this organizational structure is a particularly ineffective one—one that in its design ensures that mediocrity persists.

2

Just How Low Are Our Educational Standards?

Consider the following passage from a master plan prepared by the state agency charged with overseeing higher education in the state of Washington. After commenting on the world-class nature of Washington's system of higher education, the agency congratulates the state on the high standards in its K–12 system: "We have held on—against considerable pressure—to academic standards that ensure that our high-school graduates can read and write."[1] Perhaps for good reason the agency makes no mention of the importance of math literacy since in 2011 the U.S. Department of Education estimated that well over half of all eighth graders in the state were at or below basic eighth-grade math literacy, and almost one in four had math skills *below* what is considered basic.

If we are pleased with our expectations that high school graduates should be able to read and write, then our standards are way too low. Imagine that you were training for international competition in the high jump, but your coach only required you to jump over a two-foot-high bar during practice. Not only might your high-jumping abilities be left undeveloped, but this training regime may leave you completely misinformed about the level of competition that lies ahead—you would be in for a rude awakening when you went to compete against the rest of the world.

Something like this occurs with America's low educational standards: by setting the bar low, students both underperform and are misled about the skills and knowledge required for future success. In this chapter I take up the concept of educational standards or expectations (terms I use interchangeably), and then consider how our standards compare with those in other countries. I do this by discussing various ways that educational standards might be defined, and then examining ours in light of these differing definitions. By just about any meaning of educational standards, in the United States they are low. In the next set of chapters I will then move to discuss the costs that these low standards impose on all of us.

WHAT DO WE MEAN BY EDUCATIONAL STANDARDS?

At a very general level, we can probably all agree what we mean by the term *educational standards*: the amount of effort required by a typical student to succeed. It's the same definition used in the high-jump example above. The hypothetical coach was not holding his athletes to a very high standard when he asked them to clear a two-foot bar—for the typical athlete, that's pretty easy to do. In this sense we would probably all agree that the coach had low expectations for what the athlete could or should accomplish.

Defining and measuring "athletic standards" when referring to an athlete's training regime might be relatively straightforward; however, it's less easy to do with educational standards. That's because they are harder to observe—how do we tell if one teacher is holding her students to a higher standard than is another? Moreover, we may disagree on how we might characterize higher standards. Would higher expectations be better represented by an assurance that every student had an excellent teacher, by the requirement that every student take at least two years of algebra, or by the condition that each student is able to demonstrate mastery of second-year algebra?

So it's not straightforward what we mean by "educational standards." Without knowing what we mean, it's not clear-cut how to assess how rigorous or demanding expectations are in any one educational system. To figure this out, we might examine what institutional documents say about the purpose of education and what the system strives to achieve. This might be equivalent to assessing athletic standards by listening to the coach discuss the expectations she has of her athletes. The quote that started off this chapter is of this nature because it identifies what is expected of students.

We might also judge educational standards by looking at the required curriculum (the equivalent of examining an athlete's training schedule). Third, we might judge them by investigating the excellence of the educational environment and the level of demands placed on students in the classroom (how high the athlete is asked to jump during practice). Finally, we might inspect the level at which students have to perform in order to succeed (how high athletes have to jump to make the team, for instance). In an educational system, all of these criteria capture some aspect of what we mean by educational standards—although we may disagree on how precisely we measure and determine the relative importance of each. I'll move on now to examining how the K–12 system in the United States measures up according to each of these four different ways of assessing what is expected of students.

Educational Standards as Reflected in Stated Objectives

As touched on in the last chapter, official statements about what students should know and what skills they should have (called "learning goals," which contrasts with requirements over classes and subjects students should take) are relatively new in the United States. In fact states only began articulating what they expected of all students within their state in the late 1980s. So what do state school systems say they are trying to achieve, and what do they expect of students?

In 1996 the Fordham Institute sought to answer precisely this question. It examined what twenty-eight states said about their expectations of students with respect to English. The report's author evaluated state standards based on a long list of criteria. Here are three random ones: (1) whether the stated standards would be used as a basis for actually assessing students; (2) whether the standards were clear and specific; and (3) whether the standards were specific to a grade or a small range of grades (as opposed to generic for students of very different ages). Overall, only five of the twenty-eight states earned reasonable marks, and most fell very far short of what the author determined to be strong and clear English standards. Her main criticism was that state English standards were so vague and imprecise as to not have any real meaning (they were "toothless"), and they provided few or no guidelines on the progression of skill development. For example, one state had a learning goal that stated that students should be able to read "appropriate texts" without at all indicating what would constitute "appropriate."

Shortly thereafter, a follow-up study by the same organization looked into state standards in five different subjects. It too found that state expectations were vague or undemanding. Alaska's math standards, for example, expected high school students to "apply principles, concepts and strategies from various strands of mathematics to solve problems that originate within the discipline of mathematics or in the real world."[2] Compiling their assessment of standards in the five subjects, the authors gave each state an overall grade, with the average state earning a D+.

Since undertaking these early assessments of state standards, the Fordham Institute has continued to monitor and grade states on the stated objectives of their educational systems. In 2000 it found that average state standards had improved from a D+ to a C–, and—encouragingly—more states were earning As and Bs than were in the earlier study. Again in 2006 it updated its analysis, finding that a majority of states had been active over the intervening years updating and changing their written standards. However, judged as a whole, the Fordham Institute concluded that standards had not improved, and in fact they had declined in math and science; once again it gave states an average grade of C–.

The main criticism contained in the 2006 Fordham Institute report was the same: state goals were not specific or clearly stated enough to know exactly what was expected of students. Arkansas's history objectives, for example, stated unhelpfully that students should be able to "evaluate major turning points in history" and that the curriculum should "probe the interdependencies of nations." In Hawaii students should be able to describe "situations when addition, subtraction, multiplication, and division involving rationales" were appropriate. States were criticized for the encyclopedic nature of their standards, often indicating the goal of inclusion rather than the establishment of priorities. For instance, Idaho's fifth-grade science standards asked students to "investigate the interactions between the solid earth, oceans, atmosphere, and organisms." And in some states, you just had to wonder who possibly could have dreamed up such standards. In Idaho kindergarteners were asked to "understand the theory that evolution is a process that relates to the gradual changes in the universe and of equilibrium as a physical state." The most recent 2010 Fordham Institute report found of improvement in state standards. However, as shown in the table on the next page, twenty-one states earned a grade of D or lower for their English standards and fifteen for their math ones.[3]

Grades for State English/Language Arts, Mathematics, and Science Standards, 2010 and 2012

State	English/Language Arts, 2010	Mathematics, 2010	Science, 2012
Alabama	B	B+	D
Alaska	F	D	F
Arizona	B	B	D
Arkansas	D	C	B
California	A	A	A
Colorado	B+	C	D
Connecticut	D	D	C
Delaware	F	B	C
District of Columbia	A	A	A
Florida	B	A	D
Georgia	B+	A–	C
Hawaii	C	C	D
Idaho	C	B	F
Illinois	D	D	D
Indiana	A	A	A–
Iowa	F	C	D
Kansas	C	F	B
Kentucky	D	D	D
Louisiana	B+	C	B
Maine	C	C	D
Maryland	C	D	B
Massachusetts	A–	B+	A–
Michigan	D	A–	C
Minnesota	C	B	C
Mississippi	D	C	C
Missouri	D	D	C
Montana	F	F	F
Nebraska	F	C	F
Nevada	C	C	D
New Hampshire	C	D	D
New Jersey	C	C	D
New Mexico	C	C	C
New York	C	B	B+
North Carolina	D	D	D
North Dakota	D	C	F
Ohio	C	C	B
Oklahoma	B+	B+	F
Oregon	C	B+	F
Pennsylvania	D	F	D
Rhode Island	D	D	D

(continued)

Grades for State English/Language Arts, Mathematics, and Science Standards, 2010 and 2012 *(continued)*

State	English/Language Arts, 2010	Mathematics, 2010	Science, 2012
South Carolina	D	C	A–
South Dakota	C	C	F
Tennessee	A–	C	D
Texas	A–	C	C
Utah	C	A–	B
Vermont	D	F	C
Virginia	B+	C	A–
Washington	C	A	C
West Virginia	D	B	D
Wisconsin	D	F	F
Wyoming	D	F	F

Sources: Sheila B. Carmichael and others, *The State of State Standards—and the Common Core—in 2010*, Thomas B. Fordham Institute, July 2010, http://www.edexcellencemedia.net/publications/2010/201007_state_education_standards_common_standards/SOSSandCC2010_FullReportFINAL.pdf, pp. 9–11; Lawrence S. Lerner and others, *The State of State Science Standards 2012*, Thomas B. Fordham Institute, January 2012, http://www.edexcellencemedia.net/publications/2012/2012-State-of-State-Science-Standards/2012-State-of-State-Science-Standards-FINAL.pdf, p. 7.

In 2012 the Fordham Institute updated its 2005 evaluation of state science standards to assess the changes made to them in forty-four states. They concluded that eleven states had improved the clarity and rigor of their science standards; however, sixteen states had managed to weaken theirs. On average, states earned a C grade—the same average they earned in 2005 (see table).[4]

While strong (or weak) written standards by themselves do not assure student success (or failure), it is in theory an important starting point because clear goals could provide policymakers and educational leaders with consistent guidelines that could carry over into the quality, coherence, and rigor of the educational system, as well as what teachers expect of students. If written standards are coupled with a commitment to meeting them, and if the standards are clear on what's to be expected from students, then resources, curricular guidance, and performance expectations should follow. The written standards of states are in this way important as an indication of a state's commitment and willingness to concretely articulate its goals.

But of course statements about what you expect students to learn can be unclear, vague, and weak—perhaps even nonexistent—even if the education students receive is in fact excellent. And the reverse could likewise be true, in the same way a coach may sound great when you listen to her, yet actually be ineffectual. With that in mind, let's turn now to a second indicator of educational standards: the emphasis put on providing a high-quality educational environment. After all, providing a quality experience should be a good indicator that we have high expectations of what students can and will achieve.

Educational Requirements and the Educational Environment

In terms of the simplest measure of the quality of America's educational environment, let's turn first to the amount of time spent in school. The typical school year in America is 180 days, compared with an average of 195 in other OECD countries and 200 in East Asia. American students also spend less time per day in school—on average thirty-two hours a week, compared with forty-four in Belgium and sixty in Sweden. As the *Economist* notes, by the time U.S. students graduate from high school, such differences add up to students in some countries having spent an additional year in school.[5] Recent research shows pretty clearly that the amount of time in school matters for how much students learn, so the fact that our students spend relatively little is troubling. Moreover, budget cuts in states and districts around the nation increasingly cause them to consider reducing the length of their school year.

But "days in school" as an indication of the time our students spend learning is a misguided one. In many instances, instructional time gives way to school assemblies, substitute teachers, picture-taking days, visits from community members, health screenings, fundraising activities, preholiday celebrations, birthday parties, building renovations, and fire alarms. Extended observations at eight Chicago public schools over a three-year period estimated that such occurrences reduced the time teachers *actually* taught by about 40 percent. Another study of urban elementary schools found that students typically missed about forty-two days a year of instruction (or about 23 percent of the total) for various reasons.

And even when teachers in U.S. classrooms are teaching, instructional time is too often poorly used. It is not unusual for some teachers to spend nearly half of their time in class on noninstructional activities such as logistics and conversations of a noninstructional nature.[6] All told, the combination of nonacademic activities coupled with poor use of classroom time might leave students missing about half of the instructional time that is theoretically available during the school year. An international study commissioned by the U.S. Congress found as much, reporting that French, German, and Japanese students received more than twice as much academic instruction as did students in the United States.[7] Such an astonishingly poor use of school time should underscore the conclusion that many school systems in the United States do not appear to prioritize learning.

We also know from studies of instructional time usage that wide variability exists in how teachers use the time allotted to them for teaching. One study mentioned above found that the actual amount of time spent on classroom instruction was three times higher for some teachers than it was for others. Most often such variation among instructors occurs within the same school, not just from one school to the next. The decision over how much of class time to devote to actual instruction seems to depend more on teachers' preferences than on school-level factors such as the demands placed on teachers by the school principal or the district. It's not surprising, then, that researchers visiting different classes in one school found that different teachers approached the same subject matter in very distinct ways. In math, one encouraged students to use calculators, while another insisted that students learn long multiplication and division.[8]

I'll turn now to investigating the curricular demands placed on students. It could conceivably be true that the more limited instructional time available to students in the United States is actually better used and more demanding than elsewhere.

Unfortunately, this is not the case. For one, the American high school curriculum is significantly more relaxed in terms of the mandatory classes students have to take, particularly in the sciences and math. In 1984 the National Committee on Excellence in Education recommended that states adopt more rigorous course-taking standards for high school graduation. Of the forty-five states that establish graduation requirements, forty now meet the NCEE's standard for four years of English, thirty-six require the recommended three years of math, and thirty-one meet the recommended three years of science. In 2008 thirty states met all three subject-matter recommendations, and ten states met one or none of them.

Moreover, while states have been increasing the number of these "core" classes that students must take to graduate, until recently they have not specified what those courses should be. For example, while most states require three or more years of math, in 2011 only the District of Columbia and Ohio required all students to take a second year of algebra.[9] In science twenty states specifically required no more than one biology or one science lab course, and in some states, the science requirement can be met without taking biology, chemistry, or physics.[10]

While many states have been increasing their high school graduation requirements, particularly by adding to the number of math and science credits needed to graduate, sometimes this is accomplished by allowing students to substitute less rigorous math or science classes, rather than taking a longer sequence. As an example, of all states that have or are planning to require four years of math to graduate, only Arkansas plans to require students to go beyond the second year of algebra.[11] For the other states, then, this means that four years of required math could consist of pre-algebra, algebra, geometry, and business statistics. In many other countries, pre-algebra and algebra are taken before high school, and hence this four-year math requirement would at best amount to only two years of math in these nations.

In addition to looking at what states require students to take to gauge how demanding the educational system is, we can also look at what classes high school students actually take. Recent evidence from the class of 2004 and 2005 indicates that those high school graduates on average had taken 1.5 years of advanced math (defined as second-year algebra or higher) and 1.5 years of advanced science (defined as chemistry, earth science, physics, or advanced biology). This amount of math and science is about half a year more than graduating seniors had taken in 1990.[12] However, only one-fifth of students take a math class beyond second-year algebra, and only about 17 percent take calculus. Less than half take advanced biology, only a little over half take chemistry, and one in three takes a physics class.[13] By some estimates, one-third of graduates take no science class beyond a general biology class. Even among those expecting to earn a college degree, only 11 percent in 2004 took calculus in high school, a percentage that had remained more or less unchanged since 1992. And as we'll see shortly, such estimates of coursework based on title alone overestimates exposure to content, because course content often doesn't match what the title implies.

How does this course selection compare with other countries? International surveys provide good comparative information on the courses that fifteen-year-olds around the world have taken. The latest survey found that 17 percent of America's fifteen-year-olds reported having taken a mandatory physics class and 27 percent a mandatory chemistry class. In other OECD countries, 60 percent of fifteen-year olds had already taken a mandatory physics class, the same percent that had completed a chemistry class.[14] Not only do fifteen-years-olds in other OECD countries typically take more advanced science and math classes, but they also take these classes at a much earlier age than do our students.

High school systems in the United States demand less from students in terms of the courses they have to take. Not surprisingly, this is true in middle school as well—especially when comparing America's middle schools with those in the highest-performing countries. As one example, math classes in American middle schools focus primarily on arithmetic as opposed to geometry and algebra. A 2007 survey of U.S. eighth graders found that 17 percent were enrolled in a basic math class and 44 percent were in pre-algebra. Only 39 percent were in at least an algebra class. Two states (California and Minnesota) now require all of their eighth graders to take algebra, but the poor performance of many students has states rethinking this requirement. By contrast, other OECD countries typically prioritize algebra and geometry during the middle school years.[15]

A final way to assess differences in the quality of education different countries provide is to look at how teachers prepare for the profession. Cross-country comparisons of what we require of teachers before they start teaching reveal that we often come up short. Prospective math teachers in the United States start their teacher training program with weaker math skills, and then take fewer math classes during their training program, than do their counterparts in other countries.[16] Only about 60 percent of eighth-grade students in the United States are taught math by teachers who either majored in math or science. By contrast, in England, Scotland, and Japan, three-quarters of students are taught by someone with a math degree. In European countries as a whole, it's closer to 90 percent.[17] Nations with the highest-scoring students in math require a vast majority of future math teachers to take courses in linear algebra and calculus during their teacher training, while in the United States only about one-half of future math teachers take such coursework.[18] During training to become a math teacher, the typical American student covers about 40 percent of advanced mathematics topics, whereas teachers in Bulgaria, Taiwan, and Korea on average cover about 80 percent of these same topics.[19] One study gave future U.S. math teachers a grade of C on their math knowledge, with a good number of them demonstrating the same knowledge of math that is found in a typical future math teacher in Botswana.[20]

All told, such evidence of the mediocre educational environment we put students in is dispiriting. Unfortunately, it just gets worse.

How Hard Is It to Succeed in School? Curriculum and Demands in the Classroom

A third way to assess the expectations we have of our students is to examine what it takes for students to succeed in their courses. After all, just saying that someone took an English college-prep course or a physics course doesn't mean that they actually had to work hard in the class—just as daily attendance at track practice might entail playing the violin rather than running.*

As discussed some pages earlier, in recent years there has been a steady trend toward high school students taking more advanced math and science classes, and middle school students enrolling in algebra. In 1990 well over half of all high school graduates took a very easy math course load, whereas today only 25 percent do. Conversely, in 1990 only 5 percent took a rigorous math course load, whereas today 13 percent do.[21] But are students learning more? Unfortunately, it isn't clear that they are. As shown in the top figure on the next page, high school students today are earning more math credits during high school. Moreover, their math grades have been increasing. If students today are taking more math *and* getting better grades, logic would suggest that they must also know more math than did their counterparts from years earlier. Yet as measured by national math NAEP scores, high school students' average math skills over the last couple of decades have remained relatively unchanged, as the bottom figure on the next page shows.

What could explain this perplexing assortment of facts—more math taken, better math grades, but no evidence of better math skills? Mark Schneider postulates that schools are pushed to bolster the content of their curriculum beyond their capacity to comply, and their only way of coping with such demands is to provide an illusion of rigor: they enroll more students in classes with advanced names, while often in fact not changing the course's actual content.[22] Thus one reasonable explanation for these mystifying trends is that, while it appears students are taking and learning more math, in fact the math

---

*Which may be good for your musical talent but not for your speed—as turned out to be true for my violin-playing high school track-mate Peggy.

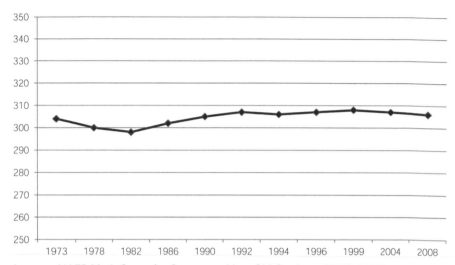

Average NAEP Math Score for Seventeen-Year-Old Students (1973–2008)
Source: National Center for Educational Statistics, "NAEP 2008 Trends in Academic Progress,"
April 2009, http://nces.ed.gov/nationsreportcard/pdf/main2008/2009479.pdf.

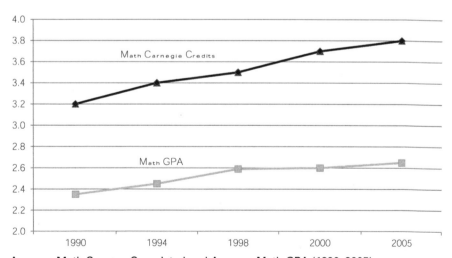

Average Math Courses Completed and Average Math GPA (1990–2005)
Source: Mark Schneider, "Math in American High Schools: The Delusion of Rigor," *Education
Outlook*, no. 10 (October 2009), www.aei.org/files/2009/10/08/10-EduO-Schneider-g.pdf.

curriculum is simply being repackaged into more math classes and credits, rather than more math. And there is other evidence that this is the right explanation. Students today who complete a second year of algebra on average graduate with about the same math skills as did students thirty years ago who took a year less of math.[23] Researchers have found a similar phenomenon with AP classes: despite the name, some AP courses appear no different from similar courses without the AP cachet.

Other evidence supports the contention that taking and obtaining credit for a particular class doesn't mean that students have learned much of what the course title would suggest. As a case in point, a couple of years ago over two thousand Ohio students who had recently completed an algebra class were tested on their understanding of basic algebra. From test results, students were ranked as having advanced, proficient, basic, or below-basic understandings of algebra. Six out of every ten of these students scored in the below-basic category—that is, in the lowest category measured. Commented one high school teacher on the problem of students learning algebra, "You've got an accumulation of deficits that are following you all the way up to that course."[24]

More evidence that many students do not learn what the course title indicates comes from the result of various states' participation in a uniform end-of-year test given to students who have just completed a second year of algebra. In the spring of 2008, about ninety thousand such students across twelve states were tested on their knowledge of second-year algebra. The average percentage of questions answered correctly ranged from 20 percent in some states to 35 percent in others. Thus in almost no state did students on average get more than one of three questions correct. Moreover, only 13 percent of all of the students tested scored in a range that would indicate that they understood the subject matter of second-year algebra.[25] And students did abysmally on questions requiring that they construct answers rather than simply choose among a select number of presented answers—only about one in ten students got these sorts of questions correct. And with respect to critical-thinking and problem-solving skills—the skills that are especially important to have and challenging to learn—these students' skills proved astonishingly weak.

While it would be interesting to know what grades these students had received in their second-year algebra class and how well course grades corresponded with their test scores, this information was not made available.

On this, though, almost half of students whose ACT score indicated that they were not ready for college math had taken a second year of algebra and had earned an A or B in that class. Similarly, about half of the students deemed not ready for college-level science based on their ACT score had earned an A or B in their physics class.[26]

It's clear that stated expectations and standards do not always match those to which students are actually held. For example, consider a study of about 1,800 elementary school students in one Florida school district. This study compared students' scores on Florida state tests with the grades they received in the subject matter. In Florida, state tests are coordinated with state standards; in theory, grades given to students in the classroom should correspond with a certain performance level on state tests. For instance, a student earning an A in math should score in the Level 5 range on the state math test, a B grade should correspond with a score in the Level 4 range, and so forth. So a student who scores in the Level 1 range (which would indicate that the student failed completely with meeting grade-level expectations) should be failing the subject matter in school.

The first thing to point out from this study is that, on average, teachers were more generous in their grades than would be suggested by students' performance on the state test. Over half of the students who received an A in a subject showed through their test score that their mastery of the subject should have merited them at best a grade of C. And over 60 percent of students who received Bs from their teacher scored in the D or F range on the state test.

The second thing to point out is that, as is common in most American schools, teachers employed very different grading standards. The reason for this is complicated, but it has to do with differences in how teachers understand their role, their own standards, as well as pressure from parents (or administrators). More importantly, it has to do with the institutional environment that allows such variation to persist; I'll say more about this in subsequent chapters. For now, I'll just stick with making the simpler point that such differences exist.

The researchers in this study found that "lenient" teachers (as identified by the researchers) were almost four times more likely to award a D student (according to the state exam) with an A grade, and five times more likely to award an F student with a B grade, than were those teachers who employed tougher grading standards.[27] Thus, despite clearly stated and measurable expectations at the state level, this study demonstrated that classroom standards in Florida were not only lax, but extremely variable.[28]

While generally less is known about the rigor of English and social studies curricula as opposed to math and science, one recent study of high school English courses by the Association of Literary Scholars, Critics, and Writers concluded that the books typically read in high school English classes were unchallenging and aimed at about a fifth- or sixth-grade reading level. Moreover, assignments deemphasized a close reading of the texts and instead asked students to address topics such as how material in books could be linked to their personal experiences.[29]

That students are often assigned texts that don't seem to be aligned with their grade level helps explain why so few students leave high school with the ability to understand complex texts. One study based on test results of over 250,000 eleventh graders found that fewer than one in three could understand difficult texts such as would be expected in college or a career.[30] When it comes to foundational skills such as reading, the educational system as a whole does not appear to establish these foundations and then develop them. Rather, what students learn and when is determined by many different local factors rather than some overarching intentional design. This means that teachers each year devote an inordinate amount of time to reviewing material. International comparative studies have found that curriculum in the United States indeed suffers from a lack of coherence, focus, and rigor, and involves a disturbing amount of repetition.[31] Comparing math taught in Singapore and several U.S. states, researchers found that American classrooms typically included twice as many topics per grade as did Singapore.[32] This should not be surprising. When students have so much choice and pursue various routes at different times, it's difficult to sequence courses. Teachers cannot rely on or assume student mastery of some foundational or background skills and instead have to reintroduce material rather than build on a common base.

For one final illustration of the lack of rigor and coherence in the U.S. curriculum, I want to turn to the students who take what is widely billed as a "college-prep curriculum" (four years of English, and three each of math, science, and social studies). Presumably, students who take this curriculum should be college ready. The organization ACT recently linked up students' performance on the ACT test with their high school coursework to see if students who take the college-prep curriculum wind up, in fact, college ready. Among those taking this curriculum in high school, ACT found that a full three-quarters were not college ready in all four subjects. Moreover, one-quarter of the students who followed the recommended algebra, geometry, and second-year algebra math sequence were enrolled in a remedial math class during their first year of college.[33]

This evidence indicates that rigor in the classroom is missing—or if it is there, meeting it is optional for student success. Before reaching this conclusion, it might be useful to have a more precise understanding of how classroom experiences in the United States compare with those in other countries. If we knew something about the level of demand placed on students and the quality of the educational experience in the classroom, we might better understand why students often don't seem to learn that much in their classes, or at least not learn what one might expect them to learn.

Unfortunately, we don't know an awful lot about this—although the previously discussed studies of how school time is used provide some indication of a lack of priority placed on learning per se. As indicated above, we also know that in the United States much class time is spent on review. In high school as much as one-quarter to one-third of time might be spent reviewing middle school material, which is why high school teachers frequently complain about the amount of time they spend teaching material that students should already know.[34]

But two studies provide an especially telling glimpse into how class time use and the quality of the classroom experience compare across countries. One involved videotaping and reviewing 231 eighth-grade math classes in Japan, Germany, and the United States. Experts reviewing these videotapes found that the average content of America's math lessons was consistent with what one might expect (based on international standards) during the seventh grade; in Japan lessons were what might be expected in the ninth grade; and in Germany lessons were aimed at just below the ninth-grade level. In other words, by the time American students are thirteen or fourteen years old, their math lessons are already two years behind the lessons that their Japanese counterparts receive and about a year behind those received by their German peers.

Students in the United States could fall behind because the progression of math (in this case) is slow or ineffective for a variety of reasons. To this end, the study above also assessed the quality of each lesson's content. To do this, researchers presented college mathematics professors with a written transcript of each math lesson in a way that kept the country of origin unknown to the reviewer.[35] Professors were then asked to review and rate the content of the math lesson as revealed by the transcript.

In their reviews, math professors rated a full 89 percent of math lessons in the United States to be low in quality; no math lesson was rated as high in quality. By contrast, only one in ten of the Japanese lessons was rated as low in quality, and four in ten lessons were rated as high in quality.[36] Lessons in the United States tended to focus on routine procedures and skills, whereas Japanese students spent time developing their underlying conceptual understanding and critical-thinking skills. This difference was also reflected in teachers' responses to what they were trying to achieve in the lesson—in other words, teachers in the United States were intentionally focusing on lower cognitive demands (such as memorizing) whereas those in Japan were working on developing students' higher-level critical-thinking skills. A typical lesson in the United States might involve teachers demonstrating a skill, after which students then practice the skill. By contrast, in Japan teachers might typically pose a problem, and students would collectively seek a solution or possible solutions to it. Another noticeable difference among the countries was the extent to which the math lessons would be interrupted: in the United States more than one in four math lessons was interrupted for one reason or another, while in Japan none was, and in Germany only about one in ten lessons was interrupted. This is consistent with the evidence presented earlier in this chapter that a good deal of instructional time in the United States is taken over or interrupted by other activities—assemblies, classroom visitors, announcements over the intercom, and so on.

Based on the same videotaped methodology, a second study undertook a wider comparison of math instruction around the world. It evaluated 638 eighth-grade math lessons from classrooms in Australia, the Czech Republic, Hong Kong, Japan, the Netherlands, Switzerland, and the United States. This more expansive study also found that math lessons in the United States typically involved more review time, and problems worked on tended to be less complex. In fact two-thirds of class time was devoted to low-complexity tasks and only 6 percent was devoted to highly complex ones. Lesson plans tended to be fragmented and undeveloped, and lessons often involved students repeating basic skills rather than developing conceptual understanding.

Over half of all class time in the United States was spent on review, twice the amount that took place in Japan's and Hong Kong's classrooms. Overall, more than half of all U.S. math lessons were judged to be low in quality—twice the average found in the other participating countries. In fact, for every single aspect of lessons evaluated—their coherence, presentation, the level of student engagement, and overall quality—reviewers gave America's math lessons the lowest ratings of all countries.[37]

As final evidence of how low demands placed on students are, some time ago researchers undertook a detailed analysis of students' homework assignments in the Chicago School District. They found that a very large percentage of eighth-grade assignments were of low quality, and almost 90 percent of math assignments offered students no more than a minimal challenge.[38]

To sum up, then, clear evidence shows that, on average, schools in the United States are not very demanding, at least as measured by the quality of the learning environment and the demands placed on students. Moreover, the rigor of coursework in our schools seems to vary in ways that are mystifying. We see this in the variability of class-time usage, classroom content, and grading standards. Such variation might help explain why students' math and science scores in the United States are practically unrelated to the amount of time spent in math and science classes—classroom time is used so differently by different teachers.[39] This also explains why parents are often so vigilant about the classroom to which their child is assigned—which is a key point in explaining the persistence of low standards that I'll return to in chapter 8.

For one final measure of our educational standards, I'll now examine the expectation levels in terms of the skills, cognitive ability, and content knowledge students are expected to reach and how these compare with what is expected in other countries.

Expectations of Student Performance

Thanks in part to the federal No Child Left Behind Act of 2001, all states now have written standards for a range of different grades and subjects. Under this law, states not only must develop these standards, but they also must test their students annually to see if they are meeting them. States must also report the extent to which their students are or are not "proficient." The standards that each state sets help us identify expectations in state school systems insofar as they tell us where states set their "proficiency" bar.

So how high or low are state standards? That's hard to say unless you have a common benchmark, as state standards are all over the map. Fortunately, we do have one reference point that many consider to be a good one. Every year or so, the federal government administers a test, called the National Assessment of Educational Progress (NAEP), to a random sample of American students. The NAEP is used to measure student skills and capabilities across the nation; NAEP results allow us to compare student performance over time, over states, and across subgroups of students (urban versus rural, poor versus nonpoor, Hispanic versus white, and so forth). In fact NAEP results are referred to as "The Nation's Report Card."

According to the American Institutes for Research, the NAEP sets its proficiency bar at a level aligned with those set by international organizations that establish and measure proficiency across countries. And the NAEP definition of proficiency is equivalent to the standards used by many European and Asian countries to gauge whether their students are measuring up to expectations. For example, one study estimated that while one-quarter of eighth-grade students in the United States meet NAEP math proficiency standards, nearly three-quarters do in Singapore, and two-thirds do in Hong Kong, Korea, and Taiwan.[40]

Comparing state standards to those embodied in the NAEP may be a reasonable first step to evaluate and compare state standards. At the least, the NAEP provides a common measuring rod. And such a comparison reveals one thing with certainty: states set their proficiency bars much lower than does the federal government. This becomes obvious when you compare the percentages of students who meet state versus NAEP proficiency standards, because wide discrepancies exist in almost every state. In 2005 for instance, 71 percent of Florida's fourth graders met Florida's state reading proficiency standards while only 30 percent met the NAEP's. Similarly, 74 percent of Oklahoma's eighth graders were proficient in math according to Oklahoma's standard, but only 29 percent met the federal standard. And so on in just about every state, subject, and grade.

As an overall indicator of the relationship between state and federal education standards, a recent study undertaken by the U.S. Department of Education concluded that none of the states' fourth- or eighth-grade reading proficiency standards exceeded the NAEP standard, and only fourteen states had established fourth-grade reading standards above the NAEP's much more lenient level of "basic proficiency." Only Massachusetts's fourth-grade math proficiency standard exceeded the NAEP one for this age group, and only two states had an eighth-grade math proficiency level that exceeded the federal government's.[41] In fact, most states typically define "proficiency" at a level the NAEP would call "basic proficiency." The NAEP defines basic proficiency as a level that "denotes partial mastery of prerequisite knowledge and skills that are fundamental for proficient work." More important, many states' proficiency standards are *below* what the federal government defines as "basic proficiency"—in fact, about half of all states reported in 2005 that a good many more of their fourth graders were proficient readers than were deemed to have just *basic* reading proficiency under the federal government's standards.

Even more disturbing is the fact that state standards have also been declining. According to a U.S. Department of Education report, between 2005 and 2007 eight states weakened their definition of eighth-grade reading proficiency while only three strengthened it; four weakened their fourth-grade math standard while only two strengthened it; and six states decreased their eighth-grade proficiency standard while only one increased it.[42] Another organization that monitors state proficiency standards also concluded that, on the whole, state standards declined between 2003 and 2007.[43] Such pressure on standards is not only a consequence of NCLB but also reflects community pressure (the perceived quality of schools affects property values, among other things) and a school system concerned about the ever-present threat of charter schools.

Not only are the cutoff points that define proficiency levels on state tests low and falling, they are also wildly inconsistent with one another. Some state standards are a full standard deviation below those in other states. According to two researchers, Georgia's eighth-grade reading standards are four standard deviations below those in South Carolina![44] Since score gaps of two standard deviations may be equivalent to the difference of four grade levels,[45] the difference between Georgia and South Carolina in this case is so large as to be unfathomable.

We might exercise some caution with measuring state standards against those of the NAEP. Some NAEP critics argue that its standards are too rigorous or unrealistic, or that they are not really aligned with the best international benchmarks. For this reason, let's examine state standards by turning to a second measure of students' skills and abilities. The Northwest Educational

Assessment (NWEA) is a test given regularly to students around the nation. NWEA assessment tests (called the MAP) are well regarded and are in regular use by over a thousand school districts; millions of students around the country take their tests each year.

A few years ago, researchers investigated how proficiency levels at the state level matched up with MAP scores. Their results showed that, on average, state standards were very low, and they were wildly inconsistent. For example, of those states studied, reading proficiency standards in the third grade averaged around the 33rd percentile range of the distribution nationwide. Some states set their proficiency levels as low as the 7th percentile of the national distribution of third graders' reading ability (Colorado), while others drew the line at the 61st percentile (California).[46] Michigan, which sets one of the lowest math standards for its students, draws its fourth-grade math proficiency level at a point below that reached by five out of six fourth graders nationwide.[47] Similar patterns exist across grades and across subject matter—in general, states set the proficiency bar low. Moreover, their standards do not remain consistent across grades—typically they are easiest to meet in the earlier grades, but harder in the later grades.

A final way to assess the level of skills and abilities that school systems expect of students is to examine the measured knowledge students must acquire to graduate.

Currently, twenty-eight states either have exit exams or will have one in place by 2012. Typically, these measure ability levels in English and mathematics. Students in these states are (or will be) required to take and pass a test or tests in order to graduate. Such tests are of two types: a comprehensive exam that tests for a range of skills and content-knowledge that students are expected to have gained by the end of high school, and "end of course" exams that students must take after completing a specific required course such as algebra, American history, or tenth-grade English. In 2010 seven states relied on end-of-course exams, with ten more intending to adopt them in the near future; a few states use both end-of-course exams as well as comprehensive exams.

How rigorous are these various state tests, whether comprehensive or end-of-course? The comprehensive exams are almost all "minimum competency tests," meaning they are designed to test the proficiency levels expected in the eighth or ninth grade. As evidence, let's turn to the findings of an organiza tion that examined six different state exit exams. The organization Achieve found that all six states covered material students should know by the tenth grade and which in other countries is typically covered by the seventh or eighth grade. The math tests tended to focus on pre-algebra and basic geometry rather than the algebra and geometry that students presumably learn in high school. On average, over half of the points allocated in the math exit exams required students to use basic recall or routine procedures. The state reading tests were similarly undemanding. Half of the content required basic comprehension and only 3 percent of the potential points that students earned required students to demonstrate critical-reading skills.[48] The figure below summarizes Achieve's overall assessment of the difficulty of these six state math and reading exit exams. The figure shows Achieve's judgment of whether state tests were testing basic, intermediate, or more advanced skills. As shown, the typical state exam allocated half of its points to questions requiring only a basic understanding of mathematics and reading.

One superficial explanation for the low level of these tests is that states develop exit exams to ensure that everyone (or almost everyone) passes. Why exactly they would do this is what I set out to explain in this book. But that states do this is evident in instances where they institute some sort of an exit

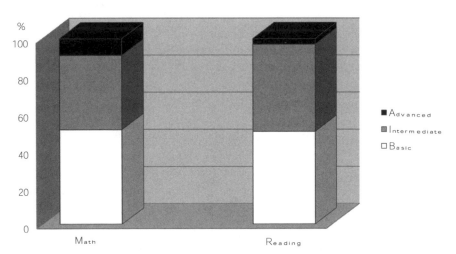

Typical Cognitive Demand of Math and Reading Exit Exams in Six States
Source: Achieve, Inc., *Do Graduation Tests Measure Up? A Closer Look at State High School Exit Exams*, 2004, http://www.achieve.org/files/TestGraduation-FinalReport.pdf.

exam; as the deadline for implementation approaches, and where past experience indicates that large numbers of students will not pass the test, states almost always back down. They do this by either lowering their passing scores, delaying the year in which the exit exams go into effect, or opening the door to alternative routes to a high school diploma. For example, despite the low level of proficiency Washington State's math exam tests for—the average cognitive demand is equivalent to seventh-grade math—the test has recently been postponed in large part because so many students were not passing it. And Minnesota recently changed its law requiring students to pass a math test before graduating; in a sort of "strike three and you walk" policy, students now are given the option of getting their degree after they fail the test three times.[49]

The fact that state exit exams are very undemanding is evident in that no college currently uses results from state high school assessment exams to determine students' level of preparation for college. No wonder. Researchers recently examined thirty-five state English/language arts exams and twenty state mathematics exams and gave them each an A, B, or C grade based on the extent to which each was able to show how prepared students were for college work. A C grade meant that the test has limited potential to provide information on college readiness, whereas a B grade indicated that the test may or may not reveal that students are college ready.[50] Grades were based on input gathered from more than four hundred university faculty members around the nation. Only three of the thirty-five state reading tests examined received an A while fourteen received a C. No state exam received an A on its math test.

Finally, what about end-of-course (EOC) exams? How do these measure up in terms of their expectations for student performance? Unfortunately, the quality of these tests, and the criteria for passing them, are also low. In 2010 the John Locke Foundation asked hundreds of college and university faculty to evaluate the quality of select test questions from one state's EOC tests for civics, economics, and U.S. history. With few exceptions, reviewers found substantial problems with the tests; as one political scientist stated, "Several [questions] are vague and leave no clear response; two do not have mutually exclusive choices; and one does not seem to me to have a correct answer as an option."[51]

In addition to being confusing, other EOC exams are just not that difficult. In Arkansas all students must pass an end-of-course exam in algebra to get a high school diploma. But if a student gets just a quarter of the questions right, his or her performance is sufficient to merit a passing grade—an abysmal standard, especially considering that much of the test is multiple choice with students choosing from four possible answers![52]

However you measure it—by what educational institutions say they are striving to accomplish in their schools, by the quality of the learning environment schools provide, by how hard students must work to succeed, or by the external standards students are asked to meet—we expect too little of our students and give them too little. In far too many classrooms and schools across the nation, little time is spent actually learning something, the quality of assignments and content of lessons is low, and high grades are easy to come by.

What is also true is that the biggest problems associated with these low expectations are, for various reasons, hidden from view. For this reason, part II turns to shedding light on them.

II

WHY LOW
STANDARDS MATTER

3

The Consequences of Low Expectations for Student Effort

Kara Miller started a stir when she wrote in the *Boston Globe* that many of her native-born college students were lazy. She complained that "too many 18-year-old Americans . . . text one another under their desks, check email, decline to take notes, and appear tired and disengaged." This behavior contrasts with the hardworking and disciplined conduct of her foreign students. Miller concludes that students schooled in America have acquired poor study habits: "By the time students are in college, habits can be tough to change."[1]

In short order, faculty members from around the nation wrote in to echo Miller's comments; they too blamed the undemanding educational system in which American students are raised for failing to instill the good study and mental habits necessary for college success. Many faculty were particularly critical of students who felt entitled to good grades for little effort.

Are America's college students really lazier and less prepared than their foreign counterparts? And if so, why? It's certainly true that many college students feel they deserve high grades for mediocre effort and performance. A recent survey of about five hundred undergraduates found that two-thirds of them believed that grades should depend on hard work, regardless of performance; one-third thought that a student deserved at least a B for simply completing all the course readings; and another one-third believed that regular class attendance should result in a B grade or better.[2] That grades should be based on the quality of work performed seemed like a novel idea to these students.

In this chapter I argue that Miller's observations are apt ones: low educational standards indeed result in students becoming accustomed to low expectations. They learn that they can get by with minimal effort, and carry these expectations with them into college. Coupled with easy access to college, low expectations in public schools allow students to succeed and enter college missing content knowledge, critical-thinking skills, writing ability, and the good study habits expected and required in college. They also allow students to choose an easy course of study in high school without much *apparent* downside.

Low expectations *lead* to low effort, poor study habits, and less learning. That is what Miller was claiming and what I argue here. Common sense would suggest this is true. Learning can be difficult and time consuming. Students, particularly teenagers, have many activities they would rather engage in than mental exertions. We probably all have some aversion to difficult mental exercises, as mastering complex or unfamiliar material is not easy. It is especially difficult when other more pleasurable alternatives exist, *and* when the benefits of your mental work are both undefined and reaped in the future. Under these conditions, you'd expect only the most disciplined, motivated, and/or academically gifted students to buckle down and toil. Otherwise most will likely engage in a strategy of "satisficing." By this I mean that they are happy meeting, but just meeting, the standard necessary for moving along without attracting too much attention. This strategy will be particularly attractive when it does not close off future options. A "satisficing" assumption is typically embedded in theoretical work that investigates how standards influence student choices.

That an association exists between effort and learning on the one hand and standards on the other seems clear. But the causal link can be disputed. Rather than low standards *causing* students to work less hard, it could be that low standards result from youth being disposed (for reasons associated with culture, family upbringing, or easy availability of technological distractions) to being lazy. Low standards (at least for some students) are necessary to accommodate a segment of the student population that is unengaged and unmotivated.

While standards and the propensity to work hard are related, people disagree about what causes what. Do low standards result in low effort, or does low effort result in low expectations? I contend that it's the former: strong evidence shows that when standards are higher, students work harder. And as a result of increased effort, they learn more.

LOW EXPECTATIONS CAUSE LOW EFFORT

That many students follow a "satisficing" strategy—they work only as hard as they need to—is obvious to anyone who listens to them. In one comprehensive survey of tenth graders, 60 percent agreed with the statement "I don't like to do any more school work than I have to."[3] In a recent survey of over 130,000 American high school students, more than half said they spent no more than an hour each week studying outside of class. And spending only a couple of hours a week on homework is generally enough for students to earn As and Bs in school.

The claim that students' attitude toward school and hard work is traceable to the expectations placed on them is also evident in what they do when expectations change. When the Chicago School District recently ended its practice of social promotion, students flocked to after-school and summer classes. A study of ten thousand American high school sophomores from around the nation found that those attending schools with stricter grading standards worked harder and learned more than did those in schools with more lenient grading standards. These instances show that students put more time and effort into their school work when more is expected or required of them.

This hunch led the sociologist James Rosenbaum to actually measure the effect of students' beliefs about the importance of hard work on the effort they expended in school. He found that students who thought that high school mattered worked harder in school, and those who believed there was no penalty for lackluster effort slacked off. Students who failed to see any payoff to hard work were much less inclined to exert effort in school than did those who thought that performance today matters for the future.[4]

A study of one Florida school district makes an even stronger case that school expectations affect effort and learning—even as early as elementary school. This study measured how much elementary school students learned each year and examined whether students' learning was related to their teachers' grading standards. Recall I discussed in the last chapter how state tests in Florida are designed so that students' scores should correspond with their school grades. A student who scores in the Level 5 range on the state test is doing what the state would consider an A grade in terms of grade-level expectations, one who scores in the Level 4 range is doing B grade work, and so forth. Researchers found that teachers employed very different standards when grading their students.

The investigators took advantage of these differences to identify hard- and easy-grading teachers. They then investigated if the grading standards mattered for student learning. After all, lenient teachers might have an easier time motivating and encouraging students than might hard teachers. What they found was that in classes in which teachers held students to a higher grading standard, students learned more. Moreover, the parents of students who had a more demanding teacher themselves spent more time helping their children with homework. The researchers concluded that parents help out their children as "co-teachers" when more is asked of their children. I'll return to this point shortly.

Low standards also influence students' effort in another way. The lower they are, the less the school engages youth. It's hard to get someone who is unengaged and bored to work hard. And how unengaged are youth in our schools? The survey mentioned above asked students precisely this question. According to their answers, the typical high school student is astonishingly bored and disengaged. Some complained that school was too difficult, but most complained that school was too easy. In fact, *half* reported they were bored in school every day, mostly because the material wasn't interesting, wasn't relevant, or was too easy.

It's obvious that boredom is not the state of mind we want in students in order to elicit their best effort. When school is easy, students learn that they can get by without paying much attention. It shouldn't be surprising that students' attitudes toward school and schoolwork deteriorate the longer they are in school. One study found that in the state of Washington, 92 percent of sixth graders reported that they try their best in school most of the time, but by twelfth grade only 69 percent reported this inclination. Over this period, the share of students reporting that their schoolwork is usually meaningful fell from nearly two-thirds to one-third.[5]

The contention that low standards elicit low effort shouldn't be a surprising one. We know that college students spend more time on classes in which it is harder to excel. When teachers make it harder to get a good grade, students work harder. There is a paradoxical trend in higher education that now may be easier to understand: over the last few decades, the amount of time students spend studying has fallen from an average of forty hours a week to twenty-seven. Yet at the same time, college grades have gone up. How can these two things both be true? A good guess is that students have responded to grade inflation by spending less time getting good grades—it has become easier to meet the *satisficing* threshold. *Why* grades have been going up in both college and high school is unclear, but it isn't because student work has improved (recall from the last chapter that average high school math credits and grades have increased while math test scores have remained flat). More likely it's that student effort has responded to the ease with which good grades can be had. By this conjecture, grade inflation may explain why the literacy rate among college graduates has been falling. Student effort—be it in elementary school, high school, or college—is influenced by where the bar is set.

Kara Miller and others who seconded her observation believed that it was Americans who underperformed in college, not foreigners. Is this true, and if so, why? For the time being, let's stick to the "is this true" part of the question. I'll pick up on the why in later chapters.

Are American students different from those overseas in terms of the effort they exert and their level of disengagement with school? Miller and other faculty members were reporting on anecdotal observations and were not comparing random American with random foreign college students. So it's not clear we can trust these observations—any more than we'd trust comparisons made between the average Chinese student and the average American student studying in China (there are a few).

We can get at this comparison through student surveys filled out by students who take international tests. These surveys measure self-reported differences among students in their attitudes and work habits. One such survey from the *Programme for International Student Assessment* (PISA) finds differing attitudes between American and other students in OECD countries. More than one-third of fifteen-year-old American students reported expending little effort in school. The percent of students expending less effort in other OECD countries was noticeably lower. In only one other country did more students report lower effort and perseverance in their schoolwork than did their American counterparts.[6] In terms of their own self-reporting, then, American students don't work as hard as their counterparts abroad. American students also report being less challenged and engaged in school.

Differences in coursework taken by American versus non-American students also make the case that our students work less hard. High school students pursue coursework that is intellectually less rigorous and demanding. Only about one-third of U.S. students take what is considered to be a set of college-preparatory high school courses—even though almost nine in ten have college plans. Amazingly, even among those students who are college bound, fewer than half follow the recommended college-preparatory curriculum. During their senior year, fewer than one in five students takes a math class.[7] Even academically elite students with the highest aspirations follow a wide array of course-taking patterns, not necessarily all of which are designed to help prepare them for college.

As indicated in the last chapter, a good part of the reason for the easier course-taking pattern is that students exercise considerable choice over their courses. They also have choice over the rigor of those courses—some courses are labeled as honors or AP for instance, indicating a more advanced treatment of the topic. But whether or not a student takes such a course is left to the student's discretion.

If our schools are doing a poorer job at engaging students and motivating them to work hard than other school systems do, we should see it not just in what students say about themselves and what coursework they pursue, but also in terms of outcomes. After all, genuine learning takes good content and teaching practices, but it can't occur without hard work. If students aren't working hard, and aren't all that interested in school, then we should see that reflected in their performance relative to those abroad. In fact this is exactly the pattern we see. The most recent international test results in math show that among fourth graders, those in eight OECD countries on average scored below those in the United States. However, among fifteen-year-olds, youth in seven of these eight countries all performed above those in the United States (with Italy the exception).[8] Our students' performance relative to those in other countries gets worse the older the age at which we compare them.

Further evidence that American students learn less as they get older comes through a close look at NAEP scores. The good news is that nine- and thirteen-year-olds' ability to read has been improving modestly over time; many fewer are functionally illiterate than had been the case not too long ago. Yet these gains come to an end in middle school. By high school, earlier improvements are not being translated into better high school performance. According to NAEP, today 20 percent of seventeen-year-olds are still unable to read simple, uncomplicated passages for specific information—a percentage that has remained unchanged over the last forty years. Such illiteracy persists despite the fact that we've succeeded in improving kids' academic skills in the earlier grades.[9]

As final evidence, the organization ACT, which administers the college-admission test by the same name, recently examined eighth, tenth, and twelfth graders' college readiness in different subjects. It found that between eighth and twelfth grade, the percentage of students not meeting *any* college-ready benchmark actually increased from 14 to 21 percent. The authors concluded that any momentum gained in students' academic abilities by the tenth grade is lost during the last two years of high school.[10] This evidence all points to the fact that our school systems fail to challenge and engage students, particularly during their high school years.

While it's very tempting to blame students' failure to learn on the influence of family, technology, or society in general, we shouldn't be so hasty. Even among those who eventually drop out of school, almost three-quarters report before doing so that education is important to them.[11] We can't escape the fact that our educational system does a poor job eliciting effort from students and communicating to them the importance and relevance of hard work. Instead, students' propensity to goof off in middle and high school, and eventually to become disenchanted with it, is partly a reflection of our low standards.

The problem of low effort is further exacerbated by the ease with which students gain access to college. Easy access allows students to treat high school as a bothersome hurdle rather than as an opportunity to take steps toward their future goals. A survey of college-going high school seniors solicited their beliefs about high school. Forty percent of respondents said they believed that high school was irrelevant. One student summed it up in the following way: "High school doesn't really matter . . . because . . . junior college is not such a big deal to get into."[12]

From the point of view of the high school student, taking easy classes in high school—and just barely passing those classes—is not problematic because the hard part about college is just getting in. Even a majority of students earning an average grade of a C or lower in high school still plan to attend college. Since entry into a community college is within reach of just about any high school graduate, many students do not worry about the costs of slacking off. In many schools this is a cultural norm that our educational system contributes to rather than combats.

MIXED MESSAGES

Why do college-bound students not take classes and exert the effort that will better prepare them for college? One explanation for the more easygoing attitude among American youth is that they don't care. But this doesn't ring true, especially given how ambitious young Americans are. In fact, the sociologists Barbara Schneider and David Stevenson refer to contemporary youth as "The Ambitious Generation" because of their high and rising educational and career aspirations.[13] A different explanation is that high school doesn't adequately convey information to students about how best to prepare for college and plan for the future. Instead, many high school students are led to believe that while college may be harder than high school, is all they need to prepare for college-level work is a secondary school degree. But as I take up in the next chapter, this is too often untrue.

Herein lies a second problem with low standards: not only do they mean that students don't have to work hard (and many of them don't), they also fail to send students accurate messages about how well prepared they are to succeed in college. To illustrate how little students know about college, in interviews with thousands of high school students, fewer than half knew the placement-testing policies for higher-education institutions in their region. While they knew admission standards (what was required to get in), they were unaware of what was required to earn college credit. This helps explain why so many students entering college end up in remedial math, writing, or reading classes—classes for which they earn no college credit—and why so many students are caught off guard when they finally figure this out.

Critics of the public school system have long argued that high schools do not adequately convey to students what is necessary for college success. In school systems abroad, this problem rarely arises because students typically follow a national curriculum aligned with college expectations. Or they pursue an academic (as opposed to vocational or professional) track in high school, the purpose of which is to get students into college. Moreover, getting into college usually involves achieving a high score on a national college-entrance (or high school leaving) exam. All students know this—they understand what is on these national exams, are aware of what type of score they need for what sort of postsecondary opportunity, and understand the connection between high school work and their aspirations.

In France, for example, students aspiring to attend college must take national exams (the baccalaureate). These exams have been compared in difficulty with advanced-placement exams in the United States. Spanish, Finnish, Swiss, and Dutch youth's eligibility for college is similarly determined by exams based on high school content. These clearly change the incentives for students to study and work hard. Students develop realistic notions of what options will await them and how best to change these options. While college-going students in the United States typically take the SAT or ACT, these tests intentionally are not directly connected with a high school curriculum. And student performance on these tests simply determines if he or she will have a shot at a competitive college, not whether college is in the cards. A vast majority of American college-going students do not attend a competitive college, thus for many the SAT or ACT scores don't carry great weight.

Since most American students attend nonselective institutions, providing students with information on how to get into college is not all that important. Consequently, many students develop mistaken beliefs about their real options. They know they can get into a college, but many lack information about the relationship between effort and performance in high school on the one hand and the college options available to them, or even their prospects for success in college, on the other. Here's one indication. One thousand high school graduates from the class of 2010 were asked a year after they graduated about their high school experiences. Nearly three-quarters reported that the workload and demand placed on them had been easy or very easy; hardly any said high school had been very challenging.[14]

That students are often unaware of the relationship between their high school curriculum and performance and their future opportunities is partly evident in their attitudes: American high school students are more ambitious than their counterparts in other countries, reporting for instance greater occupational ambition. When asked about their career expectations, almost 60 percent of fifteen-year-olds in the United States reported that they expected to be a professional. This was the highest percent in all of the twenty-seven OECD countries where this question was asked, and it compared with a more realistic average of about 40 percent in the other OECD countries.[15] Despite mediocre math skills, American youth also tend to think positively about their ability to learn math. In a 2003 survey associated with the TIMSS, U.S. students reported very high rates of self-confidence in math, while students in high-performing East Asian countries reported the lowest levels of self-confidence in math.

While there is nothing wrong with a system that provides youth with hope and self-confidence, there is if it is misdirected and deprives them of information about what is likely to be true in their future—especially when this information might result in them changing their plans, goals, and decisions (or provoking more active parental involvement). American youth today are ambitious, but too often their ambitions are at odds with their daily practices and choices. The problem is that very often youth don't recognize this.

This misalignment is apparent insofar as too many American students arrive at college with misperceptions about how well prepared they are to be there. Many later express regrets about the poor use of their high school years and are frustrated with the low standards to which they were held. Students often report that, had they known better, they would have taken more difficult courses and worked harder. The reflection expressed by one community college student that "my high school was just mostly concerned with getting us out of high school" is a common one.[16] This is a troubling indicator of the extent to which our low expectations can mislead youth. A survey of community college students conducted by the Pearson Foundation found that half of them felt that high school could have prepared them more for college by offering stronger courses and placing greater emphasis on basic skills.[17] That schools are the main source of this misalignment is apparent in the finding that high school teachers are twice as likely as college instructors to say that state standards do a good job preparing students for college-level work.[18]

Low standards coupled with easy access to college mean that students fail to get useful information on the path that their current decisions lead to. They overestimate their odds of future success. One scholar summarizes the situation as follows:

> Lured by the prospect of easy success, students choose easy curricula and make little effort. Just as some high schools implicitly offer students an undemanding curriculum in return for non-disruptive behavior, many high schools enlist students' cooperation by telling them that college . . . is easily attained by all.[19]

The information students have about their college prospects is important because gaining access to college is one of the most important reasons why students will work hard in high school.[20] Making access too easy means students don't have to work hard. But access does not mean success. That is the sequel to this story, which I take up in the next chapter.

NO ONE TO THE RESCUE

The problems created by low expectations aren't just that they result in disengaged and misguided students. In also means students make choices that are not likely to be consistent with their future goals; yet they don't find this out partly because it isn't obvious to them. Parents, guardians, teachers, administrators, even legislators—those who monitor student progress—base some of their monitoring on students' external "signals": Are they passing required tests? Are they promoted to the next grade? Are youth graduating? Do they get into college? To the extent that these "monitors" see positive signals since students graduate and enroll in college, external pressure on students to work and try hard is likely to be low. In fact, the message seems to be that all is well, even when it isn't.

It also means that when schools simply pass students along, they can be seen as successfully doing their job. This is true in far too many schools. In a recent survey of over five thousand school counselors, only 25 percent reported that the main mission of their public school is to make sure students are college- and career-ready; instead they reported that school leaders saw their school's main mission as graduating students. Even more disturbing is that in high-poverty schools, only 19 percent of counselors reported that their school's orientation was to prepare students for the future. Among private schools, on the other hand, a full two-thirds of counselors agreed that this was their school's priority.[21] Such survey data reveal how sensitive is a school's sense of purpose to the characteristics of the students it serves. It also shows how many public schools do not (at least according to school counselors) prioritize communicating to students what it takes for future success. And students who most need this information—those who have fewer means outside of school to get this assistance—are the ones least likely to be in schools that provide it. There is something amiss with a system that makes such noise about how students must be college- and career-ready on the one hand but on the other fails to itself prioritize this.

That poor information is part of the reason students fail to prepare themselves is evident where states do communicate to students, parents, and the public how prepared for college students really are. Kentucky leads the nation in collecting and disseminating information on students, starting from preschool and up through graduate school. User-friendly data reveal how high school students fare in college based on their secondary-school record. Making this information readily available to the public and being particularly proactive about making sure it gets in their hands has changed educational practices in the state. Colleges and high schools have started a dialogue about expectations, and high school coursework designed to reduce the need for remediation has been introduced. One consequence of this new information is that today more of Kentucky's high school students are graduating college ready. Remarked the executive director of an organization spearheading the data-collection effort, "You can't expect people to fix something if they don't know it's broken."[22]

This anecdote indicates that providing administrators and parents (and others) with more accurate information about how kids are doing can influence school priorities and practices. Plus, encouragement (and pressure) on students can improve student outcomes. Recall the study of Florida elementary school students discussed earlier in this chapter; it found that parents helped their children with homework more often when their child was held to higher grading standards. The researchers ruled out the possibility that this added parental effort was the effect of more homework; they conjectured instead that it was due to the "signals" their children were sending to their parents via their lower grades. This added assistance probably helps explain why some children with harder-grading teachers wound up learning more than did the children with more lenient-grading teachers: parental intervention enhanced the quality of education that the child received.

We know elsewhere from studies that parents get more involved with their children's education when they have reason to be concerned about how well their children are doing. It's reasonable to suspect that low standards have the perverse effect of reducing investments by parents and others in children's education, which further contributes to their lower academic achievement.

Here's a concrete example of how parents can become more involved with their child's education when schools are more demanding. Taiwan, Korea, and Japan are three countries known for their rigorous educational system and the high demands placed on their students. In these countries, it is common for families to ensure success by making significant investments outside of the school system. Families send struggling sons and daughters to what are called *bu xi ban* in Taiwan, *hagwon* in Korea, and *juku* in Japan. These "cram" or "shadow" schools help students keep up with the content of their school work, especially in mathematics. Noteworthy, too, is that, in these countries, students' academic performance tends to be among the highest in the world; even the "low-performing" students do quite well, usually better than our average student. It's likely that the high expectations provoke more effort from students, and also encourage families to invest in and monitor the quality of education to ensure that their children succeed.

In some sense, the claim that higher standards bring about more parental involvement is counterintuitive. One might expect that parents concerned about their children's education would make *more* rather than *less* investments in their child when standards were low—parents somehow should feel the need to compensate for a mediocre or bad education, not complement it.

It is true that low expectations *do* result in a high level of parental involvement in their child's education. Yet, as I take up a few chapters from now, this level of parental involvement in America is both selective *and* of a peculiar form. Parental investment is *selective* in the sense that it tends to be made by parents hoping or expecting their children will attend competitive colleges. It is *peculiar* insofar as it is commonly directed at insulating their children from the widespread practice of low expectations characteristic of our educational system. But more on that later.

CURRICULAR TRACKS AND BELIEFS

Before moving on, let me briefly address one other way that low standards can affect student effort and learning. In chapter 8 we'll see that one of the consequences of low expectations is that schools place students into various curricular tracks, one of which is typically a college-preparatory track. This practice often starts as early as elementary school—when, for instance, students are separated into a "talented and gifted" or "honors" class. At such an early age, this practice may in a subtle way undermine effort. This separation may establish or reinforce the belief among students, teachers, and parents that there are "smart" kids and "less smart" kids. When students are led to believe that their intelligence is fixed rather than influenced by effort, they work less hard. And they respond less constructively to academic setbacks as these are interpreted as reflecting on their fixed rather than changeable attributes. On the other hand, when students believe that their intelligence is acquired through effort, they are more apt to feel challenged and work hard.[23] Effort and work habits can be undermined in settings where school systems perpetuate a belief that academic ability is innate.

It isn't easy to get students to work hard in school. But doing so is easier when students are given clear reasons why it matters—which is something our educational system does not provide enough of. It holds students to low standards, it supplies them with poor information about their future prospects, it makes it hard for outsiders to judge how students are doing and what future opportunities are *really* available to them, and it perpetuates the belief that academic accomplishments are inherited rather than the result of hard work. For all of these reasons, student effort and performance is lower in the United States than it should be. And the standards to which students become accustomed set the bar for where students aim, as well as the work habits and expectation levels they acquire.

Perhaps the fact that U.S. students remain optimistic about their future prospects and confident in their skill levels, regardless of their actual prospects and abilities, can be chalked up to the sunny disposition and endless optimism of American youth. Students who reach the conclusion that opportunity awaits them regardless of their performance and choices in school have judged correctly: for many, exerting higher effort and investing more into their education do not have a clear or immediate payoff. To the extent that students weigh the benefit of hard work against its cost, they may reasonably deduce that effort doesn't pay. But this also means that students succeed without developing good work habits, the value of perseverance, or self-discipline. While low effort can be successful in the short run, as seen in the next chapters, it is not in the long run. But this message is one that our educational system does not adequately convey to students.

In his book *Lessons from Privilege*, Arthur Powell makes the case that at one point elite college-preparatory schools had the mission of educating an economically, although not always academically, elite segment of society. These schools succeeded even with those not inclined toward mental exertion, through a school system that provided high academic standards along with strong incentives for hard work. On this Powell comments ironically that our educational system "gave educational incentives to students who already were its more privileged, but [gave] few similar incentives to anyone else."[24]

His point remains a good one: our schools do give some students reason for hard work, and it tends to do so with students who are already advantaged. But those who would most need external reasons to apply themselves, along with the support needed for this to pay off, are often the ones who least get it.

The next chapter discusses one consequence of this: students often wind up in college both ill prepared for and unaccustomed to college standards. They also bring with them expectations of high grades for little effort. For college success and beyond, though, effort, skills, and knowledge matter. But that message isn't communicated very well. This underscores the importance of figuring out how to motivate students to work hard in school, a charge our schools have not taken on. As I'll show in the next three chapters, the consequences for all of us of students' underperformance are quite staggering.

4

Low Standards Compromise Higher Education's Mission

Low expectations in our schools help explain why America's students underperform. Let's move now to discuss why low performance matters.

In this chapter I address one reason low performance matters: it weakens the mission and effectiveness of our higher educational system. While most states now require high school students to take three years of math to graduate, few states actually require their students to *know* math before graduating. Not surprisingly, many do not. The same holds true of many other abilities and knowledge areas that students should have mastered before they enter college. When youth arrive at our colleges unprepared, it is both unfair to them because they've squandered their important formative high school years and a very wasteful way to use scarce education dollars.

As an illustration, consider Sharasha Croslen and her cohort. In 2007 Sharasha graduated from the Bronx Leadership Academy High School and was accepted into a local community college. Despite having taken three years of high school math, upon entry she found herself without the ability to solve very basic math problems. Once in college she enrolled in remedial math. Furthermore, six out of every ten students from her high school who went on to local community colleges had to enroll in such classes to relearn (or learn for the first time) what was expected of them out of high school. "I know this is stuff I should know," Sharasha said with exasperation, "but either I didn't learn it or I forgot it all already."[1]

This creates a problem for our colleges and universities: a very high percentage of students attend without having acquired the skills and knowledge expected of them as college students. While youth are increasingly attending college, stagnant performance in high school means that a growing number of them are not college ready. Between 2007 and 2009, community college enrollments alone grew by 17 percent. To accommodate the growing numbers of college students who lack adequate preparation, colleges have adjusted their policies and practices. These adjustments have been costly—both for students and for society at large.

One adjustment has been the one just described: the increasingly common practice of offering "pre-college" curriculum to students not yet ready for college-level coursework. A second trend is that colleges have been easing up on what they expect of students. But even these two trends have not been sufficient to make sure students succeed in and finish college; a third development is that more and more students just drop out.

COLLEGE PREPARATION AND THE GROWING RELIANCE ON REMEDIAL CLASSES

Despite our not having a uniform definition of what it means to be "college ready," many, likely even most, students who enter college are not. Most colleges (especially two-year schools) require newly admitted students to take placement tests in writing, math, and English to determine their level of preparation. Those who fail to demonstrate competency are often steered into taking what are alternatively called remedial, pre-college, or developmental classes in the subjects they failed to pass. Such classes are "pre-college" in the sense that credit earned in them cannot be applied toward a student's degree. Best to think of these as noncredit courses teaching high school content and skills. But students (and taxpayers) still pay for them.

Abundant evidence attests to the fact that many high school students today graduate unprepared for higher education and hence in need of remedial coursework. Recently, in California, 83 percent of students enrolling in state community colleges failed to show college-level competency in math, and 72 percent were not college ready in English.[2] In New York City 74 percent of public school graduates attending local community colleges were not college ready in English and math.[3] In the City University of New York (CUNY) system, half of all students recently failed CUNY's entrance exam.[4] More than half of the entering freshmen at the University of Alaska similarly failed various college competency tests.[5] In 2008 one-third of new college students in Colorado needed to take at least one remedial course.[6] A national study by Strong American Schools estimated that 43 percent of the students in community colleges and 29 percent in four-year colleges require remedial classes.[7] Not surprisingly, almost half of all math classes offered at some of our nation's community colleges are remedial ones.[8]

Enrollments in remedial classes tell us something about college-going skills. But we know this by other measures as well. One of the better and more consistent indicators of college readiness among the college-going population comes from the ACT, a test that measures academic achievement among high school students preparing for college. Colleges around the nation use the ACT for their admission decisions. ACT's college-readiness criteria recently indicated that one-third of high school graduates were not college ready in English, over half did not meet its expectations for college math, half did not meet its social studies standard, and 71 percent were not ready for college biology. Only one in four test takers met all four college-ready standards.

The Manhattan Institute has another way of measuring college readiness. According to its standard, only about one-third of ninth grade public school students are ready for college four years later.[9] Among Hispanic students, the figure is an abysmally low one in five.

Too many youth with college and career ambitions start college underprepared. Confronted with freshman classes lacking many basic skills, colleges have been put in a bind. One way they have responded is by expanding their menu of remedial classes. Currently, about three-quarters of colleges offer at least one remedial course in reading, writing, or math. Among community colleges all or nearly all regularly offer such courses. Nationwide, over one-third of college freshmen enroll in these classes; at the nation's community colleges more than half do. These statistics aren't a good gauge of the magnitude of unpreparedness, however, because remedial courses are not always mandatory for those who fail to show competency in a subject. Even in cases where they are mandatory, students, professors, and administrators often find ways to get around this requirement.

Moreover, typically one or two classes can't fix a student's deficiency. They often arrive with very large deficits needing consecutive remedial classes. Among students who recently entered California's community colleges, a majority was not merely deficient in math but placed two or more levels below the first-year standard. About a third also placed two or more levels below college-level reading and writing. Enrollment in multiple remedial classes is typical for students who enter with especially weak reading skills; such students will usually enroll in four or more remedial courses. For some students *an entire first year of college* consists of taking classes for which they earn no credit.

Poor preparation for college creates a dilemma: the more remedial classes students are expected to take, the less likely they are to complete them and their college degree. Of those students who take remedial classes in community college, probably fewer than a quarter of them complete their degree— half the rate of those who do not take remedial classes.[10]

Moreover, offering and expanding remedial classes to accommodate the academic deficiencies of incoming students doesn't ensure that they actually take these classes, nor does it solve the problem of unprepared students in credit-bearing classes. On the first point, as indicated above, states and individual colleges differ in their policies on remedial course requirements. In the state of Washington, for instance, students at some community colleges are seven times more likely to be enrolled in a remedial course than they are at other state community colleges. This difference is an indication of variation in policies among the state's two-year institutions, and not reflective of the distinctive characteristics of their students. As is true in Washington, many states commonly lack a uniform definition of the skills they require of new college students. This inconsistency also reveals disagreement over the best way to assess students on these skills and variation in the treatment of those students who arrive at college lacking them. At some schools, students may simply be "advised" to take a remedial class, whereas other schools will make it mandatory.

Even in states where remedial courses are mandatory when students fail placement tests, there can be exceptions to this rule. Or a lack of college-level skills may not preclude students from taking college-level courses. For instance, in California all community college students must take placement exams. But if they fail one, they are not required to enroll at their placement level, and in fact many students do not.[11] Finally, testing out of remedial classes does not always mean students are college ready; sometimes the tests are very easy to pass. Research by Michael Kirst shows how low the bar is set by colleges for requiring remediation. Thomas Bailey, director of the Community College Research Center, puts it this way: "Students who pass the placement assessments may still lack many of the skills and knowledge that are essential for success in college."[12]

Shortly, I'll take up the problem created when so many students are clueless about how unprepared they are for college, but you can see here (as well as from the last chapter) that it's no wonder why: we don't do a very good job communicating to students what it means to be college ready.

It's clearly pricey to have so many students come to college unprepared. It's costly on many fronts, but let's look simply at the expense colleges incur from having to offer these remedial courses. Such courses require faculty, space, equipment, and overhead that could have been used for other educational purposes. In the Chicago City College system, about 6 percent of the entire budget—or roughly $30 million—is diverted to such classes. In recent years in Florida, over $118 million each year in public funds has been spent on remedial classes. The City University of New York spends $33 million each year on their remedial course offerings.[13] One estimate in California put the cost to that state's taxpayers at about $300 million a year; an Ohio estimate placed it at $130 million a year in that state.[14] The organization Strong American Schools attempted to calculate the cost of remedial education nationwide for the year 2005; it placed it at about $3 billion a year in extra tuition payments. About $2 billion came from taxpayer subsidies to higher education; another $1 billion came from students' tuition payments for these classes.

The full cost of students having underdeveloped skills exceeds these numbers by a long shot though. Taking remedial classes delays graduation and the beginning of students' careers. This delay and added expense can be incredibly discouraging for students who thought they were prepared for college only to find out that they were not. Many of them eventually drop out, and dropping out comes with its own social costs. A study of the comprehensive costs associated with underprepared students just in the state of California estimated that total to be an astonishing $2 billion to $6 billion a year.[15]

The obvious point here is that we'd be much better off if students arrived at college better prepared for college-level classes. What that means is apparent, because it's clear what students have to do to beat the odds of requiring remedial coursework. High school coursework is the best predictor of which students wind up needing it. Not surprisingly, students in remedial college classes are likely to report that their high school classes were by and large undemanding. A high school student taking no more math than second-year algebra is twice as likely to take a remedial math class as is a student who took a calculus class.[16] Among students who took fewer than four years of English and fewer than three years of math, social studies, and science, only one in eight was college ready according to the ACT standard. By contrast, students taking the college-prep core during high school were more than twice as likely to be ready in both math and science.[17] Seventy-one percent of students who took calculus met the ACT math standards, while only 7 percent who took less than three years of math did. Among those students who took biology, chemistry, and physics in high school, 47 percent met ACT's science benchmark, while only 11 percent of those who took less than three years of science did.[18]

High school coursework is a good predictor of who will need remedial courses. But it's not perfect. Unfortunately, even excelling in high school and taking a "college preparatory" curriculum does not guarantee that students acquire the necessary skills and knowledge for college. A study of college transcripts among California students revealed something that shocked everyone: students who took advanced English courses through the twelfth grade were just as likely to need remedial English courses in community college as were students who stopped taking English in tenth grade. The reason for this was that high school English teachers were teaching lower-level skills than were expected in college—they emphasized story lines instead of arguments about meaning.[19] Nor are grades and class rank great indicators of whether or not students will pass placement tests. In fact, many students who wind up in remedial classes in college took the most difficult classes their high school offered, and a majority of them also had a GPA of 3.0 or higher. Clearly something is amiss when the transition from twelfth grade to what is essentially thirteenth grade is so misaligned in terms of expectations. It's possible that the culprit here is colleges with unreasonably high expectations. But that's unlikely. These too have been under pressure.

COLLEGE STANDARDS

In addition to offering remedial classes and requiring students to take them, colleges have adjusted to their students' lack of preparation another way—by lowering their own expectations. Most college students (about 80 percent) attend what are considered to be nonselective colleges. Such colleges have an open-door policy that allows just about anyone with a high school degree to attend. Community colleges in particular—which serve the role of providing all students with an open door to a college degree regardless of preparation—are under pressure to keep this door open, even for students without the requisite skills and knowledge. This is largely due to an admirable belief in the equalizing role of education and an insistence that colleges compensate for institutional, social, and perhaps temporary personal failures or shortcomings. In 2010 the president of the American Association of Community Colleges expressed this view while commenting on a proposal to end open-door admissions at Chicago's community colleges: "Community college has always been an open door for college. We have taken everybody. . . . I hate to see that philosophy—to improve quality by denying access to the most at-risk students. . . . We need to find some way to take care of these students. We can't just leave them out there."[20] His remark captures well the attitude of many who want to keep a door to higher education open for all, even if it requires making college less demanding.

While admirable and quite unique from an international point of view, the American impulse to provide such open access conflicts with the desire to protect educational standards. Remediation offers one way to negotiate this conflict. In addition, community colleges in particular—which have some latitude in defining whether and when students need to take remedial classes—may lower their standards to advance their mission of providing access and enrolling students. Particularly in our new era of declining financial commitments to higher education, the pressure to admit and retain students (thereby earning their tuition dollars) has never been higher. It would be no surprise if institutions were finding ways to lower their standards to encourage students to enroll and stay. And as discussed above, merely enrolling students in remedial courses doesn't necessarily fix the underlying problem of inadequate preparation and poor study habits.

One recent study examined changing community college practices across the nation; it concluded that faced with the growing need for remedial classes, community colleges were responding by "softening" their requirements. One way has been to allow students to take a required remedial class any time before graduation; another way has been to make requirements for remedial classes flexible so that students can bypass them. Finally, some colleges have begun offering credit for courses with high school content, such as intermediate algebra.

Commenting on such trends, the study's author concluded that "community colleges were sacrificing standards in the interest of protecting access."[21]

At least in some schools or in some portions of the college curriculum, the fall in college standards is also indicated by grade inflation, which has made failure in college more difficult. As mentioned in chapter 2, grades in college have been going up at the same time that the amount of time students spend on their studies outside of the classroom has fallen by a third. Among college seniors earning decent grades today, very few demonstrate proficiency in various tasks measuring different types of literacy expected of college graduates.

The best evidence that college graduates today are graduating with weaker academic skills comes from a periodic national study of literacy among Americans. The National Assessment of Adult Literacy (NAAL) tests participants on the meaning of texts encountered in daily life. The most recent (2003) survey of nineteen thousand Americans found that average literacy among those with a college degree declined significantly between 1992 and 2003. Fewer than one in three graduates scored high enough to merit a "proficient" stamp in literacy; this was down from 40 percent in 1992. For purposes of the study, proficient is defined as "using printed and written information to function in society, to achieve one's goals, and to develop one's knowledge and potential."[22] Another national survey aligned with the NAAL measured literacy among college students during their final year of study. It found that among students in two-year colleges, fewer than one in five was proficient in quantitative literacy, and among those in four-year institutions, only one in three had acquired this proficiency.[23]

The less demanding nature of some college courses around the nation, as evidenced by both the weaker skills of college graduates and by grade inflation, has been blamed on several different trends. Many have pointed to the rise in importance of student evaluations and the growing tendency among colleges to want to "keep the customer happy." Because universities operate in an increasingly competitive market, they are responsive to their "consumers"—students and, to a lesser extent, their parents. If students want a more flexible curriculum in which good grades are easy to come by, competing institutions eager to please them will comply. Whatever role this factor might play, it is still true that the less challenging nature of college coursework can also be traced to a less well-prepared student body and to the work habits they bring. This makes the task of developing the advanced skills expected in higher education a more difficult undertaking. The sociologists Richard Arum and Josipa Roksa report evidence of this in their recent book. They conclude that the least prepared students make little academic progress during their first two years of college, which contrasts with the significant gains made by the best-prepared students.[24]

The problem of unprepared students in college classes is not adequately addressed by colleges shifting their role toward remediation; remediation alone does not ensure that those in college have genuine college skills. Colleges and universities are dealing with this challenge by lowering their standards. But even these two trends aren't the only way low expectations in our public school system have compromised higher education's mission. A third and final trend is the most disheartening.

UNREALISTIC EXPECTATIONS: COLLEGE DROPOUTS

The third problem in higher education related to the large pool of inadequately prepared students is that of college dropouts. Currently, just over 50 percent of those who enroll in college complete a bachelor's degree, about the same percentage as graduated in 1960. In Texas only about 10 percent of those enrolling in community colleges earn a two-year degree four years later.[25] Given the rising number of students entering college, this means more and more are dropping out each year. And internationally, our dropout rate is phenomenally high; it's now one of the highest in the industrialized world. That half of college students eventually complete their degree compares with a 71 percent average among OECD countries and a remarkably high 91 percent in Japan.

As might be expected, dropping out of college is a particularly common phenomenon among less prepared students. Among students who take remedial classes, graduation rates sink to a third or a half the rate of those who don't. Graduation rates are especially low among students who take several remedial classes. Very few students who graduate from high school with a GPA of C or below and enter college wind up with a college degree. And yet most of such students want to attend college. Of those who actually do enroll, a surprisingly high number drop out before they have even earned a single credit![26] Reality hits many students quite quickly it seems.

Underdeveloped skills can cause students to drop out for two reasons. First, they often must take remedial classes that lengthen the time and expense to degree completion. Surprised by their need to take remedial classes, students can become angry and frustrated when they learn that they must take and pay for classes that don't count toward their college degree; it would be no surprise if this knowledge caused many of them to quit.

The evidence that remedial classes discourage college completion is not as strong as you might think though. There's better evidence for a second, more important reason why students drop out: low skills make succeeding in college difficult. And remedial classes often don't make up for this. Students who are simply unprepared for college-level work are often not aware of this and become discouraged by the mismatch between their abilities and interests and college expectations. In short, students leave high school and enter college having underestimated the academic rigor and dedication required for success. Once they realize this, they are prone to drop out. This, more than the cost or hassle of remedial classes, explains why unprepared students don't complete their college plans.

One reason students arrive at college unprepared for college work is that, as I have discussed, they did not choose or were not encouraged to take a college-preparatory course of study. Many of these students enter college with what sociologists term "misaligned ambitions." While ambitious, they haven't been clued in to how to achieve these ambitions. They are not well informed about college-level expectations or the extent to which their skills are inconsistent with what will be expected. High school graduates are often surprised to learn that if they do not pass their institution's placement exams, they must first take remedial courses in order to take college-level courses later. During high school, many have come to misunderstand what they must do to ensure college success. In twenty-eight different focus groups involving a total of 257 community college students, investigators asked students about their high school experiences, finding that "the vast majority expressed frustration about what they perceived to be low expectations in high school for their academic abilities and a lack of information about community college."[27]

Students in these focus groups also reported being uninformed about college expectations and requirements, and wished they had made better use of their time in high school. Students repeatedly said that their schools had not encouraged them to take hard classes. "They don't tell you [the requirements to prepare you for community college]. After you graduate from high school, you figure that out: Oh, these classes they told me were options weren't actually options," is how one put it.[28] Weak student skills and poor information prove a lethal combination for too many youth.

Lack of information means that many high school students often just infer about college what they have learned in high school: that successful completion of a course happens without significant effort. Students also bring with them expectations about standards and grades. Researchers at the University of California, Irvine (a selective institution), estimated that one-third of students there expected Bs for class attendance. One college senior put it this way: "If someone goes to every class and reads every chapter in the book and does everything the teacher asks of them and more, then they should be getting an A like their effort deserves."[29] Students arrive at college with inflated beliefs not only about their academic preparedness but also about the ease with which they have to work to get a decent grade.[30]

When through their college experience and actual performance students discover how underprepared they are, many revise their expectations and drop out.[31] Simply in terms of lost productivity, the cost to society of having such underprepared students drop out of college runs in the billions of dollars a year.[32]

Low standards lead to low student effort, with too many students leaving high school without the skills, knowledge, and abilities we expect of them. A high percentage of these underprepared students still wind up in college. The cost of reeducating them runs in the billions of dollars a year. But even with these "second-chance efforts," colleges have a hard time maintaining college-level standards; not surprisingly, these have been slipping over the last few decades.

But even lowering standards and reorienting instruction to compensate for incoming students' shortcomings are not enough to ensure that college students succeed. Instead, too many students just give up on their college plans. By international standards, our college dropout rates are a testament to this problem. These high rates alone tell us that the gap between our K–12 system and our colleges and universities is a costly one.

Not only is it expensive for everyone involved—students who are prepared, students who are not prepared, parents, taxpayers, and American society in general—but there is also a disturbing ethical dimension here. There is something unsavory about an educational system that in spirit offers opportunity to all but in practice disproportionately benefits a select, advantaged group—in terms of both those who successfully negotiate our colleges and universities and those who run them. But, without a more seamless K–16 school system, there is not much chance we'll be able to remedy these problems. In later chapters I'll turn to discussing this problem, and remedies to it, in greater detail. For now let's turn to more evidence of how low expectations in schools harm us all.

Reduced Productivity and Increased Wage Disparities

As almost everyone knows, Social Security and Medicare are on shaky grounds. Recent projections by the United States Department of Health and Human Services put the expected long-term deficit for these two programs at about $45 trillion in present-day dollars—that is, over the next seventy-five years the United States expects to spend $45 trillion more than citizens will pay into these two programs. How we should respond to this shortfall is the subject of heated public debate. Some advocate increasing the retirement age and reducing benefits for wealthier retirees, others favor higher payroll taxes and less generous benefits for everyone, and still others argue for radical changes to shift responsibility for providing health and retirement insurance from the government to individuals.

But there is another way to reduce Social Security and Medicare's projected deficit, and it is one that is rarely if ever discussed: improve the quality of education so that the working generation produces the wealth needed to pay for the elderly one.

Education has long been considered a key to economic growth and prosperity. Economic models of growth almost always include some measure of what is called "human capital" as one factor explaining economic growth over time, as well as differences in growth rates across countries. Until recently, though, empirical applications of these models have almost always measured "human capital" through *quantitative* measures of how well educated citizens are in a country—for instance, by using the average time that citizens have spent in school, or by the percent of the population with a high school diploma.

Yet new research is providing compelling evidence that the importance of "human capital" on growth and income in a country is not best measured by the *quantity* of education that citizens acquire but rather by the *quality* of that education. While on reflection this seems obvious—who would say, for instance, that a youth sitting through high school hooked up to his or her iPod the entire time makes him or her more knowledgeable or productive?—the policy implications can be quite dramatic. The assumption that duration in school is what matters leads to policies focusing on high school graduation rates and college retention. Recognizing that it is quality and not quantity that matters means focusing on what students have learned as well as how to improve that learning. Let's turn to look at what research now says about the importance of cognitive skills on an individual's and a nation's income.

WAGES AND WAGE INEQUALITY

That one's education plays a big role in how much a person earns seems indisputable. Nowadays someone with more formal education than a high school degree on average earns twice what someone with at most a high school degree earns.[1] Yet proving that education *causes* higher income isn't so easy. There are two reasons why staying in school longer could be associated with higher earnings. One is that the longer one is in school, the more one gains the cognitive and noncognitive skills (such as diligence and an ability to negotiate intraoffice politics) that are valued in the workplace. If stronger cognitive (and noncognitive) skills make citizens more productive, then we should see this reflected in wages, because greater labor productivity on average translates into higher wages: when a person acquires more of these skills through the educational system, he or she typically is more richly rewarded in the workplace via a higher-paying job or a quicker promotion. This explanation is rooted in the presumption that more time in school increases one's skills, thereby increasing one's wage-earning potential.

A second explanation for the relationship between time in school and wages is not a causal one. It's possible that people who are more productive to begin with—due to some family, genetic, or cultural advantage they may enjoy—are more likely to remain in school. The association between length of time in school and wages is simply a consequence of both being correlated with the underlying characteristics of people who are able to tolerate—possibly even enjoy—spending time in school. These underlying characteristics, rather than schooling per se, are what are really driving the relationship we see between time in school and earnings.

The first explanation—the common assumption that persistence in school improves people's productivity—leads to the conclusion that good policy seeks to retain students as long as possible. The second is less sanguine about the social benefits generated by our educational system. While somewhat at odds, these two explanations share in common the assumption that labor markets reward those with higher cognitive skills. The question, then, is to what extent can we credit our educational system with the skills acquired by those who successfully negotiate it versus credit the inherent characteristics of those who stay in school?

For the moment, at least, let's bypass this underlying, more complicated question by going directly to the link between cognitive skills—the skills we *expect* schools to teach our kids—and labor-market outcomes.

Figuring out the link between cognitive skills and labor-market outcomes has become a hot area of research; scholars have begun examining various measures of cognitive skills during youth to see if they help explain earnings sometime down the road. These studies have been pretty consistent in showing that youth who acquire greater cognitive abilities (typically measured by a variety of different test scores) earn more money as adults, independent of how long they are in school. This work supports the contention that the academic and nonacademic skills acquired during youth are important for explaining later life outcomes such as earnings and educational attainment.

The evidence for this conclusion is becoming clearer and more compelling with time. In one of the earliest studies, the economists McKinley Blackburn and David Neumark found that between 1979 and 1987 earnings among males reflected not just their educational attainment but the cognitive skills they had acquired years earlier.[2] After this publication, others quickly followed. These too have found that even very modest increases in cognitive ability during high school can result in a noticeable increase in annual earnings later on; one study estimated that over thirty-five years of work a fairly small increase in skills translated into an average of over $100,000 in additional income during the person's lifetime.[3] Another study found that the role of educational attainment per se on earnings ten to fifteen years after high school was much less significant once high school seniors' cognitive skills were taken into account; moreover, high school skills explained a good share of future college-going decisions.[4] These and other studies like it are distinguishing the separate roles played by time in school versus cognitive skills. Most conclude that cognitive skills measured early on do a better job predicting earnings than does how long students remain in school.

New York City's Department of Education recently compiled detailed information that further sheds light on the importance of youth's acquired skills on lifelong outcomes. The department examined third graders in 1999 who had (according to test scores) somewhat average reading ability to see how they had fared by high school graduation time. Very few of those students who by the eighth grade had somehow become excellent readers dropped out of high school (only 2 percent did), and a full 86 percent of these students graduated with New York State's honors diploma. On the other hand, those students who somehow by eighth grade had slipped to become weak readers were as likely to have dropped out by graduation time (19 percent) as they were to have graduated with an honors degree.

The emerging consensus based on research such as this is that even moderate increases in youth's measured cognitive skills can have a significant impact on their lives in terms of educational attainment, career, and income. And studies in countries such as the UK, Sweden, and Canada are finding that the same holds true in those countries as well.[5]

Of course none of this sheds light on the key question raised on the previous page about what *causes* some to acquire higher cognitive abilities during their youth than others. With reference to the study above in New York City, what accounts for wide variation in how much children grew academically between the third and eighth grade? Was it due to differences in their teachers or to the curriculum they were exposed to? Or did their families instill (or fail to instill) a love of reading in them? Whatever the source, we know that the level of cognitive skills kids demonstrate as early as middle school—however these are acquired—plays an important role in lifelong outcomes.

Careful studies trying to isolate the effect of schools from students' characteristics show without much doubt that schools *can* matter. And these studies also show that where education policy and practices result in students doing better—they get better grades, higher test scores, or succeed in more challenging classes—these students also wind up staying in school longer. In a sense, you could say that success in the present breeds success in the future. In fact, some researchers have concluded that acquired cognitive ability early in life goes a long way toward explaining who graduates from high school and who doesn't, who persists in college and who drops out. This means that, to the extent that schools can provide youth with a rich educational experience and successfully get them to work hard in school, students will benefit directly from higher wages as well as indirectly from remaining in school longer.

In terms of schools' contribution, we can say more than this. For one, we know that students learn more in some school systems, schools, and with certain teachers than they do with others. A recent study underscores this point. It measured the impact of fourth-grade teachers on college-going decisions, teenage pregnancy, and adult earnings; the researchers find that teacher quality influences all of these outcomes. Simply in terms of earnings, they estimate that replacing a poor-quality fourth-grade teacher with an average one results in a typical student earning $52,000 more over his or her lifetime.[6]

But it is also true that the unevenness in our school systems means that, in some schools or in some classrooms, schools don't make as much of a difference as they should or could. For instance, too many students *don't* have good teachers. This mixed answer means that simply asking the question about the relationship between time in school and labor-market outcome bypasses the crucial intermediary question of the relationship between time in school and cognitive abilities. Schools matter the most when students want to learn, when there is a strong curriculum, and when teachers are effective. For too many students, one or more of these factors is missing. The real challenge we face is to *make* schools matter.

We know that the knowledge and skills people acquire over their formative years are not evenly distributed; if it's true that labor markets reward skills rather than time in school, then outcomes such as income inequality should be at least partially traceable to the underlying inequalities in cognitive abilities within society. After all, in the United States growing wage inequality over the last few decades can be traced to the growing demand for skilled labor (leading to higher wages) and the falling demand for unskilled labor (leading to lower wages). Since 1950 the association between education and wages has been getting stronger; it has been especially strong since 1980. And the link between cognitive skills and income has also become stronger.[7] These trends are partially motivating the scramble for admission to top universities. They should also imply that differences in cognitive ability may play a larger role in growing income differences among us.

To what extent can wage inequality in the United States today at least partially be due to the underlying distribution of cognitive skills in the population? Some years back, the economists Derek Neal and William Johnson investigated wage differences between black and white males to try to explain why black males made so much less than white males. Initially, they found that race alone seemed to be the best explanation, thus suggesting some form of labor-market discrimination. But then they took into account information on these men's cognitive skills at the end of high school. Once they accounted for this, they found that the wage gap between white and black males nearly disappeared—that is, white and black males earned more or less the same *if they left high school with the same cognitive abilities*.[8] They thus concluded that the black-white wage gap was largely a product of differences in the quality of education received by youth from different racial backgrounds and was *not* primarily a product of labor-market discrimination. Other researchers using different data sets have reached similar findings: differences in measured cognitive skills do a better job explaining racial wage differences than does race per se.[9]

If differences in cognitive skills at least partially explain racial differences in income, perhaps they might also help explain differences among countries in the extent of wage inequality within their boundaries. After all, many European countries have much less income inequality than we do in the United States. Could this be at least partly due to educational systems that lead to less dispersion in cognitive skills among their citizens?

Explaining why income inequality is different in one country versus another is a daunting task. Among other factors, we'd need to consider differences in labor-market rules such as minimum-wage laws, the role and influence of unions, taxes and social spending, and so on. This is exactly what Stephen Nickell did some years ago to try to sort out the importance of inequality in cognitive skills within a country to explain why income inequality differed among countries.[10] Taking data from various OECD countries, he examined differences between the best and most poorly educated citizens in these countries (as measured by their scores on international literacy tests) and the degree of earnings inequality. The figure below reports his findings;

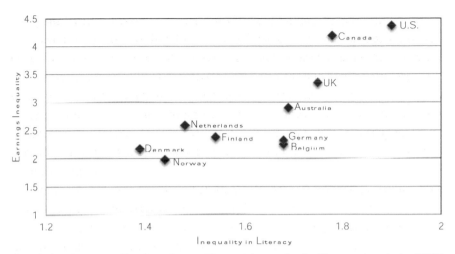

Correlation between Earnings Inequality and Inequality in Literacy Levels in OECD Countries

as shown, there is a very close correlation between the two. Here you see a measure of the range of literacy levels in countries on the horizontal axis; on the vertical is a measure of inequality in earnings. There's a clear pattern: countries with wider literacy gaps among citizens also have higher levels of wage inequality. You see, too, that America has one of the highest measures of both literacy and wage dispersion.

While highly suggestive, the figure displays a simple correlation and doesn't take into account other factors within countries that may also explain wage inequality. For instance, you would also want to take into account the different role and influence of unions. Most believe that variation in the role unions play in different countries' labor markets is a key factor explaining the degree of wage inequality within a country. Nickell explored this possibility and concluded that unions do help reduce disparities in income; however, in the large scheme of things, he found their role was a minor one, especially compared with the large role played by the underlying distribution of literacy levels.[11] While the jury is still out about whether cognitive skills are as important as Nickell finds in explaining cross-national differences in inequality, almost all studies find some role for them. Noted economist Tyler Cowen recently summed up his read of the evidence this way: "The problem [of income inequality] isn't so much capitalism as it is that American lower education does not prepare enough people to receive gains from American higher education."[12]

NATIONAL INCOME AND ECONOMIC GROWTH

If it is true that higher cognitive skills increase people's productivity and thus ability to earn more later in life, and that the distribution of these can be linked with the distribution of income within a country, then this association should also be reflected in the aggregate. By that I mean that aggregate income—income for a country, say—should be higher when citizens are better educated. Attempts to tease out the factors explaining economic growth (rising income) should find that having better-educated citizens corresponds with higher income. While many past studies support this, until quite recently all have relied on *quantitative* rather than *qualitative* measures of citizens' education. But as I discussed above, quantitative measures may not provide good information on how well educated a population is.

It's difficult to figure out the importance of cognitive skills for a nation's economic growth because finding internationally comparable measures is hard. But this problem has been significantly reduced by the growing availability of data from international tests that make cross-country comparisons of citizens' literacy possible. This availability has given rise to a burst of new research on the economic significance of educational quality.

In one of the earliest such studies, the economists Eric Hanushek and Dennis Kimko used international student test scores to try to disentangle the relationship between educational quality and growth. To do this, they measured the *quantity* of education in each country—that is, how long on average citizens spent in school—to isolate the importance of quality per se. Controlling for quantity, they found that a reasonable but not overly ambitious increase in test scores in a country (one standard deviation) corresponded with a one percentage point increase in the country's growth rate.[13] Moreover, they found that once you controlled for the quality of education in a country, quantity (how long citizens remained in school) had *no* effect on a country's growth rate. This is important because they also found that there was not always a close link between quantity and quality: some countries with relatively well-educated populations based on time spent in school scored quite poorly on literacy tests. Looking across countries, then, they concluded that the amount of time citizens spent in school is not a good measure of how well educated a nation's citizens are. Instead, to explain growth, we must look more directly at qualitative measures of education. This finding set the groundwork for a flurry of other research that now casts doubt on the usefulness of time in school for explaining economic growth.

For instance, Serge Coulombe and Jean-François Trembley evaluated growth rates among fourteen OECD countries over a thirty-five-year period to see if changes in literacy across time and across countries could explain growth rates. They found that literacy rates did a good job explaining growth patterns both across and within countries. Moreover, they too found that literacy rates were better at predicting economic growth than was the average number of years spent in school.[14]

Subsequent attempts to challenge these findings have used different data sets, time periods, and countries and employed different methodologies. In the most comprehensive study, Eric Hanushek and Ludwig Wößmann examined extensive data on OECD countries over the period 1961–2003. They concluded that measures of academic achievement in a country were strongly associated with economic growth, while the quantity of education in these countries was not.[15] Collectively, such studies have reinforced the basic message: when it comes to the importance of education on growth, it is the quality of education in a country that matters, not how long citizens spend in school. One study, in fact, estimated that if several decades ago we had embarked on a successful campaign of educational reform that had raised our students' achievement levels to those found in South Korea or Finland now, our nation's gross domestic product today would be about 10 percent higher.[16]

So far in this chapter, we've discussed the impact of educational quality on individual outcomes such as educational attainment and income, as well as on national income and its distribution in a country. The main point is that the quality of education in a country matters more for explaining these outcomes than does how long citizens persist in school. But many other outcomes associated with having a well-educated population also matter to us. On this point, research on educational quality has not yet caught up with prior work done based on educational attainment.

A few years ago, authors in a book edited by the economists Clive Belfield and Henry Levin quantified the savings that improved high school graduation rates would have on various public expenditures. Their collective findings were astonishing. The careful studies included in this volume estimated that each additional high school graduate saves the government $39,000 in health care expenses over that person's lifetime and generates $60,000 more in taxes, that a 1 percent increase in male graduation rates would save society over $1 billion a year in costs associated with crime, and that eliminating high school dropouts among women would result in an $8 billion to $11 billion annual savings in federal welfare expenditures.[17] While future research will surely tell us whether it is educational attainment per se that matters or the *quality* of that education, at this point common sense says that it is the latter. Finding a way to improve the quality of education students receive will have many more benefits than simply those associated with economic growth and reduced income inequality.

One final word before moving to this section's last chapter. Very recently, OECD researchers took on the ambitious task of estimating the economic impact of improving the quality of education in OECD countries. For each country, they simulated the effect on economic growth of very modest and attainable increases in the cognitive abilities in youth over the next twenty years (a total of one-quarter of a standard deviation improvement in each country—a quite modest increase). In America they predict that such an improvement would translate into an increase in GDP over the next eighty years of $40 trillion.[18] Compare that number with the combined Social Security and Medicare shortfall estimated over roughly the same period that I mentioned at the start of this chapter. They are remarkably similar. This estimate means that if we could achieve only modest improvements in our schools over a period of two decades, we would generate the wealth sufficient to sustain the expected Social Security and Medicare payments that otherwise threaten to bankrupt our federal government.

A second very recent study by some of the same authors asked a similar question: What if there were a gradual change in student performance over the next twenty years resulting in American citizens being as well educated as those found in today's top-performing countries? They concluded that seventy-five years from now our GDP would be 36 percent higher.[19]

So what does all this mean? It means that policies that stress retention, second chances, college access, increased high school graduation rates, and the like may not generate all that much in social benefits. That is, not unless we are sure that students learn more when they spend more time in school.

Unfortunately, for too many students, that is a big assumption to make. Our big challenge is to *make* schools matter, and that should take the top spot on education's agenda, not goals related to duration in school.

It also means that solving the conundrum of student underperformance in America not only can address our country's vexing problems of income inequality and growth; it could at the same time generate the wealth needed to help solve many other challenging public-policy problems.

6

Low Standards Harm Those We Assume Are Helped

Let's turn now to a last and most important way low expectations harm us: they harm those we *assume* they help.

Having low expectations of what knowledge, skills, and abilities students should gain means that there are substantial differences in the quality of education they acquire. It also means that educational quality becomes subject to the demands of parents, the motivation and aspirations of students, the propensities of school principals and administrators, and the ability level, knowledge, biases, and commitment of teachers. In the American context such variability means that those most in need of a quality education—those who disproportionately rely on formal education for their knowledge and skills—too often don't get it.

We all know that socioeconomic origins are closely associated with the cognitive and noncognitive skills students acquire. The question is why. There is no agreement on the complete answer to this question, and, as is easy to imagine, it's a complicated one to answer. However, a key *part* of the often overlooked answer lies in the organizational features of our educational system that fail to give students from disadvantaged backgrounds a fair shot at a quality education.

EDUCATIONAL OUTPUTS

I'll start first with documenting differences in the skills and abilities acquired by students from different socioeconomic groups. Of course, such gaps cannot be attributed solely, or maybe even primarily, to schools since schools are only one way in which youth acquire knowledge and skills: prenatal care, interactions in the family and with peers, health-care access, family expectations, and other out-of-school experiences also shape one's knowledge, motivation, work ethic, and aspirations. Genes, or innate ability, also play a role.

In all countries, students' socioeconomic background is one of the most important predictors of how well youth do in school, both in terms of specific skills acquired as well as educational attainment. What's not clear is the extent to which this association is due to factors specific to the formal educational system, versus influences outside of education such as mentioned above. We do know, though, that in some countries students' background characteristics are more influential than in others.

In particular, we know that American youth from disadvantaged backgrounds have *especially* low academic skills when compared with their counterparts in other wealthy countries. Here's some of the evidence. Every year or so, comparative test scores across nations are released, leading to much hand-wringing about the quality and *comparative* quality of a nation's school system. One such test, the Programme for International Student Assessment (PISA) assesses the skills and knowledge of fifteen-year-olds to evaluate whether students at the end of their compulsory education have acquired the knowledge and skills expected of them to succeed as adults. The PISA is a well-regarded test; for example, a student's performance on PISA's math assessment has been closely related to such later outcomes as whether or not the student completes high school or attends college.

Students who take the math PISA are categorized into one of seven groups (or levels) based on the score they achieve. The lowest score ("Below Level 1") is reserved for students whose performance on the test is so low that the test is not helpful in measuring their math competency. Students scoring in the next range, Level 1, exhibit only the most basic math literacy, such as an ability to locate information in a simple table, do addition, or compare two columns of numbers. Students who score at or below Level 1 are not considered to have the level of literacy needed to successfully function in today's society.

The 2006 PISA assessment of students' math literacy estimated that a full *28 percent* of fifteen-year-olds in America fell into this Level 1 or below category, a figure significantly above the percent in other OECD countries. For example, in Canada only 11 percent of fifteen-year-olds fell into this category.

More significant, though, is that American students from the lowest socio-economic rungs were much more likely to be "illiterate" (Level 1 or below) than they were in other countries, and this is true for both math and reading literacy. In fact, students' socioeconomic indicators have been found to be more than twice as important in the United States in predicting students' literacy levels than they are in Canada. Among thirty OECD countries, only two other countries had a stronger association between students' socioeconomic background and their science literacy than had the United States.[1]

Other studies based on different measures of students' literacy levels and socioeconomic status have likewise concluded that upbringing in America is a stronger predictor of literacy levels than is true in many or most other countries. In examining how well eighth-grade students from different socioeconomic groups did on an international math test (the TIMSS), another study found that only two countries among nineteen rich ones had a larger gap in average math literacy levels between low and high socioeconomic students than did the United States.[2]

Not only does socioeconomic background seem to matter more in the United States in terms of the literacy level youth achieve, it also seems to be a stronger predictor of how long youth remain in school. While college *aspirations* and even enrollments are much more equitably distributed in the Unites States than they used to be, this is not true of attainment. Somewhat irrespective of their background characteristics, more students today aspire to and even enroll in college. However, the characteristics of those who wind up with a college degree remain strongly skewed by class. As chapter 4 discussed, a very large percentage of students who begin a course of study in a two- or four-year institution do not complete it. Low-income and minority students are the ones who disproportionately end up dropping out.

On this score, one study of youth in the late 1980s is telling. It found that only 57 percent of those students from families in the bottom 10 percent of resources graduated from high school, compared with a 98 percent graduation rate among those students from families in the top 10 percent of resources. Among these graduates, the college-going rate for the bottom 10 percent was 34 versus 80 percent for the top 10 percent. And of those attending college, the percentage that actually finished was 32 versus 63 percent. Putting these all together, only 6 percent of youth in the bottom 10 percent of family resources graduated from college, whereas almost *half* of the youth from the top 10 percent did. While college-going rates among high school graduates from poor versus wealthy families differed only by a factor of 2.4 (34 percent versus 80 percent), this figure is extremely misleading. Missed is the fact that many low-income students don't even *graduate* from high school, and when they do and manage to make it to college, more often than not they don't finish. So more telling is that the most advantaged American youth may be *eight times* more likely to graduate from college than are the least advantaged ones.[3]

And even when they do attend and complete college, low-income students graduate from quite different institutions than do high-income students. Among the nation's most competitive colleges and universities, three-quarters of the students come from families in the top quarter of the income distribution, whereas only about 3 percent come from families in the bottom quarter. By this calculation, then, high-income students are *twenty-five times* more likely to attend one of our elite institutions of higher education than are low-income students.[4]

This difference in where students go to college matters for a number of reasons; one is that going to a select college where you are surrounded by students expecting and planning to graduate from college increases the odds that any particular student at that institution is *herself* more likely to graduate. Going to a nonselective college, on the other hand, *in and of itself* increases the odds that a student won't complete her college degree.[5] This is especially true for those attending community colleges; regardless of background characteristics, levels of academic preparedness, and aspirations for a four-year degree, students at community college are much less likely to complete their BA than are those who start their studies at a four-year institution.[6]

So where one goes to college matters. But a more important reason for lower educational attainment among youth from disadvantaged backgrounds is the inadequate preparation they get during their elementary and secondary education. Half of low-income high school graduates who apply for admission to a four-year institution may not be even *minimally* qualified to enroll in college. And unprepared students very often just drop out.

But what explains this low level of preparation? There are a couple of possible explanations.

EDUCATIONAL INPUTS: UNEVEN SCHOOL QUALITY
Why students' socioeconomic background plays a more important role in their educational outcomes in the United States compared with other coun-

tries is a puzzle. It could be that disadvantaged youth here versus those in Europe or Canada are *especially* disadvantaged, so it isn't right to equate them. American culture and an inadequate safety net may mean some American youth are particularly left adrift. There is some truth here, and I'll return to this in my concluding chapter. However, there is also a tendency among Americans to think that our problems of racial and ethnic divisions, an "underclass," a breakdown in the family, drugs, and youth who live for the now are somehow distinctly American ones. We think of Europe as consisting of homogeneous and happy populations embracing a more collectivist ethos than do we. But such beliefs are off the mark. They underestimate the degree of social division in other countries, they misjudge the success we've had with many of our immigrant populations, and they mischaracterize the degree to which Canada and Europe face less challenging problems with their youth than do we.

Another of the more popular explanations for the stronger link between students' background characteristics and their educational outcomes is that, unlike other countries, we rely heavily on local funding for our schools. This makes the quality of education contingent on community resources. Poorer communities wind up with less well-financed schools, and kids in those communities suffer the consequences of a lower-quality education.

Poor and minority students in the United States indeed on average attend schools that are less well funded and that employ less effective teachers than do their richer or whiter counterparts. Just based on dollars to school districts, high-poverty districts in the United States spend considerably less per student (by last count, on average $825 per year less) than do those districts with low levels of poverty. Comparing districts with high versus low minority enrollments, the funding gap is slightly larger: high-minority districts in the United States spend almost $1,000 less per student each year than do those districts with few minority students. Multiply this by a typical class size of say twenty-five, and on average in schools with high levels of poor or minority students classrooms have $20,000 to $25,000 less in resources.[7] One could well imagine that this $25,000 could make a noticeable difference in how much students in these classrooms learned, particularly if you account for the probability of this $25,000 more in resources accumulating over years and years of schooling.

While students' background characteristics make a difference in terms of the resources available in their district, it is also the case that resources *within* school districts are disproportionately allocated to the more advantaged students—a bias that further shortchanges minority and low-income students. This happens primarily through the allocation of less experienced (and therefore less expensive) teachers to schools with higher concentrations of low-income and minority students. Among the largest fifty school districts in California, forty spent less on teachers in their high-poverty schools than they did on teachers in their low-poverty schools.[8] A study of ten large school districts throughout several states found that in each district, low-poverty schools employed teachers earning significantly more than did the high-poverty schools. These latter schools also employed fewer teachers and staff members, and received fewer unrestricted funds, than did their lower-poverty counterparts in the district. And such differences can add up. Some low-poverty schools within a district received $1 million more in funding than did an equivalent-sized high-poverty school within the same district.[9] While surely an outlier, it is still true that funding inequities within districts result from education's unfair financing rules.

In addition to being taught by younger and less experienced teachers, low-income and minority students are also more likely to be taught by teachers teaching out of their field. In high schools across the nation, students attending high-poverty schools are twice as likely to be taught by such teachers than are those in low-poverty schools. This is particularly true when it comes to math: nationwide, 41 percent of middle school math classes in high-poverty schools are taught by teachers without a certificate or a degree in math, more than twice the rate found in low-poverty schools.[10] Such qualification gaps are especially unfair given that research findings clearly show that student achievement is directly linked to such teacher qualifications.

Low-income students also suffer from more adverse "peer effects," meaning that the composition of students in the classroom—which numerous studies find to be an important factor in explaining a student's achievement level—is less advantageous. Consider immigrant students in the United States. Studies have found that they attend schools with a much less advantaged socioeconomic mix than do immigrants in other OECD countries. On the other hand, native students in the United States typically attend schools with a better socioeconomic mix than do native students in other OECD countries. This is because sorting among schools along socioeconomic class is particularly strong in America.

Policies allocating school resources both between districts and within districts, and the way students sort among schools and districts, certainly help account for America's stronger link between students' background characteristics and their academic success. In this sense, critics are right that how we fund schools and allocate teachers among them contribute to the lower academic achievement of disadvantaged groups. However, a more important explanation is that America's schools contribute to and reinforce the achievement gap through our approach to school curriculum.

CLASS AND CURRICULUM

High school students usually have some sort of a distributional requirement—for example, they might be required to take three years of English and two years of math between ninth and twelfth grade. Such requirements can be met by taking a variety of math or English classes. Students also have a fairly wide range of electives, allowing them to take physics or physical education, calculus or business graphics, and so forth. The point is that the content, rigor, and expectations in two students' courses of study during secondary school can be very different, even when they attend the same school. By and large, low-income and minority students disproportionately take less demanding classes in middle and high school, and it is this that harms them down the road.

There are two ways that wide latitude for individual choice in one's course of study harms disadvantaged students. For one, low-income and minority students disproportionately are placed (or place themselves) in a less demanding "track" when schools offer various levels of rigor for the same class. In addition, they frequently choose less demanding or rigorous courses when permitted to do so. It may be that the more rigorous courses are not offered at a given high school, in which case it is more accurate to say that the choice of, say, an AP versus a non-AP history class was not made available to them.

Beginning in middle school and especially by high school, American students self-sort into particular curricular tracks. The practice of separating students into different tracks based on ability is justified by the belief that academically capable and high-ability students benefit from a more academic curriculum, and those with less ability or motivation benefit from a vocational or less rigorous curriculum. Offering lots of options to students allows there to be "something for everyone," which a more "one size fits all" curriculum would not do. If inheritance or earlier or ongoing environmental influences largely determine how much students are going to learn, then it may be pointless—perhaps even counterproductive—to subject some students to more rigorous classes.

In practice, though, the separation of students into tracks almost always involves more than "ability." Often you'll find that an "ability group" consists of students from almost all ability levels.[11] In his analysis of tracking practices in one school district before a court order to detrack, Kevin Welner found that controlling for GPA and test scores, white students were 2.3 times more likely than were African American students to be placed in the highest-track English class. Even among students identified as "gifted," African American students were much less likely than were white students to be in the more advanced tracks.[12] Exactly why and how race and social background come into play in these outcomes is not clear. Essentially, the question boils down to this: Why do we hold different students to separate standards? For now I'll hold off addressing this question as it is the theme of the next three chapters.

One consequence of the high degree of choice involved in both middle school and high school is that, in addition to being placed in less advanced tracks, low-income and minority students take less demanding courses than do their white or Asian counterparts. In middle school black and poor students are more than twice as likely to be in a general or pre-algebra math class than are their white and nonpoor counterparts. Children with a mother who has not completed high school are two and a half times more likely to be in a general math class compared with students whose mother has a BA or higher. Among recent high school graduates, students whose parents had attended graduate school were more than three times likelier to have pursued a rigorous course of study than were students whose parents were high school dropouts.[13] Even if you look strictly at those students in fifth grade with equivalent academic performance, by eighth grade one study found that the white students among them were almost twice as likely to be enrolled in algebra then were the black students.[14]

Black and Hispanic students also take fewer science and foreign-language classes during high school, and when they do take science, they frequently enroll in a general science class. Almost one-third of black and Hispanic graduates in 2004 took no more than general science, and they were half as likely as white students to have taken a second year of chemistry, physics, or biology.[15] White students are two to three times more likely to take precalculus or calculus than are black and Hispanic students, and almost twice as likely to take mostly honors English classes. Asian and white students take precalculus at four to six times the rate of American Indian students. Students from high-socioeconomic-status families are three times more likely to take advanced science classes than are those from the lowest socioeconomic rungs.[16]

College preparatory classes in the form of Advanced Placement (AP) courses, which are available in a majority of high schools around the nation, also disproportionately enroll white, Asian, and higher-income students. In 2005 only 6 percent of those who took AP exams were black, a percent only slightly larger than twenty years earlier.[17] Even among students with similar income, black and Hispanic youth enroll in AP courses at significantly lower rates than do their white counterparts.

While it's true that the practice of allowing students to take different types of courses does allow for greater homogeneity in ability level in the classroom—a practice that could make pedagogical sense—it's also true that it accommodates an educational system that permits a wide range of ability levels to develop. When your school (and social) system results in large achievement gaps that increase over time, the practice of separating students by "ability" allows this underlying problem to persist by accepting it instead of redressing it.

WHY AND HOW CURRICULUM MATTERS

So why does all this matter? It matters because the significance of these differences in coursework taken cannot be overstated. They are a key factor explaining our achievement gap. How much students learn and how ready they are for college depends on the classes they take. Also, the rigor of classes sets students' expectations, which can further set them behind once they enter college. Finally, the wide range of choices contributes to a fractured educational system that fails to send consistent and clear signals to students about how best to achieve their future goals. The premise that it is good policy to hold different students to different standards (starting at an early age) is not well-supported, nor is it at all consistent with what we know by looking at the experience of countries that don't engage in this practice to the same degree we do.

Importance of Classes

It should probably go without saying that what and how much students learn depends in large part on the classes they take. That much seems like common sense. Yet the belief that we should offer different students different levels of rigor and offer them choice over which classes to take is a widely held one. Underlying this is a theory that, for students to learn the most, the demands and expectations need to be in line with their ability level, and that more learning occurs when students are grouped in homogeneous ability-level groups. Many also believe that ample student choice over coursework best meets and supports students' wide range of interests and trajectories. In theory this should help students stay in school longer, learn more, and hence be more successful.

Yet the overwhelming evidence is that just about all students benefit from some period of exposure to rigorous coursework with high expectations. One key to learning is to motivate students (and parents) to make the investments in learning that are necessary for gaining the sorts of skills we want students to have. And this is more likely to happen if the curriculum is demanding and viewed as important. When low-income and minority students wind up in classes with less content, with fewer demands placed on them, and when they are headed for a nonselective college (where high school performance doesn't matter as much), these three things conspire against them.

Growing evidence supports this claim. A number of scholars have undertaken careful research to distinguish the role played by course selection in explaining how much students learn. Such studies take account of students' background characteristics and measures of their ability and knowledge, and then examine what happens when otherwise identical students take different courses. The purpose here is to try to best get at what is called in social science research "the counterfactual." That is, what *would* have happened had a student taken a *different* set of classes? Short of discovering a time machine, this question is really impossible to answer with certainty. The best way to investigate this question—or others like it—is to "control" for factors other than course selection (ability level, family income, gender, grades, and so on) that might otherwise explain why some students have learned or know more than others. Statistically speaking, once these have been controlled for, you can then identify what the effect of x is on y, *holding all else constant*. This is the best way to get at the question: What if students had taken a different course load (x)? How much would they have learned (y)?

Careful studies along these lines find compelling evidence that students who take more challenging courses learn more. One such study found that the math gap between students with low and high indicators of socioeconomic status could be almost completely explained by differences in the courses they took. That is, poorer students who pursued coursework similar to that pursued by richer students, performed almost as well on math assessment tests.[18] A U.S. Department of Education study found that even students in the bottom quarter of test scores learned more when they took college-preparatory classes than when they took a less demanding course of study.[19] Another study of twelve thousand high school students concluded that all students benefited from taking algebra in the eighth grade, regardless of their math skills.[20] Taking advanced math courses in high school also has been shown to improve students' math skills. In fact, math course selection can account for why some students learn three times more than others in high school.[21]

Accelerating instruction—moving up the age at which students are exposed to certain curricula—has also been shown to improve performance. One study found that when students take algebra in the seventh or eighth grade rather than in the ninth, they do better in math later on, regardless of their initial math ability.[22] Another looked at poor-performing eighth-grade English students to see how they did in their ninth-grade English class. It turned out that ninth graders who ended up in low-level English classes were much more likely to get Ds and Fs in English than were those who took college-preparatory English classes. In fact, students of *all* initial eighth-grade ability levels were more likely to flunk out of the low-level English class than they were a college-preparatory English class!

A final illustration shows the importance of course selection on learning. One researcher compared groups of ninth-grade students with relatively similar SAT scores and tracked growth in these scores based on their subsequent course-taking patterns. Regardless of starting point—some in ninth grade scored in the bottom quarter of the test distribution while others scored in the top 10 percent—students who took advanced-track courses did noticeably better on the SAT test three years later compared with those who took lower-track classes. For instance, among the lowest-scoring ninth-grade students (those who scored in the twenty-fourth percentile of the national distribution), those who took advanced coursework in high school on average scored in the forty-second percentile of SAT scores three year later, while those who took the least advanced coursework wound up in the twenty-ninth percentile of the national distribution.[23] Such a pattern held true for all ninth graders, regardless of their initial starting point.

In addition to how much one learns, course-taking choices can also change students' trajectory. Evidence shows that students who take harder classes wind up staying in school longer. This also influences subsequent course selection. In one study, researchers investigated the influence of a student's eighth-grade math track on high school outcomes. Taking math skills into account, they found that those students in remedial math in eighth grade consistently fell behind those who had been in a regular eighth-grade math class.[24] The main reason for the increasing math gap was the different math courses that students in the two groups took. Placement in remedial eighth-grade math classes seemed to set students on a path that caused them to fall farther and farther behind in high school. Not surprisingly, low socioeconomic students were most likely to be on this low-level trajectory. Already by eighth grade, then, these students were being launched on a track that was closing off future opportunities.

Not surprisingly, then, public schools with a more academic focus—that provide a uniform, core academic curriculum to all students—improve both overall student performance as well as reduce disparities among different social groups. In one of the best studies to date, three researchers examined data tracking the progress of over ten thousand students. They examined how much science and math these students learned between eighth and twelfth grade, focusing on the importance of schools' curricular offerings and academic orientation. Controlling for students' socioeconomic status, race, gender, starting academic skill level, and courses taken over the four-year period, they concluded that students in schools with a greater emphasis on an academic core and with less student choice learned more, and gaps among them shrank.[25]

The importance of coursework is evident too from research examining the impact of changes in countries' national curriculum. Such studies provide strong proof that requiring students to take a common academic course of study reduces disparities in academic achievement, whereas separating students into more academic and less academic tracks widens inequalities and reduces social mobility. A number of educational systems overseas formally "track" students, some at quite a young age. In these countries, students are placed in (or in some instances choose) an academic- or vocation-oriented track at some point in their school career. Compelling evidence shows that the earlier this is done, the more uneven educational outcomes are and the lower is social mobility.

Northern Ireland has an advanced academic track (called "grammar school") into which it places high-scoring eleven-year-olds. Not long ago it began allowing students to enroll in these schools even if they hadn't officially qualified. New (previously underqualified) students chose these schools, driving up enrollments by 15 percent. Substantial increases in national test scores followed, among both poor and nonpoor students.[26] On this basis, the evidence seems pretty clear that this change in policy was a successful one.

Similar changes in other countries reinforce this conclusion. In the 1970s Finland stopped the practice of separating students into vocational and academic tracks at the age of eleven, instead requiring all students to follow a common, uniform, academic curriculum until age sixteen. A recent study concluded that this change increased social mobility in Finland.[27]

In 1973 Romania increased the age at which students chose between an academic and vocational track from age fourteen to age sixteen. One immediate result was that, after a short period of time, the number of students eligible to attend Romania's universities (they had passed the university entrance exam) increased. This increase came disproportionately from more socially disadvantaged students.[28]

These and other examples indicate that countries with early tracking systems gain nothing in terms of average performance; early tracking instead seems to primarily result in greater disparity in student achievement. This explains why scholars and policymakers increasingly conclude that early tracking reinforces the association between socioeconomic characteristics of students and their educational attainment and performance. Two well-regarded scholars succinctly expressed this when they concluded that "tracking has harmful effects for low-socioeconomic students while providing no benefit in terms of average student achievement." Rather than transforming students and providing them with opportunities, early tracking replicates the existing socioeconomic order. In our own country, there is a price students pay when they choose (or are placed in) a less demanding course of study, even among those students who might not initially have highly developed cognitive skills.

Students learn more when they take more demanding classes. When they take easier classes, or when they are in lower-level tracks, they often are subject to lower expectations and fewer requirements. Teachers tend to focus their more demanding expectations on those in the highest tracks; for others, coursework is frequently more routine and repetitive. Students in higher-tracked classes benefit not so much from the fact that the curriculum is more closely associated with their ability level but that they have more opportunities to learn: the coursework is more demanding and engaging, and the classroom climate more focused. Moreover, more qualified or effective teachers usually wind up teaching these classes. As a result, more advanced classes offer learning environments that all students would benefit from. It's for this reason one scholar pithily termed tracking "the rationing of opportunities."[29]

The above comment implies that an educational system that was organized and designed to provide all with the opportunity for a high-quality, uniform course of study might look quite a bit different from ours. I'll return to this theme in the chapters ahead, but it bears suggesting that the status quo meets the needs of some segments of society, and this helps explain its persistence. It is similarly true that changes to the status quo—having an educational system where all students follow a similar curriculum—would involve significant changes to our current educational system. This too explains why it isn't easy to alter the current practice of providing different students with a distinct curriculum.

Information and Expectations

Disadvantaged students are much more likely to take less demanding classes. This has implications not just for what they learn and how hard they are expected to work in school, but also for their expectations, their aspirations, and their ability to achieve these aspirations. Once students are placed in a track or in classes of a certain level of difficulty, they usually make similar curricular choices in the future: students' willingness to pursue challenging coursework is influenced by the extent to which they've done this in the past. Students who take less advanced classes in middle school are much less likely to enroll in college-preparatory classes in high school, independent of their ability.[30] Not being in a top track seems to convince students that they do not belong there, and in consequence those who remain in the least advanced tracks fall farther and farther behind their peers. Part of the explanation for this is that putting students in lower tracks places students in a less demanding or engaging educational environment where they learn less. But it also leads students to misunderstand or misjudge the benefits of taking harder classes.

As chapter 4 mentioned, there is reason to believe that curricular tracks can influence students' self-identity and their willingness to apply themselves to their studies. But tracks also provide students with different information. High school students' knowledge about college standards, expectations, and policies—and how best to prepare for college—depends on their high school coursework. Students in lower-track classes tend to have less information about college, in part because they are not likely to be contacted by college outreach efforts. Students in more advanced classes, on the other hand, receive much clearer information about how to best prepare for college. While higher-track students receive the message of the importance of preparing for college, others receive the message that graduating from high school is all that matters for college. Such ignorance on college standards is exacerbated by the fact that those students in less advanced tracks are held to lower standards and are more likely to get good grades for subpar performance. In this way they are more likely to wind up with ambitions inconsistent with their likely path. Students with such "misaligned ambitions" are too often set up for failure.

Lower-track students also fail to get the information they need for another reason: schools aren't designed to give them this information. You may recall from chapter 3 that an extensive survey of high school counselors found that they did not think their schools were sufficiently oriented toward the mission of preparing students for college or a career. Instead, by a very wide margin, counselors (disapprovingly) reported that their high school's main mission was to graduate students. Counselors in high-poverty schools were especially prone to report this as being their school's priority. Evident here is that school mission depends on student characteristics. It's easy to imagine that especially for disadvantaged kids in lower-track classes the primary message they get in school is to finish.

These sorts of messages, coupled with an easy course load with good grades for little effort, are counterproductive. Students receive vague and contradictory signals about how best to get into and succeed in college. This leaves many students misinformed about how their high school coursework affects their later college options. Such poor information is especially disconcerting when acquired by lower-income students. Schools should play a more active role in helping them set and realize their goals than is necessary for students who have multiple sources of information about how to succeed. Because schools often fail to provide students with this information, successful college preparation depends on outside sources. But outside sources are precisely what many disadvantaged students don't have; they need it from their schools. In this way, the confluence of socioeconomic class and academic track results in some students having two strikes against them. Despite having similar college-going plans, lower-income students often don't take the right steps to get into a good college. And they work less hard in school. One scholar summed it up as follows: "[Lower income students] would have worked harder if they had realized the future relevance of high school achievement."[31]

Several chapters back I discussed the importance of students being motivated to work hard. When students understand how their actions today affect their opportunities in the future—how their actions help or harm their ability to realize their aspirations—their choices today are more likely to factor in these longer-term consequences. Those having a good understanding of how coursework and diligence in high school pay off are more likely to buckle down. When they don't have a good understanding of this connection—when they have what sociologists call "misaligned ambitions"—students are more likely to make plans and take actions that are inconsistent with their ambitions and that in fact can foreclose future options. But students may do this without even realizing it because they don't have a clear idea about how their actions today relate to their hopes for tomorrow.[32]

Of course lack of preparation could also reflect less ambition among disadvantaged students. But ambitions among lower-income students in high school are not all that different from their richer peers; while an "ambition gap" used to exist, today it is almost nonexistent. This is good news. Ambition is an important source of motivation, and students need to be motivated to do well in school. Yet low-income students' college graduation rates over the last thirty years have barely budged from below 10 percent; meanwhile, graduation rates among rich students have doubled from 40 to 80 percent. Such low graduation rates among poorer students are not for lack of ambition. Rather, it's partly because of misaligned ambitions: a full three-quarters of low-income students who start college drop out. This rate has remained unchanged since 1970; meanwhile, college completion rates among the top income group has grown from 55 to 98 percent.[33]

There is a disturbing ethical dimension to allowing students to skate through school without communicating to them the longer-term consequences of this. At one stage, our educational system sustains (unrealistic) expectations and supports high (though dreamlike) ambitions, and then at a subsequent stage it hands those students off to another part of the educational system that succeeds in showing that those ambitions really *were* dreams. The nature of the problem as described here is that it is hard to see that this is what is occurring. That's why it persists. I'll say more about this later, but here I'll simply point out that the hidden nature of the costs imposed on us all by our low (and uneven) standards is a good part of the reason why we don't condemn them more loudly.

SUMMING IT UP

The wide array of curricular offerings that we make available to students contributes to an educational system that leaves too many students inadequately educated. Allowing students ample room to choose their coursework reinforces rather than weakens the link between students' background characteristics and the quality of education they receive. This chapter is not meant to imply though that students' background characteristics in and of themselves don't matter—that good school policy can overcome the importance of influences beyond the school grounds. Nonschool factors play a large role in how youth do in school. For one, children tend to internalize the values, beliefs, and attitudes of those closest to them; in this way families can influence students' motivation, aspirations, propensity to work hard, and self-confidence, all of which influence how students do in school. And there are countless other ways that class, race, and income affect how well different students do.

Yet school policy can weaken such factors through a commitment to providing all students, for much longer than we currently do, a standard and uniform academic curriculum, accompanied by policies counteracting shortfalls in other aspects of students' lives. In the American context, a real commitment along these lines would require us to do two things. For one, it would require quite significant changes in the middle and high school curricula and policies around them. But such a commitment would also entail looking carefully at policies outside of those associated with our formal educational system to find ways to better support kids' ability to bring to school what is important for success. We could alternatively stick with an educational system in which some students get an excellent education because parents and students demand it. In this sense, when students get a good education, it isn't so much due to the design of our schools, but rather more to the luck of the draw—certainly not the way anyone starting from scratch would intend for an educational system to work.

A straightforward implication is that coursework should be more demanding and uniform for all students. This conclusion should be obvious, but it is at odds with so much of current policy.

But would *all* students be better off following an academically demanding curriculum? The answer is obviously no. Without a doubt, raising our expectations of all students would leave some worse off. How many and how worse, though, depends on exactly what changes are on the table. If we were to keep everything else the same except the courses that students were required to take, there would be little hope that this would matter much. In fact, it could conceivably end up making our educational system worse. I personally doubt this, but it is certainly possible. In many ways this is what almost all states have done and are increasingly doing to ramp up their expectations of students. On the whole, there have been very modest signs of overall improvement in student success. Some states are getting even more prescriptive by requiring (for instance) all eighth-grade students to take algebra or all of their high school graduates to take two years of algebra. But such policies are often enacted in name only, and when they are not, they *can* result in noticeable increases in student failure.

The point here is that marginal changes in the curriculum that all students have to take are not likely *in and of themselves* to have much of an effect on how students do. Students who have not developed the foundational literacy skills expected of them during elementary school, who fall short on family values for academic work, who have little internal desire or external motivation to learn, or who have teachers who lack the skills and knowledge to teach and use classroom time well could very well be left worse off with such policies. And the more that these other issues are left unaddressed, the weaker is the case for moving to high expectations for all our students.

III

WHY LOW EDUCATIONAL STANDARDS PERSIST

7

The Tyranny of Too Many Voices, or "Too Many Cooks Spoil the Broth"

Our educational system does not hold many students to high or even reasonably high standards. This creates serious problems, the most important of which the last four chapters described: much wasted time in school and low student effort; less effective colleges and universities; students misled about what steps they must take to pursue their ambitions; a less productive nation; wage inequality; and finally, an unfair educational system that limits the opportunities of too many students—particularly those who are already disadvantaged in other ways.

It's hard to see how this is anything other than a devastating indictment of our educational system. What possibly could explain our collective failure to address or change these low standards when everyone knows they exist and when they are associated with outcomes that all of us should find unacceptable?

Part of the answer is that, while there may be widespread agreement that we have a mediocre educational system, we don't all agree on what would make it better. Many problems in public life are of this nature—most agree that our health care system is a mess, Social Security is unsustainable, our Afghan military strategy is not working, and so on. But without a consensus about what should be different, we stick with existing policies that nobody really supports. America's political institutions are purposely biased against dramatic policy changes, so this too helps explain why change is hard to come by.

Another part of the answer to this question is the nature of public institutions that have a guaranteed source of revenue. Such institutions generate benefits (income, authority, power) for those in them, foremost among them decision makers. Such decision makers (Agents) develop a vested interest in the status quo and tend to resist fundamental change since that usually threatens their position and benefits. This conservative tendency is the nature of public institutions (or private for that matter) with stable and predictable revenue sources.

Yet there is much more to the persistence of the status quo in education than simply "we can't agree" or "change is resisted." Part of the problem lies in the complicated set of governmental entities with overlapping roles in schools, curriculum, and education policy. Particularly, given that these responsibilities and roles have evolved over time, the entire set of intergovernmental relations and responsibilities are neither well articulated nor well coordinated. It is no wonder education policy winds up being fragmented, inconsistent, and highly contested. Such an institutional environment makes coherent change very hard to come by.

While a stronger federal role (in setting standards, in financing) could help, political institutions in America do not promote the introduction of federal education policy in a way that is coherent across state and local governments. The most obvious agent of change in our educational system, the federal government, in practice often has a perverse effect, as I illustrate later with the example of the No Child Left Behind Act. This institutional environment undermines the effectiveness of federal policy and contributes to widespread skepticism over its efficacy.

A second reason for the persistence of low standards I take up in the next chapter: the constituency for high standards gets co-opted through our practice of offering a wide array of coursework for students. This practice permits a subset of students to be educated under higher standards while leaving the rest—those less concerned about or aware of the shortcomings associated with pursuing a less rigorous course of study—to a mediocre education. A final reason is that there is a strong but misplaced belief among many that low expectations reflect our commitment to the disadvantaged, and that strengthening them would harm the most vulnerable youth in our society—a topic I turn to in this section's last chapter.

Coaching a baseball team involves teaching a complicated set of skills. Among other things, it involves teaching the pitcher about release points, infielders about foot movement and timing, outfielders about how to play a line drive hit directly at them, and batters about where to place their hands and locate their bat when attempting a sacrifice bunt. The hardest skill is teaching youth the mental discipline to continually anticipate what might happen next. None of these are easy skills to teach or learn.

Now imagine that in addition to the coach's role in teaching these skills, there is a head coach who manages all of the coaches in the area. In particular, he takes parental and fan input into account to determine which coach goes to which team. Under a range of conditions, any one coach must consult the head coach before making decisions. For instance, a coach cannot attempt a sacrifice fly more than twice in a game before first consulting the head coach. The coach also cannot have a fielder play in the outfield more than two games a week without prior consultation with the head coach. And so on.

Furthermore, each year a state baseball organization holds meetings to determine if any of the rules of the game need to be changed. It may add rules under which coaches must consult with head coaches. Citizens can also enact rule changes via a referendum. The state also establishes rules for the amount of time that one particular skill can be practiced on any one day and the amount of consecutive innings a player can take the field. It also specifies the percent of the budget that can be spent on offensive versus defensive equipment, with local organizations charged with adding detailed rules about how to divide expenses when equipment is both. The state further establishes rules for how frequently chalk must be placed on the field and how often the infield must be groomed during a game; sanctions are imposed when these rules are not followed.

Meanwhile, a national baseball organization makes rules over the types of statistics that each manager must compile and post on a website. In addition to player statistics, the manager must also post information on drills used during practice, broken down by player position and whether or not the skills were designed primarily for defense or for offense. Coaches also must report any injury that occurred during practice or a game, with follow-up reports indicating how that injury was treated, how long it took to heal, and the steps taken to avoid a repeat injury.

This hypothetical account is of course intentionally a farcical one. But in some ways, it is not that farfetched a spoof on America's educational system. Educational policy formation in the United States occurs within a complex and complicated institutional setting involving a role for an array of government agencies, interest groups, and individuals. Many of the rules established by the educational bureaucracy have little or nothing to do with education's fundamental role of educating youth. Rather, it reflects a somewhat ad hoc bureaucratic system that lacks an overarching coherency and purpose. The large and complicated education bureaucracy makes controlling the process and seeking compliance with this process its top priority. And this comes at a cost of paying too little attention to the type and quality of content delivered in our schools.

This chapter argues that this institutional complexity as well as the degree of decentralization in it helps to explain why our low standards persist. We'll start first by examining the role that a decentralized educational system plays in determining educational standards.

LOCAL CONTROL AND EDUCATION STANDARDS

We've already established that the more democratic, decentralized way in which standards are established and monitored in the United States contrasts with how they are determined in most countries. Typically, elsewhere they are set at a national level, with national exams ensuring uniform expectations, coursework, and rigor across the nation's schools. It may even be at the national level where the final word for curricular decisions are made, including goals, content, and performance standards. But in what way does the decentralized nature of standard setting in America's schools affect the rigor and expectations found there, and hence affect student performance? Or does it matter at all?

In theory, at least, a more decentralized educational system that allows for greater citizen participation could result in a more demanding school system. Local communities may have much better information about how to best educate their youth. They may also be more invested in ensuring that their students are provided with a quality education, unlike remote bureaucracies that might be primarily interested in expanding the size, influence, and status of their organization. Greater central control over standards may also result in a more cumbersome bureaucracy that hampers the distribution of resources that best serve the interests of students. Finally, centralized decision making may mean that greater weight is placed on interest groups lobbying for their own benefit rather than those of students. These and other similar arguments are what you commonly hear today from those who argue for maintaining or strengthening local control and local decision making in our educational system.

So stronger local control and decision making could lead to higher standards and better schools—in the same way that just letting a coach manage her baseball team may lead to better baseball. Certainly, the rhetoric around the local control of education suggests that centralization results in policy paralysis and bureaucratic indifference. But does it in practice? Let's turn now to a theoretical argument, and some evidence for it, about why local control in fact could lead to lower standards.

Local Control and Educational Standards: A Theory

Some years ago, the economist Bob Costrell published a seminal article in which he developed a theoretical argument about why local control could lead to lower standards and weaker student performance.[1] His argument: First, assume that those who set educational standards are trying to do what is in the "public interest," where *public* refers to the population within its jurisdiction and *interest* refers to what affects the well-being of this population. Second, assume that higher standards (meaning that greater effort is required by students to succeed in and complete school) lead to increased student performance among some of those who clear this higher bar, which in turn increases future productivity and income down the road (assumptions supported earlier in this book). We can hence infer that more rigorous standards on average leave those who are able to meet them better off. Finally, add the assumption that higher expectations also mean that more students will fail to meet the criteria for success, and in consequence will drop out of school. Some such students would be left worse off than they would have been under lower standards if the higher ones *reduce* their future productivity and income by leaving them with a *worse* education.

With these basic assumptions, Costrell reasons that policymakers setting standards face a tradeoff: on the one hand, setting a higher bar improves the prospects of those who clear it, but on the other it can make those who don't worse off. He then asks: Where do officials or communities set the bar?

Costrell posited that students who pass higher standards are more likely to leave their immediate community than are those who fail them. If true, then the more local the point at which standards are set, the more concerned decision makers will be with the downside of higher standards rather than their upside. That's because local communities are more likely to face the consequences of, say, more dropouts in their communities and less likely to benefit from the upside (say, a more sophisticated level of literacy and civic engagement in the community)—because the successful youth tend to leave the community. Under these conditions, he predicted that a decentralized educational system will set lower standards than would a more centralized one where "leaving" is less of a concern.

To sum up, then: If you are an official in Elm Town determining the educational standards for children in your town, you put more weight on the prospect of dropouts that might be costly for your community than would officials in Washington, DC, who would be considering the consequences of standards for the nation as a whole rather than for any one community. After all, at the federal or national level, a "leaver" would be someone who left the country, whereas a "leaver" in Elm Town would include someone who moved away to nearby Mapleton.

There's a second theoretical reason why decentralization—as opposed to a more centralized educational system—may lead local officials to be reluctant to set high standards. If some local community unilaterally decided to establish high standards so that those in the community meeting them were better educated (and by assumption more productive), a problem arises: outsiders (say a college or a prospective employer) may not know that graduates from one public school system with higher standards are better prepared or better educated than are graduates of neighboring school systems with lower standards—unless of course a high-quality school district came with some sort of "name brand" recognition. Without this connection, a potential employer or a college admissions officer would have no reason to believe that José from Hard-to-Graduate School District is better educated than is Josie from Easy-to-Graduate School District. In fact, one district providing its students with a better education has a positive effect on other districts because it increases the average quality of the graduating pool—the average high school graduate now has stronger academic or work skills. This gives rise to the free-rider problem: communities want *other* communities to have high standards but do not want to enact them themselves. This is why private schools and selective colleges (as well as their graduates) work hard to maintain the name recognition of their institution so that outsiders perceive a qualitative difference between them and others.

But there is a big difference between a school (or school district) working to *maintain* a qualitative distinction and one working to *establish* that distinction. Yet a state or certainly a nation would not face this same problem: it is much easier for Massachusetts to establish a good reputation among employers and colleges for the quality of its schools than for the Framingham School District to do so. Setting standards at a more central level can in this way get around the free-rider problem identified above.

While a nice theory embodying common sense, it is worth asking if standard setters think in such explicit terms about the costs and benefits of where they set the bar. In academic discourse such as Costrell engages in, this portrayal is best thought of as a shorthand way of expressing a more complicated process whereby pressure groups and personal beliefs are responding to and formed by the costs and benefits outlined in this stylistic narrative. Community members to whom local education officials are responsive worry about the cost to their community of dropouts, while the advantages of holding students to higher standards aren't all that apparent. Their input and pressure reflect this concern even if it isn't explicitly spelled out in their own mind or in the minds of those who make decisions.

According to Costrell's early work, these factors—a preoccupation with the downside of high standards, a limited ability to capitalize on the upside, and the free-rider problem—can conspire to keep expectations set at the local level lower than they would be at a more centralized level. More central (or national) standard setting can in some circumstances lead to more rigorous ones than would be true if set at a more local level.

Costrell's later work (as well as that of others) has resulted in a more sophisticated and nuanced treatment of the theoretical relationship between centralization and standard setting than the simple story I've described here, and the theoretical conclusions are more complicated.[2] But the point remains that under some set of reasonable conditions, the local setting of standards can cause problems. We certainly see the problem of local governments being unable to do what is socially right in other policy arenas that share a commonality with those surrounding the setting of educational expectations. If you leave local communities to set air pollution standards or corporate tax rates, for instance, they will choose much lower ones than is socially optimal: the cost to the community is high, while the benefits only partially accrue to citizens within their jurisdiction. Despite strong demands for cleaner air during the 1960s—analogous to the demands today for higher educational standards—local communities and even states failed to enact any rules that had any teeth. Cleaning up the air (or water) did not happen until the 1970s, when action was finally taken by the federal government. Similarly, no local government (at least to my knowledge) taxes corporate income, while the federal government collects considerable revenue from this tax. In fact, local communities do the opposite by frequently granting corporate tax abatements and tax incentives to keep businesses in the neighborhood. In all of these examples, federal action can be viewed as the mechanism by which local communities and state governments coordinate their mutual interests when their unilateral action just doesn't make sense.

Local roadblocks to setting high standards would also explain why movements for them have almost all come at the state level rather than from unilateral choices made by local school districts. And while state governments can establish higher standards within their borders, the discussion above points to the potential shortcomings of doing so unless states around you are also following suit. Absent federal action, the only way to achieve this is for states and communities to band together to collectively agree on common standards.

It should now be more understandable why a movement across the nation seeking higher educational standards is taking the form of a set of curricular expectations developed by the National Governor's Association (called Common Core Standards), with states being asked to adopt them. This is consistent with individual states having figured out the dilemma they face when they unilaterally enact higher standards. We now see state governors banding together to try to do this collectively. Common Core Standards can thus be viewed as a solution to the collective-action problem created by decentralized standard setting that makes it hard for decision makers to set them high. In fact, almost all important educational reform movements over the past several decades have come from beyond the borders of the local school district—the standards-based movement, vouchers, merit pay, charter schools, curricular changes, and changes in teacher preparation and qualifications.

Local Control and Educational Standards: Practice

States jumping on board the Common Core Standards movement (as of this writing, almost all have) provides some evidence—albeit indirect—that the decentralized setting of standards is likely to lead to lower ones than most people would like. But is there other evidence that standards set at a more central level will lead to more rigor than those arising from local decision making? As I discussed in an earlier chapter, it is clear that U.S. federal proficiency standards (the NAEP) are more demanding than are those that states have established. But since federal standards are not actively used in policy formulation (and state ones are), it is not obvious that these would be the same ones the federal government would establish were they to be used, for example, to determine curricular content or to evaluate if students were meeting academic expectations.

Better evidence supports the claim that more centralized standards are tougher ones. Recently, researchers have looked to international data to see whether the existence of national standards is associated with stronger student performance. In one study, Ludwig Wößmann examined the math and science performance of hundreds of thousands of eighth graders in thirty-nine countries around the world.[3] As one indication of national standards, he separated countries that had national exams from those that didn't. In fifteen of the countries he examined, a central authority had final approval over the content of end-of-year exams. Wößmann found that after controlling for other factors in the country that help explain student performance—money spent on education, teacher characteristics, family characteristics, class size, parents' education, whether or not the student was an immigrant, and so forth—students in these fifteen countries performed at a considerably higher level than did those without this central government role. In fact, he estimated that this central role for setting educational expectations accounted for almost half of a grade-level difference in performance between these fifteen countries and the other twenty-four.

In follow-up studies, Wößmann and others have repeated the above analysis using different international data sets of student performance; in each study they reach identical conclusions. Consistently, they find that the increase in performance among students in countries with centralized exit exams at the end of secondary school is roughly equivalent to an additional half year of schooling. Based on these studies, Wößmann and his colleagues are concluding that countries achieve higher student performance when standards are set at the national level—and particularly when accompanied by national tests.[4]

Other factors help explain why America's decentralized approach to setting standards could result in low expectations. Local and, to some degree, state decisions over such things as curricular content means that across the nations' schools there is little consensus over what content courses must or must not contain. Diane Ravitch's *The Language Police* provides a fascinating description of the extent to which curricular decisions reflect local preferences (or the strength of local lobbies) for such things as the presence of women figures in history, Christian values in literature, and creationism in science. As a result, textbook publishers find it difficult to prepare a text that meets the demands of one audience while still being able to sell to another. Ravitch argues that text publishers have found that the best way to sell their books is to avoid writing or including anything that could be controversial. Consequently, history textbooks in particular consist of bland and often meaningless accounts of events that are written to appease warring parties rather than impart good historical content—perhaps explaining why only about one in ten high school seniors has a firm grasp of American history. After reviewing school history textbooks, historian David McCullough concurred with Ravitch, referring to them as "so politically correct as to be comic."[5]

Ravitch similarly argues that school literature texts are purged of any provocative content at all; instead, the selection of literature is done with an eye to social and political concerns over the race, gender, religion, and the actions taken by stories' characters. The textbook industry, which is simply interested in selling books, does this by producing textbooks that often offer a bland enough version of reality that no one can argue with it. In so doing, though, they fail to engage or develop students' critical and higher-order thinking skills. In this way decentralization contributes to policy reflecting the interests of particular groups rather than a clear articulation of what we want our educational system to accomplish.

Finally, for a variety of reasons, local stakeholders can have a vested interest in making sure that students appear to be succeeding even if they aren't. For one, in most communities property values are influenced by the perceived quality of the local schools. Parents, too, pressure schools and teachers to give their children good grades. And the entire local educational enterprise knows that the more there is evidence that kids struggle in school, the more vocal become advocates for some alternative, with charter schools and vouchers being the most threatening substitute.

SCHOOLS FROM AN ORGANIZATIONAL PERSPECTIVE

The more local setting of educational standards may contribute to them being set at a low level. This might help account for why our school system is less successful. But institutionally, our educational system is marked not just by decentralization, but also by the complex and fragmentary nature of its bureaucracy. In fact, "decentralized" isn't really the best way to characterize the organization of education in America. A more apt description is that it is incoherent or (as one observer puts it) a "non-system."[6] The balance of this chapter discusses our school system from an organizational perspective, with an eye toward explaining how and why bureaucratic features contribute to perpetuating low expectations.

The Organization of Schools

Beginning at the bottom, the most decentralized unit of leadership and policymaking in education exists in the more than one hundred thousand public schools across the United States. Here many key decisions are made, such as classroom and teacher assignment, curricular content and offerings, grading standards, and student promotion policies. While in all states educational standards are spelled out at the state level, without external criteria for what it means to pass, say, second-year algebra or U.S. history, in practice educational standards tend to be set at the classroom level. Indeed, principals and teachers typically choose what is covered in a particular class, and teachers are often the sole arbiters of course rigor and performance expectations.

Above the school is the school district. Roughly fifteen thousand school districts exist across the country, and these tend to have the most influence over children's educational experience. For one, districts typically provide about 40 percent of schools' funding. Districts commonly hire and assign teachers to schools, oftentimes setting salary levels as well (an important determinant of districts' ability to attract teachers). They also play a key role in determining curricular offerings and the extent of specialized programs of study offered (such as AP classes, gifted and talented classes, and a vocational education option). Districts are managed by a school board whose members are in most instances elected by the community. Such school boards appoint the district superintendent of education; together they determine and oversee educational policy within the district. The superintendent and the district staff—teachers, principals, administrators, and so forth—all carry out policies established by the school board and its superintendent. Districts also administer and carry out most state and federal policies and programs. Other countries rarely have the equivalent of a school district (or if they do, it is primarily administrative), as school policy is more directly linked to policy set by a central or regional government.

The legal authority for education policymaking lies with the state; such is typically carried out by the governor and a state superintendent of education (many of whom are elected). In recent years, state governments have come to play a much larger role in setting and financially supporting school policy. As I discussed in an earlier chapter, the state's role in coursework, testing, and some forms of accountability increased during the 1980s—although implementation of these policies is usually left to local districts. Today state legislatures provide about half of all education dollars, along with increasing oversight. Still, states vary widely in how much responsibility for and funding of education is taken at the state versus delegated to the local level. Almost all state governments establish curricular guidelines, define high school graduation requirements, set standards, and assess students to determine the degree to which they've reached these standards.

Although the federal government's role in education is limited, it too has expanded over the last few decades. Until recently, the federal government stuck to providing funds and regulating practices through a variety of programs and laws; its primary purpose was to support educational opportunities among groups that require or merit additional resources. Such programs and laws have been established at different times and are administered by different agencies, and often lack coordination. Typically, federal dollars are administered by state education agencies so that state agencies disburse funds and implement and monitor federal requirements. Frequently, a complex and not well-coordinated relationship among the various state and federal government agencies exists. Politically and legally, the federal government's role has been limited to aspects of education unrelated to curriculum and instruction, since historically this responsibility has fallen outside its purview.

Of note here is that each level of government—federal, state, and local—is subject to its own set of political considerations and interest groups. Each government (or "set of Agents," using the terminology of the Principal-Agent Problem) is independent insofar as local governments are not directly accountable to state governments, nor are state government officials responsible to the federal government (other sets of Agents). This means that federal policy typically is administered through both state and local governments; because its authority is often contested and its initiatives not welcome (the Agents don't agree), its ability to influence the content and quality of education is limited. This helps explain why federal initiatives usually take the form of providing money for noninstructional and noncurricular purposes. In some sense this also goes for state government—it usually can't make personnel changes at the local level (it can't replace noncompliant Agents).

In addition to different governments, nongovernmental agencies also actively influence education policy. Foremost are the textbook publishers, who can have an inordinate sway over what is and isn't taught in the classroom. Test-making companies also have a vested interest in education policy and tend to be vocal on education policy issues. Unions, courts, the business community, PTAs, local officials, principals, and teachers all have an ability to influence the policies and practices at the school and classroom level as well. Compared with other countries, local stakeholders play a much more active role in influencing what goes on in America's schools.

This institutional configuration in which policy is formed and decisions made gives rise to four interrelated shortcomings. All of these conspire against our ability to establish coherent and demanding expectations of students.

Poor Coordination and Inconsistency

As described above, America's educational system consists of three independent governments, each with responsibilities that are not well coordinated and often contested. While the roles of state and federal governments have been increasing of late, this has occurred in a fairly incoherent way without any mechanism by which the collective effect is examined (the Agents aren't coordinated). Taken as a whole, policy can often lack coherence. For example, at the same time that federal and state policies are introducing greater control over what goes on in schools, other state and federal policies are holding schools more accountable for school outcomes. This amounts to both insisting on calling the plays in a football match from an observers' booth while also holding the coach responsible for the outcome of the game. These dual trends are contradictory and contribute to inconsistent (and unfair) demands on schools.

Such inconsistency is common. The political nature of the education bureaucracy opens up many opportunities for different groups to influence policy (the Agents can be influenced by other Agents or Outsiders). And different groups seek to influence policy at different "entry" points. For instance at the school level, parents try to influence teachers and principals; community groups and unions seek to persuade local superintendents and school boards; the business community, legislators, and interest groups attempt to sway state officials. So many "entry points" for influencing policy (or Agents) would not exist under a more centralized system where differentiated practices and outcomes at each level are less possible, and where the political nature of decision making is confined. In more centralized bureaucracies, schools become more immune to variation in local politics and pressure groups. This is, of course, why so many Americans support local control—people have more of a say. But the greater role for democratic participation and pressures placed at each entry level comes at the sacrifice of overall policy coherence. This also explains why so many observers of our educational system comment that it serves the interests of Agents more than it does those of the Principal (society).

It is telling that an estimated 60 to 70 percent of school superintendents and school-board members nationwide believe that school-board meetings are dominated by people representing special interests.[7] Developing educational goals and policies within an institutional context that requires the accommodation of different and divergent voices and concerns helps explain why education policy is so political in America and why policy formulation involves difficult negotiations and political calculations. Moreover, the larger number of decision makers increases the number of veto points at each step, making change not just political but darn near impossible. Listen to one local superintendent describe what it takes to get a policy change through his school board:

> The process by which you have to seek approval on things . . . can become a roadblock to innovation. [Board members are] being lobbied by constituents and then we spend a lot of time . . . talking about things . . . [rather than] addressing the real work.[8]

A process such as that illustrated above helps explain why state standards tend to consist of laundry lists rather than coherent, clearly sequenced plans. Three scholars summed it up succinctly when they observed that "political compromise as an organizing principle for standards seems unlikely to be consistent with the principle of coherence."[9] Responding to all without prioritizing the important helps explain so many of the odd features of our schools: the multifaceted objectives that schools pursue, the wide range of classroom interruptions that are a part of the school landscape, the growing complexity of and inconsistency in the demands placed on schools, and the existence of much poorly thought-out coursework.

Plausible Deniability

In our school system, an uncoordinated and wide range of people, organizations, and interest groups have ways of influencing policy whether at the school, district, state, or federal level. This often means that in schools leaders and teachers wind up being pushed in contradictory, inconsistent, or even incoherent ways. If one were to follow through to the classroom level to make sure that initiatives and objectives were carried through (the "monitoring" in the Principal-Agent Problem), a problem emerges. When policies themselves are inconsistent, vague, or just impossible to carry out, monitoring of actual practices would reveal this. For instance, the goal of educational excellence in the classroom can conflict with the goal of high graduation rates, with the goal of coursework containing sex education and antidrug messages, with others seeking to develop cultural sensitivity among students, and with yet others for addressing disruptive behavior in the classroom. If one were to monitor classrooms to ensure that such multifaceted educational goals and objectives were being met, what would you look for? And what if the goals conflict, as they certainly would?

A solution to this pragmatic problem is to not monitor or inspect outcomes too closely so that inconsistencies between rhetoric and practice remain largely hidden from view. In the sociology literature of organizations, this is called loose coupling. A system that is "loosely coupled" means that components of the system operate without knowledge or the influence of other system components. As is true with the Mafia, in education this decoupling allows for plausible deniability. Not monitoring actual teaching and the content of classes too carefully means that you are freer to make claims about what occurs, while pleading ignorance if it's not true. Not monitoring also means that teachers have greater discretion over which demands they will and will not comply with. This too has advantages when the demands in practice are impossible to meet or just plain nonsensical.

In practice, this means that in various ways teachers have acquired a surprising degree of latitude in the classroom—a feature of our schools I've noted and commented on throughout this book. This permits classroom practices to not be closely bound by what other features of the educational landscape say should be happening or occurring in the classroom. And so you can succeed in meeting demands for more second-year algebra or AP history classes, while in practice not changing anything about the content of your class. This allows leaders to superficially meet demands that may be impossible to genuinely meet either because school resources or students' skills place limits on a school's ability to do so. And who would know?

Schools can and are responding this way to parents' and policymakers' demand for more college-preparatory courses by providing what one scholar termed "The Delusion of Rigor"—offering courses that in content are easier than implied by the title.[10] The fact that principals in the United States spend considerably less time observing and shaping instruction than do their counterparts abroad is one indication of the looser coupling, or teacher autonomy, that exists in our educational system.

In the complex and often contradictory policy environment of the United States, this loose coupling is functional: it provides institutional stability because it permits inconsistent practices and policies to persist, while at the same time giving the appearance of compliance and success. Relative school and classroom autonomy is functional insofar as it buffers the educational system from an institutional structure that regularly places new, contradictory, and impossible demands on schools and teachers. With this environment in mind, it's no wonder that teacher unions in the United States bargain hard to maintain teacher autonomy in the classroom and to protect teachers from "accountability" or other measures of their performance. Who would want to be held accountable for what we expect teachers to do, given the sort of institutional environment that they are in? The school bureaucracy does not prioritize support for teachers, nor does it provide them with coherent, consistent, or well-thought-out expectations. By contrast, in many other countries, teacher autonomy and insularity are often not of value to teachers.

In fact, just the opposite. Particularly in the best school systems, teachers work collaboratively with and are accountable to one another.

Hence the "loose coupling" that is characteristic of classroom practices in America can best be seen as a counterpart to our educational system's complex governance structure that accommodates too many inconsistent voices. When an organizational structure is responsive to a wide array of conflicting demands, seeks consensus, and lacks internal coherence, loose coupling allows it to continue to function in a relatively stable way. As put by some scholars, "loose coupling . . . is an organizational solution to institutional inconsistency in the education system";[11] it allows rhetoric to support whatever people believe, or want others to believe, is true about our educational system.

To see how destabilizing more information on what goes on in the classroom can be, one need look no farther than the No Child Left Behind Act. The simple practice of publishing test scores as the law requires by school, grade, and demographic subgroup set in motion an outcry from nearly every corner of the educational establishment. Clearly, keeping the information it has now revealed hidden allowed many to believe or say what they wanted to about what our schools were accomplishing. Among other things, the law spotlighted problems that are extremely difficult to address and, hence, for bureaucracies seeking stability and predictability, were best left unexposed.

While school and teacher autonomy has the good effect of letting teachers do what is right even if it isn't what they are told to do (and this is what many good teachers in America have to do), it also creates numerous problems underscored in this book. For one, it leads to practices that sociologist Charles Payne refers to as "curriculum anarchy." For instance, consider the observations of Boston principal Kim Marshall after he witnessed wide-ranging classroom practices at his school:

> While teachers in one grade emphasized multiculturalism, teachers in the next grade judged students on their knowledge of traditional history facts. While one teacher focused on grammar and spelling, another cared deeply about style and voice. While one encouraged students to use calculators, the next wanted students to be proficient at long multiplication and division.[12]

Not only were some of the practices he observed completely at odds with district standards, Marshall found that such "anarchy" among teachers made it almost impossible to encourage substantive discussion among them about classroom content and teaching practices.

Thus not only does the practice protect ineffective teachers and pedagogies as well as poor uses of classroom time, it can also lead to idiosyncratic coursework, the whole of which (the elementary years for instance) becomes less than the sum of its parts. It's hard to develop sequenced material if you can't count on other coursework guaranteeing a common, strong foundation; instead, classroom time is taken over by an inordinate amount of review. Every once in a while the bureaucracy does get it right in terms of seeking or encouraging best practices, but you can't assume these will actually take hold in the classroom.

Symbolic Compliance

Because of the peculiar nature of America's educational bureaucracy— policies in one branch of the government inevitably rely on compliance from school districts, principals, and teachers—state and federal governments have a limited ability to change actual practices. This is because local authorities and educators can use their discretion in deciding whether and how to comply with new rules. This structure promotes organizational characteristics that are poorly suited to effective school performance.

Because of this potential for noncompliance (one main point made in the section above), there is a bias in policy and rules to insist on specific practices and decision criteria that reduce the discretion of those who are carrying out these policies and rules. One important result is that schools are subject to rules and restrictions governing nearly all aspects of school life: school policy and personnel decisions, budgets, instructional methods, what teachers do and for how long, rules over how decisions are made, and who gets to make these decisions. Political scientists John Chubb and Terry Moe capture this predilection succinctly: "Given the widespread . . . opportunities for noncompliance, the most attractive solution is . . . [to] reduce the discretion of school personnel by specifying the kinds of behavior [bureaucrats] want."[13]

A number of examples illustrate how bureaucratic rules focus more on controlling process and decisions than on supporting and prioritizing outcomes. The first is the history behind the No Child Left Behind Act. Back in 1994, Congress passed the Improving America's Schools Act (IASA) along with the Goals 2000: Educate America Act. In exchange for federal funds,

IASA and Goals 2000 required and helped states to establish content and performance standards, to periodically assess students on those standards, and to identify poorly performing schools.

States, however, proved slow to comply with these new requirements. Six years later, only about half of them had developed both content and student performance standards, and few had complied with the assessment requirement. Frustrated by slow progress, in 2001 the federal government responded by taking a much more prescriptive approach in its No Child Left Behind Act. This act specified exactly when students were to be assessed, how assessment information was to be reported, and most importantly, how this information was to be interpreted in terms of identifying schools and districts that were not performing up to expectations. While it was widely fought at all levels, the fact that it left little discretion did succeed in getting states to accomplish in short order what IASA and Goals 2000 had been unable to do. This illustrates why policymakers seeking some change tend to do it in a way that prescribes the actions and limits the decision making of local authorities, who are then monitored to make sure that they comply with the rules. Lost in the bureaucratic preference for control is keeping an eye on what results or outcomes we seek. While to its credit, No Child Left Behind is ultimately about performance rather than process, its heavy-handed, rule-bound approach and its emphasis on compliance has doomed it to failure.

A second example comes from the way the public has come to think about what it means to be a public school. Unlike in other countries, America's public school system is commonly described or identified by its uniform adherence to bureaucratic rules and requirements. This is apparent insofar as one of the main criticisms of charter schools is that they fail to meet the definition of a public school as defined in bureaucratic terms: teachers aren't members of a union, the schools divert funds from traditional public schools, charter schools have fewer reporting requirements, they don't meet state class-size requirements, they don't follow rules for awarding building contracts, and so on. If you stand back a bit, you see that these are all funny things to be concerned about because it isn't clear how they relate to whether or not students in charter schools are getting a good education.

Here's an excellent illustration. Recently, the *New York Times* ran a very long front-page investigative article, about half the length of this chapter, on a charter-school movement in Texas. The article went into great detail on bureaucratic aspects of these charter schools, such as their choice of school décor, teacher pay and selection, and the process by which construction contracts had been awarded. In tone, the article suggested that something was or at least might be amiss with these schools. Yet in the entire article, only about 150 words—about the length of this paragraph—were devoted to the schools' educational practices and outcomes. You would have to have read this article very carefully to find out that the schools being investigated seemed to be doing better than the average Texas public school.[14]

Another example of how education's bureaucratic setting can undermine the quality of education in our schools comes from how state and local governments frequently respond to federal policy. State and local governments oftentimes go overboard making sure that their schools meet the letter of federal (and state) law, sometimes at the expense of practices that might improve their schools. This can be attributed to overly prescriptive federal government policies, coupled with the sanctions that stem from being "caught" out of compliance. Rules and the consequences of not following them give rise to a culture of compliance in which districts (and states) engage in "defensive spending" to make sure they remain in compliance. This culture makes sense given that failure to meet some fairly technical federal compliance requirement—not identifying the right number of features in a planning document, not maintaining close records of how much time was spent on particular activities, or failing to show that services were adequately offered to students in private schools—can lead to a loss of federal dollars. And these rules are often extremely complicated. For instance, to receive Title I funds, districts have to collect data demonstrating that the funds are not used to replace local funds. This requires a complicated set of calculations; to compile proof for federal authorities that they have complied with this rule, districts must master figuring out what revenue sources should be included and which can be excluded.

Further, when states allocate federal dollars to districts, they can add on their own compliance requirements. This means that districts across the nation commonly have different sets of conditions placed on their use of federal dollars—some from the federal government itself, and some from the state. The rules upon rules make it hard for districts to figure out how their dollars can and can't be spent, how much leeway there may be in rules that make less sense, and what parts of the rules may just reflect a misunderstanding of very complex laws. Moreover, how to interpret rules (and whether or not they can be bent) depends on what federal program is involved—each federal program has its own set of (often inconsistent) rules. The net effect is that districts become bound by multiple masters, each imposing its own set of restrictions, which collectively can squelch a district or school's ability to use money effectively or in innovative ways.[15] While such a culture is great for lawyers' pocketbooks, it also evokes images of the baseball analogy with which this chapter began. That analogy might not be so farfetched after all.

Here's yet one last set of examples. Funding rules set by state and federal governments are often such that they invite districts to "game the system." When states provide districts with more money for each student enrolled in special education, districts find ways to label more students as requiring special education. When one state determined districts' transportation budget based on the number of students riding the bus over a particular week, district leaders in one district encouraged parents to put their children on school buses that particular week.[16]

Hence complex and extremely bureaucratic rules around district and school budgets also don't serve students well. Bureaucratic rules over funding can result in Agents becoming preoccupied with how to get the most out of these rules rather than how to best serve students. And just complying with these rules makes it hard for districts to keep their eye on the ball. To fund schools, districts receive many different pots of money. They may get separate pots from the state for transportation, general education, teacher salaries, special education, and equalizing funds. From the federal government they may get Title I funds along with many smaller budgets for various federal initiatives. For each pot, districts commonly must comply with different rules about how the money can and can't be spent. This may involve dozens of different reporting requirements. Additionally, districts must figure out when they can combine different funds, and what this means for their reporting requirements. For many categories of funds, rules absolutely prohibit the mixing of funds. For this reason, districts will establish distinct offices that correspond with the funding source rather than because it makes educational sense to do so.

These sorts of budgeting rules make it difficult for districts to create a cohesive funding plan because organizational structure and information gathering are a result of bureaucratic rules, not because they make sense from the point of view of educational quality. Strategic decision making about resource use can't be made effectively because often the key questions we'd like to answer are unanswerable. Basic information—such as how much is spent districtwide on math instruction, or how much is spent at one school versus another—can be nearly impossible to figure out. Thus assessing the effectiveness of resource use can be a near hopeless task. And so is that of using money strategically to meet the district's biggest challenges or to advance its strategic goals. No organization designed for outcomes would put up with such counterproductive rules.

These examples are indicative of a general tendency. The organizational structure of our educational system leads to government policy that excessively controls the details of how our schools operate. This has extended into the public's definition of what it means to be a public school. So much attention to process and adherence to rules—which is more characteristic of school policy in America than in just about any of our peer countries—comes at the expense of paying attention to the substance of what our educational system should be trying to accomplish.

And schools will often bend over backward to be compliant, without necessarily really complying—recall that the insular nature of classrooms makes this possible. Success with classroom reform is measured not by whether students do better but by whether teachers did what was expected of them. The difficulty created by this institutional environment means that often the appearance of change is prioritized over real change. Governments make demands on school districts and schools over procedural issues because this is easy and doesn't require resources. Regulation and policy initiatives that prescribe choices (rather than provide funds) is a bureaucratic preference that can be explained by the complex and political nature of our educational bureaucracy.

Contrast this with what is more typical in countries with a strong central government role in education policy, where those who implement policy decisions are employed by the same government that made the policy. In this context, decisions over policy, funding, curriculum, teacher qualifications, and training are more likely to be made in a way that considers the overall objective of education policy. This goes some way toward explaining why other countries have been more successful reforming their K–12 system than we have.

The last two points here—about state and federal government policy limiting district and school discretion on the one hand, while substantial school-level autonomy exists on the other—are a very peculiar combination. And an especially ineffective one. Yet they go hand in hand: excessive, uncoordinated control is only possible with classroom anarchy. An alternative model for achieving both accountability (here, control) and autonomy (here, anarchy) could be achieved through accountability based on outcomes and autonomy backed by responsibility. But this model is much more difficult to realize in the American context. The combined effect is that the autonomy that schools enjoy is one of isolation rather than independence, and autonomy for the purpose of insulating rather than educating is not the sort of autonomy we want in our schools. I'll elaborate more on this in the concluding chapter.

Lack of Uniformity

A fourth and final illustration of how the organizational structure of our schools leads to weak and uneven educational standards is that districts' capacity or desire to respond effectively to new policies can vary significantly. To complicate matters further, even school-level responses to new policy can differ within the same district. That's because the impact of new policy initiatives and the rate of adoption depend on local conditions since districts retain considerable control over their schools. This means that there will always be unevenness in school-level capacity that limits the ability to implement policy initiatives in a uniform manner.

As an illustration, some years ago, researchers examined how schools in two different districts responded to a new state policy designed to improve children's reading skills. Even within the same district, schools varied significantly in how they interpreted and responded to this policy. This was in part because of variation in how school principals understood their district's guidance, but it was also because the district itself failed to provide consistent guidance on the new state policy. Such inconsistency in understanding state (and federal) policies is common because such policies tend to be intentionally ambiguous, for the reasons discussed above. Implementation depends on how that ambiguity is interpreted, how much leeway there is in implementation, as well as how much capacity a school has. It is common for administrators, principals, and teachers who do not agree with some policy change to ignore it.

Such discretion left to the local level particularly disadvantages poorer districts because they often lack the resources and capacity to respond to initiatives. The sociologist Charles Payne superbly describes this potential in great detail in his book *So Much Reform, So Little Change.* He argues that urban schools are especially prone to low capacity and weak leadership, and thus have a high potential for being driven by dysfunctional dynamics. Because of the wide latitude that schools are often given, it is possible for a weak professional climate to take hold in schools; in Payne's words, schools can become personality driven.[17] When this happens, the ability to address the problems of a failing school falls on local stakeholders. But local stakeholders are not equal in their abilities to do this. In some communities they can be organized, vocal, and demanding of effective schools; in others they can be apathetic, skeptical, and uninformed.

A lack of uniformity in what is taught in different classrooms, as well as the decoupled nature of teaching just described, creates a problem with sequencing coursework from one grade to the next—an eighth-grade math teacher is dependent on students' having already learned seventh-grade math in a different classroom, and so on. We can respond to this lack of uniformity across schools and classrooms in a couple of different ways. We can expect teachers to adapt to student variability—because foundational skills and knowledge cannot be assumed—by building a lot of review into coursework. Or we can rely on curriculum that does not require a clear sequencing of courses or development of specific skills.

Our schools do both, and each compromises the quality of students' education. Rather than relying on curriculum that develops depth in an area of knowledge or in particular skills, courses emphasize breadth since breadth can be achieved without the need for sequenced coursework. A recent study comparing math and science curricula across countries found that in the United States each grade covered a much wider range of topics than did classrooms in high-achieving countries. Moreover, once introduced, topics remained in the curriculum for a significantly longer period of time, rather than fading out and being replaced by new, more advanced topics. The authors concluded that "the organizing principle (if one can call it that!) seems [in math and science to be to] include almost every topic at almost every grade."[18] In addition to focusing on breadth in their classes, teachers adapt to different levels of student preparation by building a significant amount of review into their courses. This is useful for those students who (unfortunately) need it but is redundant and boring for those who do not.

To sum up then, without a more closely coupled educational system and a coherent governance structure, policy changes will often lead to individualized responses, depending on things such as a teacher's understanding of what is sought and why, principals' beliefs about the policy, who in the educational bureaucracy a principal discusses a policy with, the district's capacity to comply with the policy, the degree of insulation, and so on. And so reforms introduced at the state or federal level are unlikely to change what goes on in the classroom, or at least certainly not in a uniform way. To be effective, federal and state policies must either be consistent with what is politically feasible at the local level or be overly prescriptive—and the latter option simply invites symbolic compliance. Even when we see clear evidence that change is needed, making change happen is difficult. This is because the bureaucratic options for reform almost always ensure that intent will be different than practice. The effect of No Child Left Behind on actual practices is the most spectacular illustration of that.

In this way, the organizational structure of our educational system contributes to a system in which establishing and supporting strong educational standards is an extremely difficult undertaking. Weaker standards in turn reinforce organizational features of our educational system—decoupled teaching and classroom practices that allow the educational system to accommodate competing demands—that themselves make the introduction of higher standards extremely difficult. The process by and institutional environment in which standards are set tend to encourage breadth over depth, so that students at best gain only a shallow understanding of complex topics and advanced thinking skills. The ability of the existing system to transform education at the classroom level is limited, and until this is addressed there is not much room for policy to improve student performance.

I'll end with a personal anecdote that I believe underscores some of this chapter's themes. A few years ago, I attended an open house at my son's school. In one classroom, I found prominently posted on the wall the state's GLEs (Grade Level Expectations) for that class. These were impressive-sounding expectations set by the state containing ambitious goals; for instance, my seventh grader would be expected to analyze causal factors that have shaped major events in history. Documents sent home by this teacher also made reference to the centrality of these GLEs in her class. Later, when inspecting the work my son brought home, I found no recognizable connection between it and the course's stated GLEs. The main skill his class was developing seemed to be the ability to color maps according to the teacher's preferred coloring scheme—the ability to analyze major turning points in history seemed to have been transformed into the ability to follow instructions.

Being a parent not unlike Eric Zorn (you'll be meeting him in the next chapter), I contacted my son's vice principal and asked him to explain why the school's learning goals were so inconsistent with its actual practices. After a lengthy discussion where I diplomatically did my best to get a direct answer from him, he finally admitted that there wasn't much he could do to influence classroom practices. He also hinted that the real problem was the organizational strength of teachers that left classroom practices beyond his control.

But unions are only a symptom of the larger problem. The governance system of our educational system is such that it makes it extremely difficult to fix problems, even when it is obvious that they exist. We have a school system that insulates classrooms and often prioritizes symbolic compliance with laws and policies.

This chapter has sketched out one set of reasons that helps explain why low standards persist. Let's now move to a second by introducing Eric Zorn.

8

Exit, Voice, and the "Something for Everyone" Curriculum

There is tension in the premise that we hold our students to low standards; even a cursory acquaintance with high school students tells you that the competition for college spots can be ferocious. Countless parents go to extreme lengths to give their children a leg up in this competition.

Take Eric Zorn of the *Chicago Tribune*, for instance. Eric recently lamented the steps he was taking to ensure that his son succeeded in school. Calling himself the "pushy, enabling father," he argues with teachers and even his son's principal over minor grade disputes; he runs out in the rain at seven in the morning to get a blank DVD for his son who had neglected to do so himself (thereby helping his son avoid turning in a project one day late); and he pays hundreds of dollars to enroll his son in an after-school program so that he will do better on an upcoming test. This is all part of his strategy to get his twelve-year-old into one of the nation's best colleges or universities.[1]

I'll explain shortly how Zorn's preoccupation with his son's success is consistent with a school system that doesn't expect all that much from students. But first, let me make the point that Zorn is pretty typical of many parents. Parents today spend considerable time and money investing in their children's future. Consider, for example, that today's college-educated mothers spend a full *nine hours* a week more on child-care related activities than they did a couple of decades ago. The researchers who uncovered this trend attributed it to parents' willingness to devote more time to improving the odds that their children have a good shot at a competitive college. These extra hours can be primarily attributed to mothers driving their children around to their various extracurricular activities.[2] That is, this extra time is explained by parents' growing willingness to do things for their kids (like arguing with vice principals and principals) that they didn't do before.

In many ways, all of this extra time and effort by parents makes sense. As top students know, the most competitive American colleges and universities are becoming increasingly difficult to get into; and even the "second-tier colleges" have become so competitive that they are now sometimes referred to as "the new Ivies." This trend is occurring because more students want to get into top colleges, but space in them has not grown much.

Several reasons explain why more students are seeking admission to top colleges. For one, the number of students going to college has grown. Students are also more mobile and are willing to travel longer distances to attend college; many top students who in the past would settle for a good state or regional college are increasingly applying to the nation's top colleges. More parents can afford private or out-of-state tuition and are willing and able to make higher investments in their children's education. Finally, there is at least a perceived increase in the rewards from admission to the nation's top colleges. This increased competition for fewer top college slots means there is an almost frenzied competition among students and parents for their children to succeed; that's why many parents will identify with Eric Zorn's compulsive efforts to ensure that his twelve-year-old does well in school.

Here's the tension though: If so many parents are willing to spend time, energy, and money indirectly on their children's education, why don't we see this demand translated into an excellent school system? After all, the most straightforward way to secure oneself a spot at a good college is to score well on the ACT or SAT and to get high grades; these are two of the most important criteria that competitive colleges use in their admission decisions. Not surprisingly, students seeking spots in top colleges obsess over their grades and SAT or ACT scores. To improve their SAT scores, students frequently repeat the test; in fact, today more than half of all students taking the SAT take it more than once. And not only do students increasingly retake the SAT, but they also spend a lot to improve their score. Currently, about 15 percent of all SAT takers invest at least $400 on test preparation material and courses. Students at younger and younger ages—even years before they expect to enter college—are increasingly signing up for SAT-preparation classes. The test-preparation business now reportedly takes in about $1 billion a year.[3]

And test preparation isn't the end of it. Endless websites and books counsel students on the best strategies for gaining admission to top colleges. Students and parents are increasingly strategic in their efforts to best position themselves and their kids for gaining a spot at a desired university. Newspapers are full of stories of teenagers padding their college application with club memberships, volunteer activities, sports teams, music accomplishments, exotic travel adventures, and so on. It is even not all that unusual in some circles for families to go to the extreme of hiring an "admissions counselor" who then becomes responsible for guiding the student through the application process—a process that may start several years before an actual application is filed. Such counselors typically cost thousands of dollars, and some parents spend upwards of $40,000 on one.

Nor has the potential for seeing profit in parents' frenzy over college escaped the attention of entrepreneurs. According to its website, College Admissions Assistance "is a private educational-service organization that provides expert college planning help to students and families nationwide." Its letters to parents address a very competitive, compulsive, and anxious audience. Here is a sample of what it says to the parents of a ninth grader:

> Colleges are now identifying prospective students as early as the 9th grade for admissions and financial aid assistance. Therefore you need to attend [a group presentation followed by a personal interview] in order to receive assistance in making critical decisions that will arise in the next few months. [Your child's] future is too important not to attend.

Of course, the assistance offered by this organization comes with a stiff price tag.

Parents' and students' frenzy over applying for admission to a competitive college—and the entrepreneurial activity that it has spawned—seems at odds with my argument that we provide our students with a low-quality education. If indeed there is a growing constituency of parents willing to spend considerable time and money on their children's future educational prospects, why don't they just lobby for and demand excellent schools? My last chapter argued that local communities and states will establish less demanding educational standards than would the national government. But if anyone were to be more responsive to this large, growing, and vocal constituency, wouldn't it be elected school-board officials and the local superintendent as opposed to the U.S. president? Doesn't this competition for college admission result in parents (and students) demanding higher educational standards so that they have a better shot at one of those desired spaces in competitive colleges?

The answer is yes, the educational system has and does respond to citizens' voices seeking a solid preparation for college-level work. But this demand from parents like Zorn seeking excellent credentials for their children has been met in a peculiar way that harms the overall quality of our schools.

WHY RISING DEMAND FOR A HIGH-QUALITY EDUCATION IS CONSISTENT WITH LOW EXPECTATIONS

Forty years ago, the political economist Albert Hirschman described how a poorly performing educational system is perfectly consistent with the existence of a segment of society seeking and demanding a high-performing one. When firms or organizations (such as educational organizations) fail to provide customers or members of their organization with the type of product, service, or policies they seek, these customers or members can attempt to change the organization in one of two different ways: they can "exit," or they can use their "voice." The exit option is illustrated by leaving, no longer supporting, or otherwise disassociating oneself from an organization, or by no longer purchasing a product. The voice option is reflected in customers or members trying to change the existing practices, policies, and products of the firm by voicing their dissatisfaction. Hirschman explained the voice option in the following way:

> Voice is . . . any attempt at all to change, rather than to escape from, an objectionable state of affairs, whether through individual or collective petition to the management directly in charge, through appeal to a higher authority with the intention of forcing a change in management, or through various types of actions and protests, including those that are meant to mobilize public opinion.[4]

Let's apply Hirschman's exit-versus-voice framework to expressing dissatisfaction with our school system. When parents are dissatisfied with the quality of education their children are receiving, they have two options beyond simple resignation: they can leave the school system (exit), or they can alert or otherwise put pressure on others to change existing school policies and practices (voice).

In Hirschman's view, the decision regarding voice-versus-exit (or even resignation) depends on the opportunities for exit on the one hand and the effectiveness of voice on the other. If exiting is easy and fairly painless and voice is hard or unlikely to be heard, then people will choose to exit. Don't like all the caraway seeds in that loaf of rye bread? Better to switch brands (exit) than exercise your voice option by writing to the bread producers asking them to reduce the amount of seeds they put in their loaves.

Hirschman also pointed out that the effectiveness of the voice option may depend on the number of discontented people willing to join forces. In this sense, choosing the exit option may weaken the voice option for others because the effectiveness of voice depends on numbers. One person complaining about a school policy is a crank, several become an inconvenience, but a crowd at a school-board meeting can become a problem that needs addressing. In this sense, the mere existence of an exit option may make change more difficult because it can soften or quiet the collective voice for change. Alternatives to an inferior status quo may in this way help perpetuate an undesirable state because fewer people complain about it.

Hirschman uses the case of Nigerian transportation during the 1950s and 1960s to illustrate how exit can quiet voice. He argues that the existence of a private truck alternative to the public rail system allowed the continuation of poor service in Nigeria's railway system, despite its crucial role in delivering exports to Nigeria's ports:

> The presence of a ready alternative to rail transport makes it less, rather than more, likely that the weaknesses of the railways will be fought rather than indulged. With truck and bus transportation available, a deterioration in rail service is not nearly so serious a matter as if the railways held a monopoly for long-distance transport.[5]

Important for our subject at hand, he then goes on to argue:

> This may be the reason public enterprise . . . has strangely been at its weakest in sectors such as transportation and education where it is subjected to competition: Instead of stimulating improved or top performance, the presence of a ready and satisfactory substitute for the services public enterprise offers merely deprives it of a precious feedback mechanism that operates at its best when the customers

are securely locked in. . . . For the management of public enterprise . . . may be less sensitive to the loss of revenue due to the switch of customers to a competing mode than to the protests of an aroused public that has a vital stake in the service, has no alternative, and will therefore "raise hell."[6]

Addressing education in particular, Hirschman argued that the effect of the exit option in public education—private schools—may on balance weaken the voice of those who seek a more effective public school system:

This "exit" [to private schools] may occasion some impulse toward an improvement of the public schools; but here again this impulse is far less significant than the loss to the public schools of those member-customers who would be more motivated and determined to put up a fight against the deterioration if they did not have the alternative of the private schools.[7]

Hirschman thought that private schools robbed the public school system of the most vigilant consumers (the "hell raisers") of education, and thus deprived schools of the "most active, reliable, and creative agents of voice."[8] In this way, private schools *contribute* to the perpetuation of an inferior public school system. Not only do they allow parents who might be the most vocal critics to leave the public system, they may also silence other critics simply because there is an *opportunity* to leave. As Hirschman put it, "the presence of the exit alternative can atrophy the development of the art of voice."[9]

Hirschman is exactly right: exit options reduce pressure on our school system to improve the quality of education that students receive, and so these opportunities work at cross-purposes with efforts to increase our expectations of students. This helps account for why low standards persist despite the existence of a growing number of educational zealots, such as Zorn, who should be out decrying our schools' lax standards.

The existence of private schools helps explain our collective acquiescence with a poorly performing educational system. However, Hirschman also didn't anticipate today's larger reason for it. In limiting his discussion to the private school exit option, his account doesn't consider how available exiting is today. Our educational system is more entrenched in mediocrity than when Hirschman wrote, even though so many more people seek an excellent education. In fact, there are at least three additional ways that American students and parents can "escape" a poorly performing school system. But let's start first with briefly examining the traditional "exit" option of the private schools with which Hirschman concerned himself.

Private Schools

Today, one out of every ten K–12 students in the United States attends a private school. Who is it that chooses the private school option? Since private schools are not subsidized by the state, one obvious general characteristic is high income. And also not surprisingly, parents with children in private schools are on average more critical of the public school system than are other parents. Based on this alone, it is easy to see that the existence of private schools probably does drain away some of the "voice" of those who would otherwise be more critical of public school standards than are those left in it.

Of course there may not be a general consensus among these exiters of what exactly they don't like about the public schools. But we do know that those who enroll their children in private schools have children with significantly higher test scores. And this is true in all grades, beginning in elementary school and continuing through high school. We also know that a high percentage of private school students attend Catholic schools, which typically require a college-preparatory course of study for everyone. A good inference is that those in private schools seek a more challenging and advanced curriculum than is typically found in the public schools.

There is no doubt students in private schools on average take more challenging and advanced classes than do their counterparts in the public schools. While fewer than half of all graduates of public high schools take a math class beyond second-year algebra, three-fourths of those in private schools do; moreover, students in private schools are twice as likely as those in public schools to take a calculus class. Only two-thirds of public school graduates have taken a science course above general biology, but nearly nine out of ten private school graduates have.[10]

In sum, those attending private schools have higher test scores and take more advanced coursework. It is reasonable to conjecture, then, that Hirschman was right: some of the potentially most vocal advocates for a challenging and demanding curriculum in the public schools are siphoned off by the private school alternative, thus muting the voice for change.

While Hirschman emphasized the role that private schools play in the persistence of a mediocre (or worse) public school system, it is still true that only 10 percent of the school-going population attends private schools. One might expect there still to be an active constituency among the remaining 90 percent lobbying for higher standards. After all, Zorn's son attended a Chicago public school.

And indeed there are a lot of frenetic parents like Zorn who send their kids to public schools. However, their voice is muted by alternative available "exit" options—options provided within the public school system itself. Let's move to discuss the three most important of these.

Location as a Form of Exit

The first way that an "exit" option is available within the public school system is through choice of school. In part due to the decentralized nature of our educational system, the type of education received in different districts— and even among schools within the same district—can vary significantly. As a result, parents can and do play a role in picking the funding level, course offerings, staffing, and instructional practices in their district, and even in a school within a district. Parents can *opt out* of a poorly performing school or district by shopping around and moving elsewhere.

This way of opting out of (exiting) certain districts or schools via residential choice is especially available here because in America the public school to which students are assigned is mostly based on the student's home address. And this way of determining what school one's child attends is fairly distinct to the United States. A recent international survey estimates that 81 percent of students in the United States are assigned their school based on their home address, about twice the average in other OECD countries. Numerous studies document the higher housing prices parents are willing to pay so that they can send their kids to schools with good reputations. Some parents have even been known to risk jail time to (illegally) send their children to a school that is not their assigned neighborhood school.

Residential choice hence provides some amount of exit opportunity from our school system insofar as it provides a means to escape a poorly performing school or school district by choosing another.

Parental Pressure as a Form of Exit

Aside from selecting the school or district for their child via residential choices, another way parents can actively influence the quality of their children's education is by influencing the teachers or coursework to which their child is assigned. As I have noted and explained in these pages, American schools have very clear variation from classroom to classroom in the quality of instruction and teachers. I have also noted that the amount of time teachers within the same school actually spend teaching during class can vary by a factor of three. Another illustration: teachers using the same text often vary dramatically in their expectations of what students should learn or what constitutes excellent work. Courses with the same title in the same school can be taught differently, and teachers can expect students to learn different things. Decentralized standards and the extent to which classroom practices are decoupled from each other permit such variation to persist. In the extreme, these practices leave classroom rigor and content up to the teacher.

The vigilant, involved parent (such as Zorn) knows that this variation within his child's school exists; he can often rely on an accommodating school system to cater to the demands that his child be assigned a specific class, teacher, or curriculum. As an indicator of the influence that parents have on the educational experience of their child within a school—and thus how public schools can accommodate differential parental demands—a survey by the U.S. Department of Education found that, in the majority of public high schools, parents play a moderate to large role in the school's instructional practices. In fact, compared with parents in other OECD countries, those in America are nearly twice as likely to influence their school's instructional content. An international survey of school principals moreover found that about one in eight fifteen-year-olds in America attends a school where parents influence staffing decisions—a level of influence three times higher than in the average OECD country. Even *students* in the United States are two times more likely to influence staffing decisions than are students in other OECD countries.[11]

Parents and students in the United States actively seek to influence classroom assignment, course offerings and content, and standards and expectations, much more so than in other countries. This means that parents and students have more ability to seek out pockets of excellence—or at least escape mediocrity—than is possible in other countries. In other words, variation in educational quality in the United States, coupled with a greater ability to influence what portion of it one's child experiences, means that vigilant parents can in some ways steer their children through the worst practices, teachers, or curriculum within a particular school, thereby in a sense escaping it. In an educational system in which change is hard to come by, allowing complainers a way to escape internally is a much easier way to handle those who otherwise might "raise hell."

Exit through Coursework

The final and most important way that the voice option for improving our educational system is muted is through our practice of delivering different coursework to different students. As I've discussed throughout this book, flexible and varied curricular offerings that provide students with significant choice over the courses they take are the hallmark of America's high schools and are a fairly unique practice (at least to the extent that they begin at such an early age). One of the more common ways that variation takes place is through the practice of "parallel tracks." This means offering all students more or less the same course, but providing some of them an "enriched" or "accelerated" version of it. Providing select students as early as elementary school with Talented and Gifted (TAG) courses is one example. TAG courses are common throughout the United States, with every state except Vermont enrolling large numbers of students in them. These programs are almost exclusively the result of state and local policy since the federal government offers almost no money to support them. So policies supporting TAG classes depend to a large extent on local citizens' demands. Some states enroll ten times more students in TAG classes than do other states. It is even common to see different practices among districts within the same state. The National Association for Gifted Children acknowledges this when it laments, "In many instances, gifted students must rely on a persistent parent, a responsive teacher, or an innovative school administrator to ensure that they are adequately challenged in the classroom."

But community demand for a TAG curriculum is clearly widespread. In 2006, 7 percent of public school students nationwide were enrolled in a TAG program.[12] Students demonstrating exceptional ability or potential for their age are generally the ones who enroll in these classes. A frequently stated belief is that 5 to 7 percent of school children are in need of such enriched curricula and activities not normally provided by the school. In other words, the common belief is that the standard school curriculum does not serve students with the strongest ability levels very well. To this end, school districts will use

TAG programs, particularly in the early grades, to provide such students with a more demanding or complex curriculum.

A second example of the existence of a parallel track in public schools is the availability of courses that purport to offer more advanced treatment of certain subjects. Course offerings designated as honors, Advanced Placement (AP), or International Baccalaureate (IB) classes reflect this practice. Such designations generally indicate that the topic is treated in a more advanced or demanding way than would be a course without such a designation. Schools nowadays are increasingly pressured to offer these courses because competitive universities are more likely to rely on "advanced" course labels to distinguish students for admission purposes; students and parents see these classes as a path for entry into a good college.

AP courses are the most common way for high school students to become exposed to a more advanced treatment of a topic. At least three-quarters of high schools offer such courses. After taking a particular AP course, students can take a national exam covering the course content; some colleges accord college credit to students who have passed an AP test. Each year over one million students take AP examinations, and this number is growing at a steady clip. As might be expected, more advantaged students tend to enroll in these classes. For instance, a recent study of course selection in Texas high schools estimated that about 15 percent of white high school students had taken an AP class over the year, about twice the rate of black and Hispanic students.[13]

Aside from AP courses, high schools (and sometime middle schools) offer a much more loosely defined course labeled as "honors." Roughly one-third of graduating seniors take some form of an honors English class during their high school years, with about half of these students taking almost exclusively honors English during their high school years.

International Baccalaureate (IB) courses are another example of parallel courses offered by a few high schools around the nation. These are somewhat similar to AP courses insofar as an optional uniform exam is made available to all students who take a particular IB course. The IB curriculum is billed as much more rigorous and demanding than typical high school courses, with tests intended to enforce that uniformity. Because the curriculum is set by bodies external to the school system, schools and local communities have little say over its content. The IB degree that students can earn entails a two-year program of study taken during a student's junior and senior years. In part because of the extra expense, IB courses are much rarer than are AP courses; in 2003 only 2 percent of high schools offered any. But these courses come with an important cachet indicating that the student has met international college-going expectations. For this reason some parents go to considerable lengths to locate and enroll their children in an IB program.

In addition to the parallel tracks of gifted, AP, honors, and IB courses, another way that different students can pursue a very different course of study in middle and high school is through the common practice of schools offering what might be considered "vertical" tracks. Students typically choose among a wide array of courses to create individualized routes toward meeting graduation requirements—routes that entail considerable differences in terms of their rigor and coherence. Such variation occurs because states and districts generally require students to take a certain number of years of instruction in a subject, or a certain number of electives, without specifying which specific courses a student should take.

This variation differs from the previously discussed parallel tracks in that students can meet a requirement—such as a math, science, or an elective course—by taking classes that are very different in their content and performance expectations. It is mostly left to students (and parents) to choose which specific class they would like to take to meet a particular requirement; parent and student choice looms large in determining what expectations a student is expected to meet.

While primarily a high school phenomenon, this practice of vertical tracking also occurs in middle schools. One study of eighth-grade course-taking patterns in math found that both across and within the same school, eighth graders took very different math classes—in fact, they took a total of thirty different ones! While many were enrolled in algebra, in some schools as many as 70 percent were enrolled in a remedial math class.[14] Nationwide today, 30 percent of eighth graders take algebra, 30 percent take pre-algebra, another 30 percent take "regular math," and the rest all take something other than these three options.[15]

Such variation in the coursework that students take helps explain why, in terms of ability to understand and apply scientific knowledge, American fifteen-year-olds are on average not all that different from their OECD counterparts. Yet almost one-fifth exhibit very low levels of scientific knowledge, compared with one-tenth or less in Canada, Finland, Japan, and Korea.[16] And even after controlling for students' socioeconomic background, science scores in the United States remain much more variable than they are in almost all other OECD countries. This also explains why very large differences in math and science knowledge exist among students attending the same school: students just down the hall from one another can pursue very different coursework. In most other countries, there's not nearly as much variation in what students have learned within the same building as there is in our country.[17]

From gifted classes for young students, to AP and honors classes for high school students, the educational system in the United States provides some excellent opportunities for more rigorous and challenging coursework. It is fair to say that the educational system has been and is responsive to a segment of the public's increasing demand for a quality education. The problem is that the system has responded in a way that satisfies the demands of some while leaving those students who are less interested, motivated, or informed (or who have less pushy parents) to an otherwise mediocre educational system. Arthur Powell, Eleanor Farrar, and David Cohen perfectly sum up the dilemma this leaves us with:

> In a universal public service where those who push for more can usually get it and those who will settle for less can pass through without penalty, incentives for fundamental change are minimal.[18]

The problem we are left with is having a school system that is trapped in inertia and that provides very uneven opportunities. Those who are "pushy" and seek advanced course offerings tend to already be socially advantaged. As chapter 6 discussed in great detail, coursework options particularly harm those from disadvantaged backgrounds.

That there is great support for this practice though—and conversely, that an educational system without it would elicit much more criticism—is evident in cases where educators attempt to remove and reduce their importance. When one public high school announced plans to end honors classes, a ruckus ensued. Students complained that class rigor had to be matched to ability. Said one sophomore, "There is a big difference between someone who doesn't like math and can't grasp it well and someone who is motivated and can do it well."[19] And this sentiment was expressed in a highly competitive public school that bills itself as being a college-preparatory academy.

These curricular practices permit a watering down of the curriculum that would have to be reversed if the practice were abandoned. A thorough study of "detracking" in four districts documented parents' (and teachers') strong resistance to court-ordered mandates to detrack the district curriculum. When courts have ordered a school to detrack, schools have tended to respond by accelerating the curriculum, a change suggesting that tracks result in students being taught less advanced material or taught at a slower pace than would otherwise occur.[20]

This aspect of school policy illustrates exactly what Hirschman predicted: the collective or "voice" process has been seriously weakened by numerous opportunities to exit. While Hirschman was right that parents can and do seek out good schools through private schools and through their locational decisions—thus allowing them to opt out of school systems that do not meet their standards—a more important way that America's school system permits parents and students to exit undemanding curricula or low standards is by taking advantage of variability within schools. By influencing which teachers their kids have, or what is taught in their kids' classes—or more importantly, by making sure that their children gain access to various enriched curricular options that schools make available to some—parents can escape the worst that our educational system has to offer. In this sense, the voice option is directed at managing the options available to some rather than improving them for all.

By making exit options for potential hell-raisers relatively easy, the voice option in education has been muted. The wide range of coursework available to students makes it difficult to generate sustained and genuine discussion over what we should expect from all students. The numerous options for exit weaken the voice of those who otherwise would be raising hell. Without these voices and the strong political pressure that would follow, there is not enough demand to compel the far-reaching changes needed in our school system. So Hirschman was right: exit options in our educational system reduce the effectiveness of voice to address the poor quality of education that students receive today. This helps account for why low standards in our schools persist despite the growing ranks of educational zealots such as Zorn who should be out decrying the poor quality of our schools.

There is an even less favorable interpretation of this practice of offering different coursework to different students. Some have argued that, when school districts and states lack the capacity and resources to provide an excellent education for all (and the support that entails), they may choose to respond only to those voices that demand it. By offering a demanding education for the elite few, school districts and states can satisfy that segment while economizing on their limited resources. This explanation places more of the "blame," if we wanted to call it such, on the low funding of schools. While this may help explain the strange and varied way we deliver education to students, the practice has not really ebbed and flowed with education dollars. Moreover, history reveals that this movement was at least partly motivated by a strong belief (and as I argue in the next chapter, a belief still with us today) about the equalizing effect that low standards have.

Before moving to this final explanation for why raising the educational bar is difficult in the United States, it is worth noting that Eric Zorn's preoccupation with helping along his son's academic career was not directly about getting his son into a top college. Rather, he was trying to get his son into one of the selective public high schools offered by the Chicago Public Schools three years down the road (although surely the reason for *that* desire had something to do with college). According to a member of an educational watchdog group in Chicago, such elite Chicago high schools make for a "two tiered [educational] system . . . [the purpose of which is] to keep advantaged families in the city."[21]

These elite schools are yet another form of exit, created to keep families like Zorn's from exiting the Chicago school system on the one hand, or from staying and voicing loud objection on the other. Selective schools are just one more way that districts have been accommodating the interests of some to keep pressure off a system in need of comprehensive rather than partial solutions. You could say that such schools serve as an escape valve. They divert parents like Eric Zorn from mobilizing support for improving Chicago's educational system to instead making a desperate early-morning dash for a DVD to help his son exit the mediocre (or worse) aspects of its public schools. Hirschman got it exactly right: people's decisions between exit and voice are shaped by the options available to them. And in education, the exit option is an all too available one.

Soft America Meets
Hard America

The Perceived High Costs and
Low Benefits of High Expectations

My previous two chapters have identified factors working against high standards. I argued that two characteristics of our school system help explain why
low expectations persist. One reason has to do with its organizational and
institutional features: our educational governance structure is both decentralized and complex; this design serves to undercut the sorts of policies we need
to support high standards. A second reason is that the practice of offering different coursework to different students quiets the public voice calling for high
standards, thereby also serving to perpetuate the status quo.

This chapter turns to a third explanation for the failure of high expectations to take hold. This time the cause lies outside of our educational system.

A few years ago the journalist Michael Barone wrote a book titled *Hard
America, Soft America*. In it he describes what he considers to be competing
forces in America, some for "soft" policies and others for "hard" ones. Here's
Barone's basic idea: "Hard" policies are those that do not protect us from mis-
fortune or the bad consequences of our own actions. A hard policy would be
one leaving homeless people to their own devices. "Soft" policies do the opposite. They protect people from fate, luck, or plain bad choices, for instance
by providing the hungry with food or retirees with a pension. Barone claimed
that societies need both hard and soft policies; moreover, for a country to be
successful it must achieve the right mix of these two types of policies—some

amount of protection from and some amount of exposure to the hard knocks of life. Overdoing it in one direction (too much "hardness" for example) will prove costly and is bound to lead to countervailing policy changes; in the end, America always tends toward some equilibrium among the nation's package of hard and soft policies.

What Barone's account does not do is spell out how and why our soft and hard policies tend toward some balance. For example, how might a "three strikes and you're out" policy in our criminal justice system (on the hard side) result in some offsetting policy on the soft side, and why would this occur? On this score, political economists have long developed theoretical explanations for why some configurations of social policies occur in some time periods and not others, or in some countries and not elsewhere. A stated premise is that individuals' preferences for different types of policies—toward the homeless or veterans or aged—are influenced by broader features of society. Policy choices reflect these underlying preferences. For instance, people support policies that invest in the poor when their fate is more closely tied to that of the underprivileged (perhaps as a consequence of more integrated residential patterns), or citizens are more supportive of redistribution when political instability looms large.

As another example, some time ago two economists explained why education policy in the United States is "elitist." Their premise was that America offers a good education to the few and a poor education to the rest, whereas in East Asia and Western Europe education policy tends to be more "egalitarian"—schools offer a decent education to everyone. The two argued that, unlike in the United States, these other countries encourage productive work among the poor. As a consequence, citizens there prefer policies that educate the poor.[1] Whether convincing or not, their basic undertaking is to explain and establish theoretically how specific policies in one area can influence those in another, and why different policy configurations come to exist in different countries. By being precise about the how and why, research in this vein allows us to grapple with understanding and critiquing why a specific "balance" between two different policy types can or might occur—in this particular example, between education policy and labor-market policies. More importantly, with such an approach one can make predictions over and judge the social desirability of one way balance is achieved versus another. Again, with reference to this particular instance, what's better, elitist or egalitarian education policies?

What's true in all of this is that one can't really think straight about education policy in the United States without taking into account the larger policy environment in which it plays out. For sure, some sort of balance is established between education policy on the one hand and related policies on the other. For example, we have policies that address what happens if people (say because of a poor education) end up economically unproductive. Such laws form part of the landscape in which discussions over school policy occur. In the specific case above, our policies toward the unproductive tend not to be very generous. You could say they tend toward the hard side: we leave those who are economically unproductive to the mercy of a fairly unforgiving labor market and welfare system. Knowing this, support for low standards (or at least weak voices calling for higher ones) could make sense as a soft counterpart to these hard policies: in theory, low expectations give people plenty of room to *become* economically productive (or so we think).

Contrast our education policies with those abroad: those in Europe and Asia could be characterized as holding students to higher standards insofar as they typically require all to take a much more uniform course of study (usually until age sixteen), and exams or some sorting process are used to determine who gains access to higher education. Those who don't meet the nation's college-going criteria are out of luck. Compared with ours, this sounds like hard policy. Yet these countries also have more generous (that is, soft) labor and welfare policies. I think these two sets of policies—education policies on the one hand, and labor and income support laws on the other—are linked. And once established they tend to reinforce one another. That's the argument I advance in this chapter.

Let's consider the pros and cons of expecting more from students. Two important considerations come to mind. First, there is the prospect (or fear) that fewer students will meet those higher expectations and thus will drop out. For some, then, higher standards would be costly insofar as they leave those who fail them with a *worse* education than would have been the case had less been expected of them. Second, there is the "what's the big deal?" factor. What's to be gained from holding students to higher standards? I believe that for most, or at least many, Americans the gains to be had from higher standards are not all that obvious. My contention is that this "payoff structure" to high standards—the perceptions of high costs and low benefits that I elaborate on below—undermines support for higher standards because people think that overall they'll leave us worse off as a nation.

Our low educational standards are an example of what is termed in economics "a low-level equilibrium." This means that the status quo serves to reinforce itself (hence the "equilibrium" part), but that it is stuck at a solution that leaves us worse off (thus the "low-level" component). Think of being trapped in a pit where you can see the light of day, but forces (in this case gravity) keep you from escaping, and you'll get the idea of a low-level equilibrium. The dilemma posed by any low-level equilibrium in social life is figuring out how to get out of it; the problem, by its nature, involves forces that conspire to keep us there. With respect to our educational system, my previous two chapters have described what I consider to be the most important of these influences. In this chapter I depict how beliefs about the costs and benefits of moving to high standards further contribute to our educational system being trapped in a low-level equilibrium.

The problem with the beliefs I discuss below is that it's hard to see that things could be better—we don't realize we're in that pit. Many believe that maintaining low standards is our best option available. Part of the reason is that we overestimate the costs and underestimate the benefits of high standards—in short, we have *mistaken* beliefs. To make this case, let's examine separately how people tend to think about the costs and benefits of moving to high expectations.

THE HIGH COST OF FAILING TO MEET GRADUATION STANDARDS IN THE UNITED STATES

Many people believe that expecting more of students would increase social and economic inequality. They assume that if higher standards make it harder to graduate from high school, then the pool of those who do is smaller and the pool of those who don't is larger. All else the same, in labor markets the pay gap between high school graduates and nongraduates will likely widen since there are fewer graduates and more nongraduates. Several observers have even postulated that egalitarian motives may be partly behind low standards because they help the low performers—students who are disproportionately poor or socially disadvantaged in other ways. You might recall the quote I cited much earlier in this book from the president of the American Association of Community Colleges. He argued against a policy of community colleges "improv[ing] quality by denying access to the most at-risk students." This concisely sums up the tradeoff many people perceive with higher standards: improving quality (higher standards) comes at the expense of the disadvantaged.

All school systems and modern democracies pay at least lip service to providing equal opportunity for all. If high standards disproportionately harm the already disadvantaged, then low expectations may reflect the weight in policymaking given to this group. Such egalitarian motives could explain why, even if the gains to higher standards greatly exceeded their potential costs, any push to strengthen standards faces an uphill battle. And this would be the right priority.

Before reaching that conclusion, though, let's explore two interrelated questions that arise from the position above. First, *are* high standards inequitable? That is, would higher expectations disproportionately harm more underprivileged groups in society while at the same time bestowing benefits on more advantaged groups? Second, if that indeed is the case, then what explains why most of the developed world pursues supposedly inegalitarian educational policies (i.e., higher standards), while America—which prides itself on its individualistic ethos—pursues egalitarian ones? After all, among our peers we're the country that in almost all categories spends the least on the downtrodden, expecting them instead to pick themselves up by their bootstraps.

On the first question—whether high standards are inequitable—chapter 6 explained why *I* don't think so. To the contrary. But it *is* certainly the case that higher standards are *perceived* as being inequitable. The fear of bad consequences for marginal students (primarily, that they'll drop out) has led to the remarkable extent to which our public school system ensures that students persist in school and graduate. Recall that the fight for "opening up the curriculum" that led to our varied curricular options occurred over the first half of the twentieth century and came under the banner of equal opportunity and social justice. And there's little doubt that this was the real sentiment that motivated those advocating for this change. To some important degree, this belief persists with us today.

Today's emphasis on retention as opposed to educational standards is clearly motivated by concern over those who would otherwise fail. To this end, students who are flunking high school are given numerous alternative ways to earn high school credit. Credit "recovery" or "retrieval" options allow them to earn credit by attending weeklong sessions, completing online questionnaires, enrolling in a web class, or attending after-school remediation classes.[2] In Florida, a full 17 percent of high school students now enroll in a state online class because they failed a high school graduation requirement.[3] A recent *New York Times* article on New York City's credit recovery options discussed the city's attempt to provide more oversight over the quality of this coursework. But such oversight has its critics. A city education official is quoted in the article as complaining that "if we become too prescriptive here, then we also run the risk of not being able to have students acquire the credits that they need. We want to ensure that our students stay in school, that they are engaged in school, that they don't drop out."[4] With a graduation rate of about 56 percent, perhaps it is reasonable to expect that New York City's officials would prioritize persistence in school for the other 44 percent rather than the quality of education students get.

The growth of "alternative schools" is yet another example of the importance placed on student retention motivated by a concern over potential dropouts. Alternative schools are typically high schools distinct from the mainstream that are geared toward addressing the needs of students who otherwise will drop out. Enrollments in such schools have grown at a steady pace over the last couple of decades; today over 1 percent of all public school students attend one of the nation's eleven thousand alternative schools. And finally, of course, there is the unusual "second chance" that we offer those who never gained their high school diploma. In America anyone at any time can earn a high school equivalency degree, called a General Educational Development (or GED) degree. Today almost one in ten young adults has a GED.

Our educational system clearly places a high priority on persistence in school—at least as measured by the extent to which we provide alternative options for students to attain a high school degree or its equivalent. My next, concluding chapter revisits this practice and considers alternative ways to achieve the same objective. But for now it is easy to see that people think that higher standards will only worsen the dropout problem. My point is simply that many people think low standards help disadvantaged kids, and our education policy reflects that assumption.

Let's move to the next question: Why in the United States? Why are Americans in particular so concerned about the fate of the marginal student? And why doesn't this same concern for the underprivileged manifest itself in more generous public assistance policies for the poor? Why low standards but not low-income housing?

Two facts explain why in America we prioritize high school graduation at the expense of what we expect of students. For one, America's students are much less likely to complete secondary (high) school than they are in Europe and other OECD countries. Our high school dropout rate is roughly 25 percent;* by contrast on average about 13 percent of students drop out in Europe. Compared with European youth, those in our country are twice as likely to not complete high school. And while the last ten years have witnessed an increase in graduation rates across Europe, they have not budged here. Moreover, the Unites States has a stronger link between socioeconomic status and the probability of dropping out. Dropout rates among black youth are over 50 percent higher than they are among white ones, and Hispanic youth fail to complete high school at four times the rate of white youth. Among students in the top quarter of the income distribution, only 3 percent drop out; among those in the bottom quarter, about 17 percent do.[5] Youth from low-income households are thus *six times* more likely to be high school dropouts than are kids from upper middle-class and rich families.

So one explanation for our policymakers' preoccupation with the downside of high standards is the magnitude and social dimension of the dropout problem—a problem few could stomach seeing made worse.

In addition to the size and distributional impact of our high school dropout problem, we're preoccupied with it for a second reason: the *cost* to individuals of dropping out is especially high. Between 1971 and 2008 the median inflation-adjusted earnings of male high school dropouts with full-time employment *declined* dramatically from over $40,000 to about $27,000. Over this time, median earnings among those with no more than a high school degree also fell and today is about 20 percent higher than among those without a high school degree. Meanwhile, full-time young workers with a college degree typically earn almost $60,000, or twice what high school dropouts can expect to earn. And this earnings differential has been getting larger each year.[6]

---

*This figure doesn't include GEDs; taking these into account puts us more in the ballpark of graduation rates across Europe.

The returns to education in America (or conversely, the costs of dropping out) are high. And the economic gains to education are especially high in our country. Recent figures from the OECD show that the average adult male high school dropout in the United States earns 62 percent of what high school graduates earn—an amount noticeably less than the 78 percent average across OECD countries. On the other hand, America's college graduates earn on average 90 percent more than do high school graduates; among OECD countries the equivalent earnings premium for college graduates is a more modest 64 percent.[7] Thus both the cost of dropping out and the returns to college are higher here than they are in other rich democracies.

The economist Kalpana Pai investigated trends in the returns to education over the 1990s and compared them across a number of different countries. Her research represents a more careful comparison than the OECD comparisons above in that hers accounts for unemployment spells and age. She found that over the period 1986 to 2000, the returns to education across all countries grew steadily. Moreover, the gains from more education were very high in our country as opposed to the comparison countries of Germany, the Netherlands, Italy, and Spain. In our country wages among those with a high school degree but not a college degree were 89 percent higher than among high school dropouts. The equivalent high school premium in Germany and the Netherlands was 50 percent, in Italy 21 percent, and in Spain 23 percent.[8]

What is noteworthy here is that the higher returns to education in the United States versus elsewhere reflect differences in public policies: in America an individual's wages and income are more dependent on his or her individual characteristics than is true elsewhere. Our policies do less to insulate individuals from labor-market fluctuations and forces than is true in other countries—in Barone's terminology we follow harder labor-market policies. Other countries, on the other hand, tend to regulate labor markets so that their outcomes are less dependent on individuals' characteristics—such as their educational levels. To give just one example, minimum wages are typically 30 to 40 percent of average wages in the United States, whereas European countries usually set these at around 50 to 60 percent of average wages.[9]

Differences in labor-market policies account for only part of the reason why those who are less well educated fare better elsewhere. In addition to labor-market policies such as minimum wages, income is influenced by tax and transfer policies: how much the government takes from you and how much in turn it redistributes back. This factor helps explain why the cost of being undereducated in America is higher here than it is abroad. In our country "welfare" policy is less generous toward those with low income, entailing much less redistribution than occurs in most European countries. As a percent of GDP, European Union countries spend over five times more than we do on unemployment and labor-market programs. And they spend over three times more than we do on family benefits.[10] While relative poverty rates before taking government taxes and transfers into account are very similar in the United States, across Europe and in Canada they are quite different once you factor in these taxes and transfers. Once accounted for, our poverty rate rises to nearly two times the rate found across Europe and in Canada—17 percent here versus an average of 10 percent there.[11] In the United States, then, our tax and transfer policies don't achieve nearly as much poverty alleviation or protection from labor-market risks as they do in other countries. Observers frequently comment that such differences are in part ideological: Americans look to social institutions to provide equality of *opportunity*, whereas Europeans look to theirs to ensure equality of *outcome*.

In America, then, youth face a lethal combination of a high probability of dropping out of high school—an outcome that occurs disproportionately among those from disadvantaged backgrounds—together with a very high personal cost in terms of the lost income associated with it. In part for reasons of compassion and in part for those of ideology (our commitment to equal opportunity mentioned above), there is significant political support for an educational system that emphasizes retention. The fact that those who fail to complete our educational system face harsh consequences ("hard" policies) partly explains why. And so our school system provides individuals every opportunity to "succeed," in the sense that success consists of completing high school. One can understand this emphasis as reflective of our commitment to equal opportunity and our belief that society should provide a level playing field. Moreover, graduating from high school keeps all future options available to students; that is, youth can still achieve whatever ambition they set for themselves. Providing students with every occasion to complete high school assures us that we have fulfilled our commitment to equal opportunity. And, crucial for my argument, it supports our belief that those who do not succeed fail for personal and not institutional reasons.

If this conjecture is right, it means that the focus on retention permits us greater ease of conscience when we leave citizens to our hard labor-market and public-assistance policies. Soft education policies are in this way a counterpoint to our hard social policies. They form a package deal. So why low standards but not low-income housing? Low standards *permit* us to see a lack of housing options for some as a reflection of their personal failure.

Another reason why Americans emphasize retention is more practical: those who are poorly educated (that is, fail to attain a high school diploma) are quite likely to be poor. In the United States they are *especially* likely to be poor, and thus more likely to be desperate or disenfranchised and resort to crime or other socially deviant behavior. Several scholars in fact explain features of our educational policies in terms of our fear of "predation" by the poorly educated.[12] To the extent that higher standards are believed to exacerbate the high school dropout problem, a movement toward introducing them into our school system raises concern among some about the additional cost to society of those who will (it is believed) fail and, in consequence, impose costs on us all.

There is good reason for this fear too. In chapter 5 I highlighted the cost to society of more dropouts: higher health care costs, more crime, additional welfare payments, and fewer tax dollars. But recall, too, the main message of chapter 5: we confuse quantity with quality. For all of the outcomes associated with our educational system that we care about, the underlying *causality* is not how long people spend in school but what they learn and what skills they acquire. Yes, we should be extremely preoccupied with the fate of youth. But our focus on retention is misplaced when it is taken to mean that retention should trump quality. Furthermore, prioritizing retention distracts us from the harder job of preparing students instead of simply graduating them.

There is a final component of this story about how wider policy and ideological beliefs conspire to support low standards. This is where America's system of higher education factors in.

HIGHER EDUCATION AND THE ECONOMICS OF SECOND CHANCES

Any analysis of standards in our K–12 system must keep in mind the expectations in the 13–16 system that follows. After all, changes in one will at the least influence discussions in the other. Today almost nine in ten high school students aspire to college. Compared with most countries, this is a very large share of the potential college-going cohort. Almost 80 percent of America's fifteen-year-olds expect to complete a bachelor's degree according to a recent international survey conducted by the OECD; in most European countries, only about half do.

Educational aspirations are particularly high in the United States when one takes into account these same fifteen-year-olds' academic performance. Among Americans who scored at the lowest level on an international math test, almost *half* expected to complete their bachelor's degrees; in other OECD countries, only about one-fourth of these students had similar expectations. And low-scoring American students have professional aspirations not all that different from average-scoring students.[13] As has been highlighted throughout these pages, low performance in high school does not appear to dampen American students' ambitions and expectations.

This is a curious phenomenon: What accounts for *international* differences in educational aspirations? As I've argued, one explanation is that public higher education in America has a very large "nonselective" sector. More than three-quarters of students who attend college attend institutions that admit more or less everyone who applies.

Such open admission policies exist because of the belief that such practices raise the number of students who eventually graduate from college. In short, they "make college accessible to all." And an open admission policy advances our ideological commitment to equal opportunity. It contributes to an educational system that provides opportunity and the means for social mobility—even to those who barely passed high school. Growth in college-going over the last couple of decades has been almost exclusively met by growth in our nonselective two- and four-year institutions.

The existence of a large open-access sector in America's higher-education system means that students who meet low standards here—that is, who are not college ready—are not nearly as disadvantaged as they typically would be in Europe and Asia, at least in terms of their access to college. In other countries, access to public colleges and universities is usually determined by test results and high school performance. For those who don't do well, they can attend private institutions at home or go abroad (American institutions would be keen to welcome them!), but they generally have few opportunities for a publicly funded higher education in their home country. By contrast, in the United States just about anyone can find a subsidized college to attend.

Of course there are costs to this open-admissions approach. Among other things, colleges must engage in a significant amount of remediation. Providing publicly funded colleges for all students regardless of ability level means that students who gained only poor or mediocre skills during high school are not all that disadvantaged; for them, a state-sponsored college still awaits. This is the "what's the big deal?" factor I mentioned earlier. The gains to higher standards—higher student performance—are not that obvious or immediate because, either way, youth have access to college. And thus in theory they have access to the same set of lifetime opportunities.

In terms of our ability to accurately and clearly consider the costs and benefits of higher standards, we're further hampered by the fact that the costs of low expectations are not at all evident to us either. The first half of the book documented this in great detail. The cost of having mediocre schools only becomes apparent down the road, and even then the problems documented—slower economic growth, growing inequality, less effective colleges, and so on—are not easily or readily traceable to our K–12 system. Having costs that are hidden, that occur down the road, and that are not easily traceable to the educational system—no wonder there is only weak political pressure to strengthen low expectations. In Europe and Asia, by contrast, low achievement levels in teenagers often dramatically limit their immediate future opportunities. This immediacy and clear link with public education serves to focus the attention of students, teachers, parents, administrators, politicians, and policymakers on educational quality. While I don't want to overstate this difference between here and abroad—in one way or another all countries are dealing with challenges created by our ever-changing global economy—it is true that citizens in the United States voice much less objection to low graduation standards and achievement than do citizens elsewhere because the costs here are less apparent. And our system of higher education is part of the reason why this is so.

My claim then is that low standards persist because of labor-market and social-assistance policies. On the one hand, we provide paltry support to poor and low-wage workers; this makes us especially attuned to the dire consequences faced by those who fail to complete high school. Driven by that concern, we go to great lengths to make sure youth graduate: we provide students with multiple easy ways for them to "succeed" with their education. Making it as easy as possible also means that, should they fail, it is easier to conclude that this failure was their fault—and therefore easier to leave them to our stingy labor and social-assistance policies. Our colleges and universities are also complicit insofar as they accommodate youth who have not acquired college-going skills.

The cost of such a forgiving educational system with such low expectations—the costs that the first half of this book went to lengths to describe—are not all that obvious nor easily connected with the fact that so many youth wind up (as a result) poorly educated. Finally, an excessively forgiving educational system reinforces beliefs among many that failure in American society is not for lack of opportunities to succeed. In this way, our country's social and educational policies have conspired to give us the worst of all possible outcomes: a lousy school system coupled with policies that punish those who too often are simply its victims.

The challenge posed by any low-level equilibrium such as the one in which our school system is currently trapped is figuring out how to get out of it. That's where we're headed next.

IV

THE WAY FORWARD

10

Getting from Here to There

Our educational system is in need of change. Students aren't learning, we're falling behind other countries, and many of our college graduates are even functionally illiterate. We offer our kids a weak and poorly thought-out curriculum; too many teachers do not make good use of classroom time and follow lesson plans that are superficial and repetitive; almost all state governments define "proficiency" at low levels of competency; and because kids with very uneven skills populate a classroom, teachers spend considerable time on review before introducing new material. This dismal picture should be tempered by the fact that the hard work and dedication of countless teachers and administrators means many students get an excellent education. But it doesn't temper it much. As a group, even our top students are not as strong as are those in a large majority of other rich countries.

This book promised not just the usual litany of complaints but also a reform agenda. Yet to generate the widespread support necessary for dramatic change, citizens must be convinced that our school system achieves far less than it could and understand why mediocrity in our school system persists. That's been two of my purposes in writing this book. I'll turn now to the third, which is to outline the sorts of reform our educational system needs.

The problems with America's schools are neither new nor caused by a lack of public dollars or public attention: they continue despite several decades of intense efforts to remedy them. Recall the 1983 report *A Nation at Risk* I discussed in the first chapter; this report rocked the nation and put "educational reform" on the headlines. It concluded that our school system came up short in four different areas. In terms of content, the high school curriculum was weak and lacked purpose. The authors put it this way: "We have a cafeteria style curriculum in which the appetizers and desserts can easily be mistaken for the main courses." Expectations were too low: there were too few rigorous course requirements, and students had easy access to college—regardless of high school performance. School time was not used well, and schools fell short on developing good study skills. Finally, the report concluded that the teaching profession failed to attract the best and brightest.

Thirty years later, these criticisms still ring true. While the primary mission of our school systems has become "reform," it isn't clear we've progressed much. For this reason alone, we must come to grips with why problems identified thirty years ago continue today. Without addressing this persistence, the countless initiatives that advocates claim will be the silver bullet for education's problems are (like most of their predecessors) doomed to fail. Such failure deepens cynicism about the ability to improve our schools—pessimism that stems from an unintentional institutional design that traps our schools in mediocrity.

My book's argument can be summed up as follows: Education's institutional environment does not provide the right incentives to both establish and support high expectations for all students; the lower standards we have lead students to underachieve. This underperformance is very costly for all of us. Yet despite such costs, our schools continue to expect too little from students. Four factors help explain why this problem with our schools is so difficult to tackle. When we establish educational standards (at least de facto ones) at the local level as we do in our country, advocates of high standards confront an institutional environment not designed to enact or support these.

Another reason is that our educational governance structure is complex and poorly articulated. This leads to multiple and inconsistent agendas that collectively lack coherency, teachers deciding what and how they teach with little oversight or accountability, schools insulating classroom practices from outside inspection, and wide variation in classroom rigor and practices. Such an institutional environment does not foster the sort of decision making, policy choices, and daily practices that support educational excellence. This governance system is accidentally designed to block change rather than pro-mote student success. A third factor explaining the persistence of mediocrity is that schools offer students too many choices, and in so doing satisfy the demands of education's "hell-raisers" by letting them "defect." Finally, an inadequate social safety net makes many of us all too queasy about the fate of those who fail our schools. Not asking too much of students is a counterpart to our unease.

Thus low standards persist because of institutional failure. Even the best people with the best of intentions are not likely to enact policies or make deci-sions supporting high expectations if institutional incentives don't support, encourage, and facilitate such policies. The ineffectual institutional context in which we educate our children imposes exceptionally high costs on all of us—costs that are especially high for disadvantaged groups. These include wasted time, poor incentives for students to work hard in school, a less ef-fective mission among our institutions of higher education, misled students who fail to realize how choices today affect their futures tomorrow, a less productive nation, greater wage inequality, and an unfair school system that limits the opportunities of too many students—particularly those who are already disadvantaged. My purpose in this book has been to stress these costs, as well as to explain how they can be traced to education's bureaucratic and institutional environment.

And so our educational system is stuck in a low-level equilibrium. As I mentioned in the last chapter, the trick with such dilemmas is to figure out how to get out of them. Unfortunately, simply pointing out that a better solution exists doesn't help much. If it did, corrupt governments would turn honest and Americans would embrace a single-payer health-care system. The nature of a low-level equilibrium is that forces conspire to keep us there; recall the last chapter's analogy of being stuck in a pit. Figuratively speaking, our schools are trapped in that pit. The challenge then is to identify specific steps that would weaken the forces that keep us there—in a sense, find ways to build a ladder out of the pit. But to do this we must address the underlying forces that explain why we're stuck. It's for this reason that I have devoted considerable space in these pages to describe what I think these forces are. If I succeeded, the changes needed should be apparent.

For our schools to be both excellent and equitable, we must make four changes: (1) dramatically reform our education's governance structure,

(2) establish high expectations for all students, (3) provide adequate support to meet those expectations, and (4) introduce strong incentives for students to work hard in school so they do their part in meeting higher standards. I discuss below each of these four requirements in greater detail. Together these would create the combination of policies required to weaken our education system's destructive dynamics.

REFORMED GOVERNANCE STRUCTURE

To have any hope of escaping the dilemma posed by our educational system, we must start by reforming its governance structure. Without doing this, providing all students with challenging coursework taught by excellent teachers will be difficult, slow, and probably unsuccessful. Our governance structure has two fundamental shortcomings, both having to do with the Principal-Agent Problem the preface introduced. Recall that the Principal-Agent Problem in education is that of getting the people and institutions that run the organization called "public education" (the Agents: federal, state, and local officials; school boards; school principals; teachers; unions; textbook publishers; and PTAs) to collectively make decisions that reflect the Principal's (society as a whole, but parents and students in particular) interests. Education's governance structure has too many Agents with overlapping and contradictory agendas, and too many multilayered Agents. This weakens the Principal's (society) ability to get Agents (the educational system) to make decisions consistent with our educational goals.

Another problem is that collectively we haven't agreed what society's interest is in education. In this, the Principals disagree. Without a clear agenda, the educational bureaucracy tends to accommodate all voices large and small—especially the large. Indeed, political accommodation drives much of education policymaking.

From the perspective of the Principal-Agent Problem, then, the two problems with our education's governance structure is that the Principals are conflicted and the Agents poorly coordinated. This alone is enough to render our educational system pretty ineffective.

In their influential book *Politics, Markets, and America's Schools*, political scientists John Chubb and Terry Moe argue along similar lines; they conclude that the problem with America's educational system is that there is too much democracy. Too many dissenting voices lead to a bureaucratic structure not conducive to effective schools. By accommodating divergent voices, schools become saddled with pursuing too many diluted goals, causing them to lose their sense of mission.

There is no doubt our school systems are burdened by multiple opportunities for special interests (those of parents, unions, textbook publishers, and so forth) to influence education's Agents. Parents lobby teachers to limit homework or school principals to assign their children to particular teachers, unions determine the conditions under which a teacher is reassigned, and textbook publishers influence course content. Without a clear and purposeful vision of our educational objectives, pretty much anything can and does go. Partly for that reason, of all school systems, ours tends to be the most faddish—a hallmark of our school system is the constant rolling out of new initiatives, only to have Agents kill time until the new scheme dies away.

A possible solution—and one with significant and growing support—is dramatic decentralization. Chubb and Moe support this, as do advocates of charter schools and vouchers. Such proponents contend that our school systems would be vastly improved were they to rely on market forces (choice) rather than democracy (government). That's because this puts parents and their children in direct control over the Agents (school administrators and teachers) without an intervening bureaucracy (more Agents). Moreover, greater competition means that Agents will be motivated to make schools effective because if they don't, the Agents may lose their jobs as parents go elsewhere. Schools will become innovative, and practices will move in the direction of those that best serve the interests of parents and their children. This is the "miracle of the market" perspective. End of story.

And it's a compelling one. The problem, though, is that parents' interests in their children's education are not always identical with those of society. Some parents (and kids) may not make the sorts of choices we'd like them to make; we see this today in their choices over coursework, or in the strong advocacy of some parents for the interests of a few at the expense of many—for example, lobbying for expensive gifted and talented programs or for selective district schools that accommodate the elite. Under complete decentralization, schools would have every incentive to continue catering to the interests of the vocal and vigilant families. Resource use in schools would reflect this. The elite may find themselves with better options and teachers, but there is no guarantee that everyone would. Leaving choices completely at the (very) local level would most likely worsen uneven opportunities and outcomes in the exact same way that "exit" options today have had this effect. And as argued throughout these pages, a lack of basic uniformity in expectations and coursework among our nation's schools and classrooms imposes a very high cost on us all.

People who argue for complete decentralization often point to the successful model of America's system of higher education. They believe the world-class nature of our colleges and universities can be attributed to the decentralized decision making and market-driven forces that govern them. But this specific example of an educational model—one with strong accountability to some interests but without much in the way of social accountability—speaks to its weakness. That is, there is a tendency for Agents in higher education today to engage in opportunistic behavior when they aren't closely monitored and when outcomes are not transparent. A recent study of America's colleges concludes that almost half of college students learn little during their first two years.[1] And a slate of other books cast serious doubt on the extent to which our colleges and universities prize educational excellence above athletics, competition for the top students, retention, national rankings, fundraising, prestige, future alumni contributions, and so on.

There is thus an important role for the government to do more than simply fund schools and then leave them to "market forces." We have a common interest in ensuring that all students receive a quality education. We also share an interest in guaranteeing that our schools provide a level (or at least a reasonably level) playing field. The Principal in education is more than just parents and students; we must make certain that our school system upholds these shared social goals. Accordingly, a strong case exists for centralized decision making over what we expect of all students. In particular, we need national standards that set uniform and high expectations of all students.

This position will strike many—maybe most—as a clear example of federal overreach. Yet just about anyone's definition of the purpose of our educational system will invoke national interests, foremost prosperity and equality of opportunity. National standards would provide information on whether or not students are achieving and learning what is expected of them. They help guarantee that schools prioritize outcomes rather than process and compliance, or alternatively goals with little social value (such as promising high GPAs or a good shot at the NBA). Pragmatically, then, they would require periodic national exams for students at key ages, maybe along the lines of the NAEP today—once each in elementary, middle, and high school. And we must not only monitor students' progress through school, we must also monitor the monitor—the national exams. This means regularly compiling information on how well these exams (and the expectations that motivate them) align with the adult outcomes we really care about—to name the most important, college, careers, income, and civic engagement.

Some question whether we require *federal* policy to achieve national educational objectives. I want to be clear about the purpose of national standards. Foremost they articulate *the* most important goal of our educational system: to achieve well-educated citizens who can think critically and tackle messy problems, are creative, can write cogently, and have developed the foundations for lifelong learning. They also ensure uniform expectations across our nation's schools and classrooms. As argued in earlier chapters, establishing standards at a more decentralized level leads to large disparities among localities and schools. Essentially, decentralized decision making over expectations allows us to escape making clear what skills and abilities we want of all youth.

It's also not true that national standard setting requires the federal government to determine schools' coursework, textbooks, hiring choices, or even instructional practices. In fact, the existence of national standards could eliminate the need for much of what the current education bureaucracy does—which is to seek control over process and compliance with directives often tangential to educational quality. The task of carrying out national expectations—the specifics of class size, hiring practices, length of school day, budgeting, curricular offerings, pedagogy, textbooks, assignments, and so on—could be left to schools. Federal standards would simply make sure that school and classroom policies and decisions prioritize those that work best.

Still, there is widespread fear of a larger federal role in education. I've argued here that this can be attributed to the overly prescriptive role that the federal government plays today: it spends considerable bureaucratic effort monitoring compliance rather than supporting goals. Such practices mean that compliance (often only symbolic compliance) sets the tone for how our educational system operates. A stronger yet narrower role for the federal government would make this outcome less likely. But to make certain that an institutional culture of performance replaces our current one of compliance and political compromise requires that we make other changes in education's governance structure.

To this end, we must combine a larger federal role with a stronger role for schools. That is, join federal standards with considerable increases in school authority and responsibility. Devolving authority to schools could on balance tip control and responsibility to the most local of all levels—schools. School autonomy means school leaders and teachers would be freed from their current concern over compliance and meeting competing objectives, and would be able to focus on innovative and effective ways to teach.

Such an institutional configuration would result in a very different approach to the twin objectives of schools offering choice for parents and accountability for society. Currently, we don't have enough of either. Parents' choices are limited, and school accountability is perverse. Choices are limited because we don't allow enough genuine decision making at the school level. Without that, schools are merely idiosyncratic and uneven, and don't offer true choice among alternatives. Accountability is clumsy insofar as it not tied to meaningful outcomes and disingenuous because schools and teachers can't really be held accountable for outcomes subject to so much control.

Let's return to the baseball analogy I developed at the beginning of chapter 7. If the hypothetical baseball bureaucracy demands excessive compliance—thereby diverting coaches' resources and constraining their choices—it wouldn't be fair to then hold them responsible for outcomes. If kids failed to master the art of short-hopping a ground ball or reading a curve ball under the hypothetical conditions I described, could you honestly say it was all the coach's fault? To hold coaches—or schools—really accountable requires that they have genuine authority and discretion over their coaching practices. Combining a central-government role of setting expectations with school autonomy for meeting them means you can have both real choice among schools and also hold them responsible for the results of their autonomy.

Again referring to the analogy: baseball can't be played if you leave each decision up to the coach. A central organization must set the rules—for instance, what happens if the catcher drops a third strike, a hit ball bounces over the left-field fence, or the score is tied after nine innings. Coaches around the nation coach under the set of rules that define the game. The analogy with schools is that governments set the rules (in this case the expectations), and then schools figure out the best way to meet those expectations. This allows room for local preferences, knowledge, values, conditions, and priorities to be factored in, at the same time making certain that everyone plays the same game and seeks common goals. In baseball this governance structure leads to players from all parts of the nation (as well as Japan and the Dominican Republic) sharing a tremendous amount in common. They also develop a remarkably similar set of skills—even though they have been coached under conditions of complete local control. It's hard to see why the same wouldn't be true in education. This combination of central control over expectations but local decision making over how schools meet them would allow a balanced role for the two main Principals—the national interest and parents' interests—while significantly reducing the complex and conflicting roles Agents play in our school system today.

It's natural to think that such a dramatic change in our schools' governance structure would be impossible to achieve in practice. But a devolution of authority to schools such as I advocate here has been occurring throughout the world. In England various reforms over the last couple of decades have introduced a national curriculum accompanied by considerable school authority over decisions such as budgeting, management, school schedule, hiring, and so on. These reforms have changed England's school system to one with a stronger central-government role, a weaker school-district-equivalent role, and considerable new school-level authority. And it's made a difference. When some English schools accepted greater autonomy before others, these schools significantly outperformed the others.[2] A recent report singled out England, as well as several other countries around the world, for its changes in education policy that have led to sustained improvements in student performance.[3]

France too has recently turned some budgeting decision-making authority over to local schools. In the Netherlands responsibilities previously under the central government's control have been turned over to schools so that they now have greater authority over personnel, curriculum, and budget decisions. Sweden has loosened central regulations and given schools significantly more freedom over coursework and resource usage. Over the last few decades, Finland too has transferred considerable authority over course content and teacher recruitment to schools. Most recently, Poland extended the time required for students to remain in an academic track and introduced new national exams; these changes were accompanied by transferring central control over school finances and administration to the building level. Similar trends have taken place in New Zealand, Chile, and parts of Australia. Even here in

America, charter schools have been sprouting up, with some providing school leaders with real autonomy.

There's a reason this pattern of decentralization is occurring throughout Europe. Like ours, countries elsewhere are grappling with reforming their school systems to improve the quality of education that all children receive. Almost all face the same problems we do of quality and equity—although most don't suffer from both poor and unequal outcomes to the same degree that we do. These countries are paying close attention to what is happening around the world and replicating what works. Mounting evidence indicates that greater school autonomy offers an inexpensive way to achieve significant gains. Another reason for this trend is that many European countries have suffered from *too much* centralization. Educating youth takes building personal relationships, responding to opportunities, identifying roadblocks, seeking creative solutions, and designing innovative lessons. It's increasingly recognized that students perform best when their schools are given the latitude (and support) to make their own decisions over hiring, pay, curriculum, and teaching methods.[4] A central government can't tell teachers how best to teach students any more than it could tell a baseball coach how best to make ball players out of his kids.

For both of these reasons, school systems around the world are moving in the direction of greater school autonomy. It tends to be the governance structure found in countries with the best-performing students. In our own country, some charter schools have been able to demonstrate phenomenal success, and a recent report profiling outstanding public high schools in America pointed to the key role played by building-level leadership and responsibility.[5]

School Choice

Along with school autonomy, a new governance structure should feature increased school choice. Most OECD countries provide public subsidies to nonstate schools regardless of their philosophy, religious orientation, or pedagogical commitment. Such practices are based on a theory of educational freedom that protects citizens from the state's power to otherwise determine the type of education that children receive.[6] When policy permits schools significant leeway in how they educate their students, government control and oversight focuses more on establishing common standards, and then on overseeing school outcomes. For these reasons alone, we should allow parental choice over a wider array of schools than is currently available (including charter schools and under some conditions private schools). If we want an educational system more focused on outcomes than on process and compliance, we must have one that allows schools greater independence and variation in how they educate students—provided they achieve the common outcomes we seek. Referring again to the earlier analogy, if we want kids to master the game of baseball, we should leave it to the coach to decide how best to do that, but then also watch to see how successful he is. To successfully build a governance structure that prioritizes common goals, then, we must first specify what these goals are, but paradoxically also couple this with considerable freedom and choice at the school level.

HIGH EXPECTATIONS

A second requirement for moving our schools in the direction of high standards for all is to establish national expectations of what is taught in all schools and classrooms across the nation. Defining these expectations will necessarily be intensely political. There will be compromises, and the results are unlikely to match anyone's ideal. But if there is a consensus on raising standards, there are many places we can look to for guidance. Examples abound of world-class standards that could at the least serve as a strong starting point. Finland has them. Many Asian countries expect an enviable level of performance from their students. We also have our own federal NAEP standards, which are mostly viewed as tough and solid, and they've been in place for decades. While all somewhat different, expectations embodied in the three main international tests (PIRLS, TIMSS, and PISA) are also widely respected. Plenty of reasonable starting points out there already reflect the long, hard, and thoughtful work of many, many people. The prospect of having high expectations of all students doesn't mean we have to reinvent the wheel nor that another round of reform must turn into a lifetime project.

ADEQUATE SUPPORT FOR MEETING HIGH EXPECTATIONS

No one believes that a reconfigured governance structure together with high expectations will suddenly cause students to start learning more. These will only be useful if they are matched by the money and capacity necessary to meet them. Some years ago, the Chicago Public School system ended the practice of enrolling low-performing ninth-grade students in remedial math and English classes; instead, all were placed in a college-preparatory course of study. But with few other changes accompanying this policy, it is not surprising that its impact was at best minimal.[7] Districts have been besieged by similar policies, many of which I've discussed in earlier chapters. While most have had good intentions, they have all failed to address education's underlying problems. So we need more than a coherent governance structure coupled with high expectations.

Curriculum

The most important additional factors are a strong curriculum, effective teachers, adequate funding, and supportive social policies. Regarding the first, there is ample, perhaps even overwhelming, evidence that students learn more with a strong and carefully thought-out course of study. It is hard to achieve that with the amount of classroom-to-classroom, school-to-school, and district-to-district variation in expectations that we have. National standards would help establish guidelines for what, as an example, all students should be able to read and comprehend by the end of the fifth grade. To meet these expectations, schools and teachers need good teaching materials, lesson plans, assignments, and pedagogical skills. But there is wide variation in the effectiveness of these. Russ Whitehurst of the Brookings Institution recently reviewed the literature on how differences in the content of teaching lessons affect student learning. He concluded that students exposed to a more effective way of teaching a subject did much better than they would have had they instead been in a smaller class.[8] What is remarkable in Whitehurst's scholarship is the implication that so many classrooms across the nation rely on teaching practices and curricular content that are noticeably inferior to others. Teachers and schools need to use the ones that work; the best way to accomplish that is to reduce Agents' control over the process of delivering education, while increasing both our expectations of schools and their responsibility for meeting these.

To this end, the federal government could continue its nascent work in funding projects and evaluating research on what courses, content, skill sequencing, and pedagogies work best, and provide this information to states and schools. Such work on comparative effectiveness is becoming more and more necessary in health care, and for the same reasons it should also be extended to educational practices. To avoid duplication, the federal government would be the natural governmental level to undertake this role of providing schools with research on best practices. Such a role would be consistent with a governance structure designed primarily to support effective practices in schools and classrooms.

Teachers

Teachers are the most important feature of a school system. Without good teachers, nothing else will work. To improve teaching means addressing two separate issues. The first is the autonomy of teachers in the classroom. By that I don't mean that teachers need to be closely supervised, but rather we must redress the decoupled nature of teaching. The best school systems in the world rely on teachers who collaborate with one another and collectively maintain authority over what goes on in the classroom. This is true too in America's high-performing schools, which typically rely on such a collaborative teaching culture.[9] Previous chapters have discussed the problems created when classroom practices are not closely connected with schoolwide aims and objectives. Teachers' autonomy in the classroom causes there to be wide variation in student outcomes, in large part because ineffectiveness goes undetected and unaddressed.

A collaborative working environment is one important way to address this. Countries with top educational performance offer a model. They tend to treat teaching as a more professional enterprise; teachers work collaboratively on lesson plans, watch and comment on others' teaching, and revise lessons and assignments together. Collaborative teaching practices, in fact, are an important way that many countries maintain accountability: they foster a professional culture where teachers work together to collectively improve the quality of their classes. Such a process in Finland, for example, has led to a rule of thumb that about 40 percent of a lesson plan should involve lecture and about 60 percent should involve students' active participation in the lesson. In Japan teachers conduct school-level research by introducing and assessing new lesson plans. Teachers and principals constantly discuss new ideas, and those that are successful replace those that are less so.[10]

Centralized standards help foster this approach to teaching. They guarantee that lessons learned in one part of the country can inform practices anywhere else and so contribute to a nationwide dialogue among teachers, administrators, researchers, and policymakers about what works best— in the same way that the web is full of instructional videos on how best to teach specific baseball skills. Transparency in teaching aids this discussion as well, at the same time as also reducing variability in class-time usage and curricular effectiveness. You might recall from chapter 7 the comments made by Boston Principal Kim Marshall. He observed how "curricular anarchy" among teachers made it almost impossible to engage them in substantive discussion over teaching practices. Conversely, teaching in a transparent environment has the opposite effect.

Teachers in the United States increasingly recognize the advantages of such a collaborative approach to teaching. A recent report prepared on behalf of the National Education Association—America's largest labor union representing a large share of our public school teachers—called for "seismic changes" in the teaching profession. Above all else the report called for collaborative teaching along the lines discussed above.[11]

Genuine school autonomy (coupled with real accountability) should foster these changes. Schools would have greater latitude to determine school culture and practices. To the extent that schools become more result as opposed to rule oriented, they'll be much quicker to adopt practices that work. Collaborative teaching practices would be an obvious example. In the next decade, over half of the nation's teachers will retire, creating an opportunity for making far-reaching cultural changes in how teachers teach.

The second issue with respect to teachers surrounds their pay. Creating a more professional work environment and meeting high expectations means we must pay a professional salary. Without this we'll never attract and retain the best, brightest, and most effective people to the teaching profession. And where do we find this money? The federal government.

Schools, the Achievement Gap, and Funding

I haven't spent much time in this book discussing the role that student and family-background characteristics play in determining student outcomes, aside from how this influences their formal education. The challenge of engaging disaffected youth can't be underestimated. It's very difficult to overcome the pull of a drug culture, the influence of a dysfunctional family, or a genetic disability. In many cases, it's a battle that won't be won, certainly not through education policy alone.

There are many reasons so many of our nation's youth are at risk for drop-ping out or marginalizing their education. Some come from high-income but abusive families. Many have serious emotional or physical limitations. Others live in horrific home environments. And yet others are part of families that—if they are lucky—live paycheck to paycheck. Those who are most in danger have not one but multiple such risk factors. Local schools and their commu-nities are best placed to understand the specific problems students face and, with the help of research, figure out what interventions may help. But for schools and communities to do this, they need both capacity and resources.

This raises the issue of school funding. In a school system design such as sketched here, having autonomy and being responsible can only be meaning-ful if schools have the resources and potential capacity to exercise autonomy and be held responsible for what they do and don't accomplish. Local funding can't promise that; even state funding is problematic given the wide variation in states' capacity to raise education dollars. And so academic excellence also requires a significant new financial commitment from the federal govern-ment. Schools that face more challenges need greater capacity to overcome those obstacles. There is lots of evidence that some interventions with high-risk kids can help them beat the odds. For example, programs that help them develop relationships with adults outside of the home and community centers that provide family-support networks have in many instances proven effec-tive; so have programs that provide youth with enriched summer activities and opportunities. But it also means these schools need more resources.

To this end, the federal government should set target amounts of resources needed for a school based on its student composition—with more money for low-income students, special education, and nonnative speakers—along with the amount required to pay teachers a professional salary. And it should make a commitment to meet a large share of those expenses. Such a "weighted stu-dent" formula would ensure that schools with more challenging kids have the resources required to get the additional help they need. Almost all successful school systems in other countries invest more in schools where the challenges are greatest and also try to get the best teachers into these schools.[12] That we don't do the same is indicative of the failure of our school-finance laws to support our educational goals. Of course, a weighted-student formula does mean some schools will be funded more generously than will others. But with greater school choice, any parent who wishes to could opt for one of those better-funded schools.

Social Policy

There are two reasons we must revisit social policy. An educational system that places more demands on students could be one that leads more to fail. While I've argued here that this needn't be so, some research findings admittedly support this claim. At least in the short run, it's a real possibility. To this end, more generous assistance to poor and unemployed citizens would help counter the unintended consequences of high standards and would strategically weaken resistance to them.

But a more important reason for revisiting social policy is that education policy alone cannot overcome the challenges that some youth and their families face. A genuine commitment to equal educational opportunity means that we must reconsider the more pervasive opportunity structures embedded in American society. This means reexamining our health-care, early-learning, drug, family-support, and labor-market policies. Such policy arenas are rarely examined from the perspective of how they affect kids and their progress (or lack thereof) through our educational system. But they should be. State governments should develop and report measures of childhood opportunity, and we should compare states based on their progress on these. Currently, such data hardly exist. This means policymakers are unable to answer basic questions about the well-being of children in their state, let alone evaluate the effectiveness of measures to improve it. Some states are making progress toward developing such indicators and then measuring and tracking young children's skills and abilities. But such efforts have been slow and results uneven.

Good social policy matters for children's longer-term outcomes; that's why we need to prioritize it. Finland's educational system stands out not just for its excellence but also because socioeconomic differences among students are less correlated with adult outcomes than they are in many other countries. This is not as surprising once you know that America's children are over four times more likely to grow up in poverty than are Finland's and that America's children fare considerably worse on such indicators as access to infant and preventative health services and deaths from accidents and injuries.[13]

While it's important that America's social policies complement and support our educational goals, we should not make the mistake some do of thinking that equity in education depends on first addressing these other forms of inequality.[14] I personally don't share the belief that the most effective and logical starting place is addressing the conditions giving rise to the achievement gap—social policy, health policy, preschool policy, family-support policy. While it's natural to think that prevention would be more successful—and morally defensible—than is seeking a cure, such a position underestimates what education policy can achieve. Italy, Estonia, and Hong Kong achieve reasonably equitable educational outcomes despite income inequality equal to or larger than our own.

On a pragmatic note, too, the position that social policy should precede educational policy prioritizes a political agenda that is very unlikely to succeed. My own sense is that the best way to advance the political agenda of more equitable social policies is to establish high standards for all and to show convincingly the limitations of education policies alone to achieve these outcomes—and the importance of social policy to complement this agenda. Not only have we not come anywhere near having done that, but evidence here and abroad shows that these limitations are not nearly as large as we think. I hope that in these pages I have succeeded in making this case as well.

STRONGER STUDENT INCENTIVES FOR HARD WORK

An effective educational system is one that provides students with strong incentives to take advantage of the opportunities presented to them in school. Except for those seeking admission to select colleges, schools provide too few American youth with strong incentives or much motivation. Our educational system simply builds on existing interests and natural curiosity, and doesn't encourage students not otherwise inclined to work hard or to discover their unknown and undeveloped abilities. To change this we must provide students and parents with a clear understanding of the likely connections between the skills and abilities students are acquiring and the opportunities available to them in the future. This is the sort of "accountability" that our current educational system almost completely lacks. State governments could significantly help by providing good longitudinal data on the relationships among coursework, grades, performance on national tests, and higher education outcomes—including what college (if any) students attended, how long they persisted, what coursework they pursued, and so on.

State governments should be charged with not only providing this information but also making it publicly available in a form that is easily accessible to parents, students, educators, the press, and administrators. Some states are already making promising moves in this direction. The state of Washington, for instance, now tracks students from kindergarten to college and will soon be adding information on career outcomes. Currently, this database includes student-level information on high school test scores, coursework pursued, college attended, remedial coursework, and college outcomes. The state intends to collect and track similar information on high school dropouts, including information on their adult outcomes.[15] If widely distributed in a format that is accessible to the average citizen (currently, Washington's is not), such data can be instrumental in helping students understand how their choices and performance today line up with their long-term aspirations. This information would also encourage parents to play a more active role in their children's progress through the K–12 system, such as has been the case in Kentucky.

To really strengthen incentives for student effort though, we need to address the problem created by the mismatch between expectations in K–12 and those in our colleges and universities.

The Gap between K–12 and Higher Education

One of the real oddities of America's school system is the lack of coordination between our K–12 system and our institutions of higher education. This gap is understandable once you know something about educational history and the public schools' governance structure. At one point a close link existed, but that link was weakened with the introduction of various nonacademic tracks. It has been further undermined by the growing emphasis on enrolling increasing numbers of students (regardless of preparation) in college. With wide variation in standards and expectations allowed in our schools, the gap between high school and college has become unbridgeable for far too many. The practice of remedial education has had the effect of making invisible the fact that so many high school graduates are not college ready.

It would be fairly straightforward to reestablish this link. But it's also a tough sell. One way would be to follow the practices of most other countries and base access to public colleges on rigorous national tests that leave many ineligible. There is no doubt that in these countries having access to higher education so determined motivates a lot of hard work (and anxiety) among students. Short of nationalizing all state institutions of higher education, in the American context there is no way to make this happen though. Another way would be for state governments to stop paying to educate students who take remedial college courses. Spreading this cost between students and their high school would be one feasible way to make sure that both students and their schools understand what is expected of college-bound students; it would also put considerable political pressure on schools when this does not happen. Such a policy would require that states set their own uniform standard of what being college ready means and insist that students meet the standard before taking credit-bearing coursework. This alone would substantially improve awareness among students about what being college ready means.

Vocational Education

Learning about Elizabethan literature and first derivatives doesn't excite everyone. So what happens to those who are more turned on by computer graphics or bookkeeping?

College certainly isn't for everyone. Nor should it be. The problem arises when the college-going decision is made for youth (through their schools' deficiencies rather than each student having a fair shot at higher education). There is lots of evidence that exposing more students to a college-preparatory education can lead to more students being both college ready and successful in their postsecondary career. Recent reforms in Poland, Finland, and Romania mean that students today spend more time following an academic track; in all three countries these reforms have resulted in noticeable gains in student achievement.[16]

School systems around the world have some feature in their design to account for the fact that all youth need a good education but not all will or should attend college. Countries usually use one of two different approaches. The first is found in the United States, England, and Scotland; students within the same school follow different "tracks" but wind up with the same qualification (i.e., a high school degree earned after completing a certain number of credits). Some students can and do get a more vocational education, but they still graduate with the same credentials as do students pursuing the academic track. In the United States students in comprehensive high schools can graduate with one curricular option called Career and Technical Education (CTE).

Students first must meet uniform state graduation requirements, but then can take CTE classes to satisfy electives. Since CTE coursework is optional, students vary in the intensity and coherence of the vocational classes they take. In the United States perhaps one-fifth of students graduate with what could be characterized as an intensive CTE-track option.

A second approach is more common. Some countries offer distinct high school diplomas that distinguish among the available curricular options that students can pursue. Austria, Germany, Japan, the Netherlands, Denmark, Finland, France, and Italy, to name just a few, in some way or another use this approach. Typically, about one-third to half of all high school graduates in these countries finish with a vocational (or professional) as opposed to an academic degree. In Finland, Denmark, Switzerland, Germany, and Austria, over 40 percent of the population of high school graduates have a nonacademic degree.[17] Often different programs of study are associated with distinct high schools. In many countries with such separate paths to graduation, vocational tracks are associated with particular employers or craft associations and provide a fairly certain pathway to employment opportunities. They are often also criticized for this feature because they are seen as directing students into less rewarding work and cutting off college opportunities.

Despite this important downside, there is a close correlation between a country's overall high school graduation rate and the percentage of those graduates who complete high school with a vocational (CTE-like) degree. Countries with more vocational graduates (such as Germany, Sweden, and Austria) have much higher overall graduation rates than do countries with fewer students graduating with vocational credentials (such as the United States, Australia, Spain, and Italy). International evidence suggests that countries that emphasize and prioritize vocational education do a better job of getting students to complete their high school degree.[18]

International evidence also indicates that graduating more students with vocational credentials doesn't have to come at the expense of educational quality. Many countries have done a good job creating degrees that combine practical skills with the knowledge and abilities we expect of citizens. In fact, countries with the largest number of vocational students are also slightly more likely to have fifteen-year-old students with higher math scores than are those countries (like ours) with fewer vocational students.[19]

Some countries have even managed to combine a vocational track with links to the academic one so that graduates still have a college option available to them. This is usually done (for example, in Sweden) by maintaining a common set of expectations across degree types. Thus, regardless of degree type, all high school graduates can qualify for college. Whether or not students actually choose to go to college is their choice, but the educational system prepares all of them for that option.

A strong vocational high school degree option, beginning at age sixteen, has some distinct advantages. For one, it provides students with a much clearer idea of how their coursework is related to or may limit future career options. For another, providing students with solid work-related skills is infinitely better than our current strategy of handing out diplomas to apathetic and disengaged students based on time served in school—just so that our graduation rates look more respectable. And doing so may succeed in persuading more students to stick with their education. Finally, vocational education doesn't need to be equated with setting a low bar; several countries abroad offer examples of approaches for creating rigorous and meaningful alternatives to our current high school diploma.

PUTTING IT ALL TOGETHER

The principles sketched out above can be summarized as follows: We need a much simpler governance structure, one that capitalizes on the fact that our federal government can best articulate (and finance) national goals, while allowing schools to determine how to put these into practice. To complete the package, we need a significant increase in school choice, national-level expectations for all students, assurance that schools with the most challenging students are the best-funded ones, social policy that expands the opportunity sets of young children so they reach kindergarten ready to learn, uniform standards (at least at the state level) of what college ready means, a good curriculum matched by a new culture surrounding teaching practices, professional pay for teachers, stronger reasons for students to work hard in school, and finally the introduction of a solid vocational curriculum.

At the heart of the principles identified above are changes in education's governance structure. The changes proposed are consistent with those being made in countries around the world. Combining central goals with local autonomy and school choice promises a much better institutional configuration, one that offers school systems the right combination of two things needed for success: autonomy and accountability.

In addition to a dramatic change in education's governance structure, we must increase our reliance on federal funding for our schools. This is necessary to guarantee that challenges at the school level are matched by resources and that we pay teachers a salary commensurate with what we should expect of them. Education will never be a national priority if we don't back it up with national-level funding. This new federal role should also be accompanied by a more expansive safety net designed with a particular eye on the well-being of children and youth.

Finally, students need stronger incentives to work hard in school. To this end, we should end the practice of publicly financing remedial education. If students do not leave high school ready for college, that result should no longer be concealed or subsidized by taxpayers. Combined with meaningful vocational opportunities, this should provide students with greater understanding of why school matters and how their current choices affect their future options.

This package is ambitious. But it may not be as impossible as it sounds. To escape a low-level equilibrium, we don't so much have to escape in one jump as we have to set change in motion.

England provides a model for how we might proceed. And its example is especially relevant. Until the 1970s the English school system was organized in a fashion quite similar to ours, with local district control and a hands-off approach to curriculum and standards. Beginning in the 1970s, England started permitting their schools greater autonomy. In the 1980s all public schools were given the choice of "opting out" of local government control through a vote by school stakeholders. If a vote passed, the school was granted considerable autonomy (over leadership and staffing, teacher pay, and facility-usage decisions); in return, the school switched to being primarily funded by the national (as opposed to local) government. About 20 percent of English high schools voted for this degree of independence. Since then England has taken further steps to strengthen central control, weaken the role of districts, and provide schools with greater authority. Public school across England increasingly look like our private or charter schools in their degree of independence, although all are held to the same national standards. As mentioned some pages earlier, England's success with its reform has attracted international attention.

We could conceivably follow in their footsteps through some districtwide or perhaps even statewide experiments. With no school districts and very low student scores, Hawaii might be a good candidate. Especially when districts and states are increasingly strapped for cash, the prospect of federal funding for schools could be all it takes. Some districts may agree to participate and allow schools to convert to a system whereby they are financed by the federal government, held to federal standards, and at the same time granted considerable school-level autonomy. Such a reconfiguration might also be sought with new charter schools (or existing private schools); these could become chartered by the federal government along the lines outlined above.

While pragmatically some sort of a wholesale conversion of our governance structure is out of the question, smaller experiments such as these are within the realm of possibility—again, particularly when state and local governments are increasingly receptive to policies that reduce their fiscal obligations. A few successful experiments could be what it takes. Build a ladder halfway out of a pit, and we're much more likely to see how to get all the way out.

What appears to be a much more centralized governance structure is really not if it is coupled with genuine authority and responsibility at the school level. Other countries are increasingly moving toward a combination of central guidance and local autonomy as evidence of the effectiveness of this governance structure grows. In the U.S. context, greater autonomy and greater choice—including a redefinition of what it means to be a publicly funded school—would tip the balance toward schools becoming more rather than less responsive to their local constituents. Strengthening the role of the federal government at the same time as that of local schools has a strong pragmatic appeal as well: it provides a solution that could circumvent ideological divides that confuse and distort debate over what we want our educational system to achieve.

The reformed governance structure and other practices outlined here would result in an educational system that is significantly less complex and better designed to serve the interests of all Americans. It also redesigns institutional support and incentives in a way that moves us much closer to the level playing field that is a core American value. Most importantly, it would undo the forces that currently conspire to trap our schools in mediocrity.

Epilogue

America's twentieth century stands out for its remarkable commitment to expanded educational opportunity for all. From elementary school to high school and college, we experienced an amazing broadening of access to education. During the first half of that century, Americans enrolled in high school at twice the rate that Europeans did. Education became our way of advancing a value quintessentially American—equal opportunity. Like no other institution in American life, our public education system came to embody this commitment and aspiration. In fact, education—whether through general access, the desegregation of schools, the GI Bill, special education, subsidized school meals, Title I, or programs for kids whose first language is not English—came to be an important, if not *the* important, way of redressing our country's social ills. Our schooling system's emphasis on access became a model that the rest of the world first emulated and now has copied.

As testament to this continued vision of education's equalizing potential, today we have more colleges than any other country in the world. To a very great extent, we have prioritized providing citizens at any stage of their life with opportunity after opportunity for personal and career growth. Almost all Americans have access to higher education, regardless of their past performance, age, or life trajectory. The repeated opportunities we provide high school students as well as the widespread availability of subsidized colleges to all citizens is a phenomenon in which we can all take great pride. Even today, no country in the world offers anything quite like the opportunities for advancement that we do.

But as is true of all important social movements, changing times require changing visions. Today our continual commitment to equal educational opportunity and social justice means we must develop a renewed focus on educational quality for all. The original vision of public education—one that would unify a diverse population and provide equal opportunity for kids from very diverse social backgrounds—is surely no longer true, if ever it was. Rather, schools have become complicit in holding children from different social and economic backgrounds to different standards and have allowed failure to persist. In far too many cases, low expectations have reinforced social norms and a school culture where failure is expected. Partly because of this, educational excellence for all has come to take a backseat on the agenda.

Maybe we've been lucky to have escaped the high social costs associated with this model of a schooling system. One might even argue that for the times the model worked—that it fostered social mobility and reduced social inequities. Today this premise is impossible to sustain given that our country has one of the highest levels of social immobility in the developed world and that disparities in access to and success in higher education by students' social standing are both gaping and increasing.[1]

Education nowadays plays the largest role in life's chances. If our educational system is to provide real equality of opportunity, we must hold all kids, regardless of starting point, to high expectations. And getting there is perhaps one of the bigger challenges of our time. Taking on reform is politically difficult and expensive. But as I've also emphasized, the costs of *not* doing so are so much higher. Our country's economic malaise, the looming costs of an aging population, and disturbing trends in social inequality give us abundant reason to dramatically rethink our educational system. If coupled with widespread understanding of why we need systemic reform, such awareness together with bold political leadership may be enough. With the right confluence of conditions, we can finally put behind us the stinging criticisms *A Nation at Risk* made of our schools a full three decades ago.

Notes

INTRODUCTION

1. Of all branches of the military, the Army sets the lowest academic standard for its recruits. Education Trust, "Shut Out of the Military: Today's High School Education Doesn't Mean You're Ready for Today's Army," December 2010.

2. Justin D. Baer, Stéphane Baldi, and Andrea L. Cook, "The Literacy of America's College Students," American Institute for Research, January 2006.

3. Lois Romano, "Literacy of College Graduates Is on Decline," *Washington Post*, December 35, 2005.

4. Erkki Aho, Kari Pitkänen, and Pasi Sahlberg, "Policy Development and Reform Principles of Basic and Secondary Education in Finland Since 1968," World Bank Education Working Paper 2, May 2006; OECD, "The Impact of the 1999 Educational Reforms in Poland," OECD Working Paper 49, 2011.

5. Although once you factor in the large number of students who earn a high school diploma through the alternative route of passing a General Educational Development (GED) test, graduation rates in the United States are about average compared with those in other OECD countries. Chris Chapman and others, "Trends in High School Dropout and Completion Rates in the United States: 1972–2009," U.S. Department of Education, National Center for Education Statistics, NCES 2012-006, October 2011.

6. Alexandria Walton Radford and others, "Persistence and Attainment of 2003–04 Beginning Postsecondary Students: After 6 Years," U.S. Department of Education, National Center for Education Statistics, NCES 2011-151, December 2011; Andreas Schleicher and Vivien Stewart, "Learning from World-Class Schools," *Educational Leadership* 66, no. 2 (2008): 44–51.

7. For a suggestion that it might, see Richard Rothstein, *Class and Schools* (Washington, DC: Economic Policy Institute, 2004), 95ff. However, Rothstein offers no evidence, and is primarily concerned with the perverse effect that could or does result from fixating on test scores. "Fixating" on cognitive skills is not the same as fixating on test scores; the key is not to confuse the two.

CHAPTER 1: A HISTORICAL AND COMPARATIVE PERSPECTIVE ON THE UNITED STATES' EDUCATIONAL SYSTEM

1. Thomas Toch, *In the Name of Excellence* (New York: Oxford University Press, 1991), 43.

2. Robert Hashway, *Assessment and Evaluation of Developmental Learning* (Westport, CT: Praeger, 1998), 7–8.

3. Quoted in Herbert Kliebard, *The Struggle for the American Curriculum: 1893–1958* (New York: Routledge Farmer, 2004), 93.

4. Arthur G. Powell, Eleanor Farrar, and David K. Cohen, *The Shopping Mall High School: Winners and Losers in the Educational Marketplace* (Boston: Houghton Mifflin, 1985), 267.

5. Mortimer Smith, quoted in Diane Ravitch, *The Troubled Crusade: American Education, 1945–1980* (New York: Basic Books, 1983), 72.

6. Powell, Farrar, and Cohen, *Shopping Mall High School*, 252.

7. Some, such as Linda Darling-Hammond, argue that this curricular model was responding to other perceived challenges as well. She writes that the "historical origins of tracking systems in the United States were beliefs in differential intelligence held by eugenicists and some educational reformers in the early 1900s, which translated into . . . specific vocations assigned by socioeconomic status." Linda Darling-Hammond, *The Flat World and Education* (New York: Teachers College Press, 2010), 53.

8. Ravitch, *Troubled Crusade*, 7.

9. Ibid., 311–12.

10. For an excellent three-volume examination of school systems around the world, see Charles Glenn and Jan de Groof's *Balancing Freedom, Autonomy and Accountability in Education* (Nijmegen, Netherlands: Wolf Legal Publishers, 2005).

11. Asia Society, *Math and Science Education in a Global Age: What the U.S. Can Learn from China* (New York: Asia Society, 2006).

12. William H. Schmidt and Richard S. Prawat, "What Does the Third International Mathematics and Science Study Tell Us about Where to Draw the Line in the Top-Down versus Bottom-Up Debate?" *Educational Evaluation and Policy Analysis* 21, no. 1 (1999): 85–91.

CHAPTER 2: JUST HOW LOW ARE OUR EDUCATIONAL STANDARDS?

1. Higher Education Coordinating Board, *2008 Strategic Master Plan for Higher Education in Washington*, December 2007, 5.

2. Chester E. Finn Jr., Michael J. Petrilli, and Gregg Vanourek, "The State of State Standards," *Fordham Report* 2, no. 5 (1998): 7.

3. Sheila B. Carmichael and others, *The State of State Standards—and the Common Core—in 2010*, Thomas B. Fordham Institute, July 2010.

4. Lawrence S. Lerner and others, *The State of State Science Standards*, Thomas B. Fordham Institute, January 2012.

5. "The Underworked American," *Economist*, June 13, 2009, 40.

6. BetsAnn Smith, "Quantity Matters: Annual Instructional Time in an Urban School System," *Educational Administration Quarterly* 36, no. 5 (2000): 652–82.

7. David Baker and others, "Instructional Time and National Achievement," *Prospect* 34, no. 3 (2004): 313.

8. Charles Payne, *So Much Reform, So Little Change* (Cambridge, MA: Harvard University Press, 2008), 33.

9. Achieve, Inc., *State College- and Career-Ready High School Graduation Requirements*, July 2010.

10. ACT, "Rigor at Risk: Reaffirming Quality in High School Curriculum," 2007.

11. Achieve, *State College- and Career-Ready High School Graduation Requirements*.

12. Jennifer Laird, Martha Alt, and Joanna Wu, "STEM Coursetaking among High School Graduates 1990–2005," *MPR Research Brief*, December 2009.

13. Ibid.

14. OECD, *PISA 2006: Science Competencies for Tomorrow's World*, (Paris: OECD, 2007), table 5.16.

15. William H. Schmidt, "What's Missing from Math Standards? Focus, Rigor and Coherence," *American Educator* (Spring 2008): 22–24.

16. William H. Schmidt and others, "The Preparation Gap: Teacher Education for Middle School Mathematics in Six Countries," Center for Research in Mathematics and Science Education, Michigan State University, 2007.

17. Ina Mullis and others, *TIMSS 2007 International Math Report*, TIMSS and PIRLS International Student Center, 2008, exhibit 6.3.

18. Center for Research in Mathematics and Science Education, *Breaking the Cycle: An International Comparison of U.S. Mathematics Teacher Preparation*, 2010.

19. Schmidt and others, "Preparation Gap."

20. Center for Research in Mathematics and Science Education, *Breaking the Cycle*.

21. National Center for Education Statistics, "America's High School Graduates: Results of the 2009 NAEP High School Transcript Study," 2011.

22. Mark Schneider, "Math in American High Schools: The Delusion of Rigor," *Education Outlook*, no. 10 (October 2009): 4.

23. Ibid., figure 5.

24. "Ohio Students Face Stricter Math Standards," *Teacher Magazine*, January 5, 2010.

25. Achieve, Inc., *American Diploma Project: Algebra II, End of Course Exam: 2008 Annual Report*, August 2008; Sarah D. Sparks, "Case in Point: Setting the Bar for Algebra," *Inside School Research*, Education Week blog, http://blogs.edweek.org/edweek/inside-school-research/2010/10/setting_the_bar_for_algebra_ii.html.

26. ACT, "Rigor at Risk."

27. David N. Figlio and Maurice E. Lucas, "Do High Grading Standards Affect Student Performance?" *Journal of Public Economics* 88 (2004): 1815–34, table 1.

28. Of course, there is another interpretation: the Florida state tests are nonsensical. However, given the degree of scrutiny they are subject to (as compared to scrutiny surrounding teacher grading), this is unlikely to be true. For reports examining Florida's tests and their validity, visit http://fcat.fldoe.org/fcatpub5.asp.

29. Liana Heitin, "Study Challenges 'Idiosyncratic' High School Reading Selections," *Teacher Magazine*, October 28, 2010.

30. ACT, "A First Look at the Common Core and College and Career Readiness," 2010.

31. Gilbert A. Valverde and William H. Schmidt, "Greater Expectations: Learning from Other Countries in the Quest for World-Class Standards in U.S. School Mathematics and Science," *Journal of Curriculum Studies* 32, no. 5 (2000): 651–87.

32. Alan Ginsburg and others, "What the United States Can Learn from Singapore's World-Class Mathematics System: An Exploratory Study," American Institutes for Research, 2005.

33. ACT, "Rigor at Risk," 20.

34. Ibid.

35. To guarantee that reviewers were "country blind," reviewers were provided with written descriptions of the classroom lessons and the conversations that took place, with all indicators that could reveal the country in which the lesson occurred removed from the description.

36. James W. Stigler and others, *The TIMSS Videotape Classroom Study: Methods and Findings from an Exploratory Research Project on Eighth-Grade Mathematics Instruction in Germany, Japan, and the United States*, U.S. Department of Education, National Center for Education Statistics, NCES 1999-074, April 1999, 70. Reviewers rated the mathematical content of lessons as either low, medium, or high. In Germany, 34 percent were rated low in quality and 28 percent were rated high.

37. James Hiebert and others, *Teaching Mathematics in Seven Countries: Results from the TIMSS 1999 Video Study*, U.S. Department of Education, National Center for Education Statistics, NCES 2003-013, March 2003.

38. Fred M. Newmann, Gudelia Lopez, and Anthony S. Bryk, "The Quality of Intellectual Work in Chicago Schools: A Baseline Report," Consortium on Chicago School Research, October 1998.

39. David Baker and others, "Instructional Time and National Achievement," *Prospect* 34, no. 3 (2004): 311–34.

40. Gary Phillips, "Expressing International Educational Achievement in Terms of U.S. Performance Standards: Linking NAEP Achievement Levels to TIMSS," American Institutes for Research, April 2007.

41. Victor Bandeira de Mello, Charles Blankenship, and Don McLaughlin, "Mapping State Proficiency Standards onto NAEP Scales: 2005–2007," U.S. Department of Education, National Center for Education Statistics, NCES 2010-456, October 2009.

42. Ibid., tables 11, 12, 17, and 18.

43. Paul E. Peterson and Frederick Hess, "Few States Set World-Class Standards," *Education Next* 8, no. 3 (2008): 70–73.

44. Ibid.

45. Gary W. Phillips, "International Benchmarking: State Education Performance Standards," American Institutes for Research, October 2010.

46. John Cronin and others, "The Proficiency Illusion," Thomas B. Fordham Institute, October 2007, 11.

47. Ibid.

48. Achieve, Inc., *Do Graduation Tests Measure Up? A Closer Look at State High School Exit Exams*, 2004.

49. Emily Johns, "Minnesota Must Pass Math Test Goes by Wayside," *Minneapolis Star Tribune*, May 30, 2009.

50. Sean Cavanagh, "Many State Tests Said to Be Poor Indicators of College Readiness," *Education Week*, October 29, 2003.

51. Quoted in John Locke Foundation, "Survey of End-of-Course Test Questions," *Spotlight* 393 (2010): 3.

52. Ian Urbina, "As School Exit Tests Prove Tough, States Ease Standards," *New York Times*, January 12, 2010.

CHAPTER 3: THE CONSEQUENCES OF LOW EXPECTATIONS ON STUDENT EFFORT

1. Kara Miller, "My Lazy American Students," *Boston Globe*, December 21, 2009.

2. Ellen Greenberger and others, "Self-Entitled College Students: Contributions of Personality, Parenting, and Motivational Factors," *Journal of Youth Adolescence* 37 (2008): 1193–1204.

3. John H. Bishop, "Signaling, Incentives, and School Organization in France, the Netherlands, Britain, and the United States," in *Improving America's Schools: The Role of Incentives*, ed. Eric A. Hanushek and Dale W. Jorgenson (Washington, DC: National Academy Press, 1996), 124–25.

4. James E. Rosenbaum, *Beyond College for All: Career Paths for the Forgotten Half* (New York: Russell Sage, 2001).

5. Washington State Department of Health, "School Achievement and Climate," Washington State Department of Health Adolescent Needs Assessment, January 2010, http://www.doh.wa.gov/cfh/assessment/docs/assessreport/schoolach10.pdf.

6. Mariann Lemke and others, "Characteristics of US 15-Year-Old Low Achievers in an International Context: Findings from PISA 2000," U.S. Department of Education, National Center for Education Statistics, NCES 2006-010, October 2005, table B-16.

7. George D. Kuh, "What Student Engagement Data Tell Us about College Readiness," *AAC&U Peer Review* 9, no. 1 (2007): 4–8.

8. National Center for Educational Statistics, "Average Performance of U.S. Students Relative to International Peers on the Most Recent International Assessments in Reading, Mathematics, and Science: Results from PIRLS 2006, TIMSS 2007, and PISA 2009," http://nces.ed.gov/surveys/international/reports/2011-mrs.asp#reading.

9. National Center for Educational Statistics, "NAEP 2008 Trends in Academic Progress," NCES 2009-479, April 2009, figure 3 and table 5.

10. ACT, "Rigor at Risk: Reaffirming Quality in the High School Core Curriculum," March 2007.

11. National Center for Educational Statistics, "Issue Brief: Characteristics of GED Recipients in High School: 2002 2006," U.S. Department of Education, NCES 2012-025, November 2011, table 2.

12. Rosenbaum, *Beyond College for All*, 60.

13. Barbara Schneider and David Stevenson, *The Ambitious Generation* (New Haven, CT: Yale University Press, 1999).

14. Hart Research, *One Year Out: Survey among the High School Class of 2010*, College Board, 2011.

15. Lemke and others, "Characteristics of US 15-Year-Old Low Achievers," table B-21.

16. Andrea Venezia, Kathy Reeves Bracco, and Thad Nodine, "One-Shot Deal? Students' Perceptions of Assessment and Course Placement in California's Community Colleges," WestEd, 2010, 6.

17. Pearson Foundation, "Second Annual Pearson Foundation Community College Student Survey," 2011, http://www.pearsonfoundation.org/downloads/PF_CC_Survey_2011_Summary.pdf.

18. ACT, "Rigor at Risk."

19. Rosenbaum, *Beyond College for All*, 56.

20. John H. Bishop, "Nerd Harassment and Grade Inflation: Are College Admissions Policies Partly Responsible?" Cornell University, Center for Advanced Human Resource Studies, School of Industrial and Labor Relations, 1999.

21. Hart Research, *2011 National Survey of School Counselors: Counseling at a Crossroads*, College Board Advocacy & Policy Center, November 2011.

22. Caralee Adams, "Data Driving College-Preparation," *Education Week*, November 15, 2011.

23. Jennifer A. Mangels and others, "Why Do Beliefs about Intelligence Influence Learning Success? A Social Cognitive Neuroscience Model," *SCAN* 1, no. 2 (2006): 75–86; Claudia M. Mueller and Carol S. Dweck, "Praise for Intelligence Can Undermine Children's Motivation and Performance," *Journal of Personality and Social Psychology* 75, no. 1 (1998): 33–52.

24. Arthur Powell, *Lessons from Privilege* (Cambridge, MA: Harvard University Press, 1996), 138.

CHAPTER 4: LOW STANDARDS COMPROMISE HIGHER EDUCATION'S MISSION

1. Jennifer Medina, "Schools Are Given a Grade on How Graduates Do," *New York Times*, August 9, 2010.

2. Andrea Venezia, Kathy Reeves Bracco, and Thad Nodine, "One-Shot Deal? Students' Perceptions of Assessment and Course Placement in California's Community Colleges," WestEd, 2010.

3. Javier C. Hernandez, "Amid Complaints of Students Sliding by, New York Attempts Regulation," *New York Times*, July 13, 2009.

4. Anna M. Phillips and Robert Gebeloff, "In Data, 'A' Schools Leave Many Not Ready for CUNY," *New York Times*, June 21, 2011.

5. Associated Press, "More than Half of UA Freshmen Require Remedial Work," *Tacoma News Tribune*, September 18, 2010.

6. Associated Press, "In Colorado, 1 in 3 New College Students Need Remedial Classes," *Community College Week*, January 25, 2009.

7. Strong American Schools, "Diploma to Nowhere," Delta Project on Postsecondary Education Costs, Productivity, and Accountability, 2009.

8. Lisa Fodero, "CUNY Adjusts Amid Tide of Remedial Students," *New York Times*, March 3, 2011.

9. Jay P. Greene and Marcus A. Winters, "Public High School Graduation and College-Readiness Rates: 1991–2002," Manhattan Institute, Education Working Paper 8, February 2005.

10. Thomas Bailey, "Rethinking Developmental Education in Community College," Community College Research Center Brief 40, February 2009.

11. Venezia, Bracco, and Nodine, "One-Shot Deal?"

12. Bailey, "Rethinking Developmental Education in Community College."

13. Fodero, "CUNY Adjusts Amid Tide of Remedial Students."

14. Henry M. Levin and Juan Carlos Calcagno, "Remediation in the Community College: An Evaluator's Perspective," Community College Research Center Working Paper 9, May 2007; Christopher Magan, "Ohio Universities to Drop Most Remedial Classes," *Education Week*, October 11, 2011.

15. This includes the costs of remediation, the additional costs to businesses for training, and lower earnings. Vicki E. Murray, "The High Price of Failure in California: How Inadequate Education Costs Schools, Students, and Society," Pacific Research Institute, July 2008.

16. Clifford Adelman, "The Toolbox Revisited: Paths to Degree Completion from High School through College," U.S. Department of Education, February 2006; Strong American Schools, "Diploma to Nowhere," Delta Project on Postsecondary Education Costs, Productivity, and Accountability, 2009.

17. ACT, *ACT Profile Report, National, Graduating Class 2009*, 2009, tables 2.9 and 2.10.

18. Ibid., table 3.2.

19. Brad Phillips and Bruce Vandal, "Standards: A Critical Need for K-16 Collaboration," *Education Week*, November 1, 2011.

20. Caralee Adams, "Community Colleges Rethink 'Open Door' Admissions as Remedial Costs Rise," *College Bound*, Education Week blog, http://blogs.edweek.org/

edweek/ college_bound/2010/08/chicago_considers_ending_community_college_
open_admission.html.

21. Dolores Perin, "Community Colleges Protect Both Access and Standards? The
Problem of Remediation," *Teachers College Record* 108, no. 3 (2006): 370.

22. Doug Lederman, "Graduated but Not Literate," *Inside Higher Ed*, December 16,
2005.

23. Justin D. Baer, Stéphane Baldi, and Andrea L. Cook, "The Literacy of America's
College Students," American Institute for Research, January 2006.

24. Richard Arum and Josipa Roksa, *Academically Adrift: Limited Learning on
College Campuses* (Chicago: University of Chicago Press, 2011).

25. Fodero, "CUNY Adjusts Amid Tide of Remedial Students."

26. James E. Rosenbaum, *Beyond College for All: Career Paths for the Forgotten Half*
(New York: Russell Sage, 2001).

27. Venezia, Bracco, and Nodine, "One-Shot Deal?" 6.

28. Ibid., 6–7.

29. Max Roosevelt, "Student Expectations Seen as Causing Grade Disputes," *New
York Times*, February 18, 2009.

30. Ralph Stinebrickner and Todd R. Stinebrickner, "The Causal Effect of Studying
on Academic Performance," *BE Journal of Economic Analysis & Policy* 8, no. 1
(2008): article 14.

31. Ralph Stinebrickner and Todd Stinebrickner estimate that at one college about
40 percent of students who drop out do so because they have figured out that they
are not as well suited for college and college work as they had originally thought.
Todd R. Stinebrickner and Ralph Stinebrickner, "Learning about Academic Ability
and the College Drop-Out Decision," National Bureau of Economic Research
Working Paper 14810, November 2009.

32. See Cecilia E. Rouse, "The Labor Market Consequences of an Inadequate
Education" (paper presented at the Symposium on the Social Costs of Inadequate
Education, Teachers College, Columbia University, New York, NY, October 24–25,
2005); and Mark Schneider and Lu Yin, "The High Cost of Low Graduation Rates:
How Much Does Dropping Out of College Really Cost?" American Institute for
Research, August 2011.

CHAPTER 5: REDUCED PRODUCTIVITY AND INCREASED WAGE DISPARITIES

1. Cecilia E. Rouse, "Consequences for the Labor Market," in *The Price We Pay: Economic and Social Consequences of Inadequate Education*, ed. Clive R. Belfield and Henry M. Levin (Washington, DC: Brookings Institution, 2007), 99–124.

2. The payoff to more schooling was especially high among those with higher academic ability. McKinley L. Blackburn and David Neumark, "Omitted-Ability Bias and the Increase in the Return to Schooling," *Journal of Labor Economics* 11, no. 3 (1993): 521–44.

3. The $22,000 in 1972 dollars in the authors' study is about $113,000 in 2010 dollars based on the CPI inflator. Richard J. Murnane and others, "How Important Are the Cognitive Skills of Teenagers in Predicting Subsequent Earnings?" *Journal of Policy Analysis and Management* 19, no. 4 (2000): 547–68.

4. Ibid.

5. Eric A. Hanushek and Ludger Wößmann, "The Role of Cognitive Skills in Economic Development," *Journal of Economic Literature* 46, no. 3 (2008): 607–68.

6. If one were to discount the stream of income to the age of twelve, it would amount to about $12,500. Raj Chetty, John Friedman, and Johan Rockoff, "The Long-Term Impacts of Teachers: Teacher Value-Added and Student Outcomes in Adulthood," Executive Summary of National Bureau of Economic Research Working Paper 17699, December 2011.

7. Richard J. Murnane, John B. Willett, and Frank Levy, "The Growing Importance of Cognitive Skills in Wage Determination," *Review of Economics and Statistics* 77, no. 2 (1995): 251–66.

8. Derek Neal and William Johnson, "The Role of Premarket Factors in Black-White Wage Differences," *Journal of Political Economy* 104, no. 5 (1996): 869–95.

9. Murnane and others, "How Important Are the Cognitive Skills of Teenagers?"; Richard J. Murnane and others, "Do Different Dimensions of Male High School Students' Skills Predict Labor Market Success a Decade Later? Evidence from the NLSY," *Economics of Education Review* 20, no. 4 (2001): 311–20.

10. Stephen J. Nickell, "Poverty and Worklessness in Britain," *Economic Journal* 114, no. 494 (2004): C1–C25.

11. For supporting evidence, see Hanushek and Wößmann, "Role of Cognitive Skills in Economic Development." Some investigating this topic, however, have

not shared this conclusion. See Francine D. Blau and Lawrence M. Kahn, "Do Cognitive Test Scores Explain Higher US Wage Inequality?" CESifo Working Paper 1139, 2004; Dan Devroye and Richard B. Freeman, "Does Inequality in Skills Explain Inequality in Earnings Across Advanced Countries?" Centre for Economic Performance Discussion Paper 552, 2002.

12. Tyler Cowen, "Why Is Income Inequality in America So Pronounced? Consider Education," *New York Times*, May 17, 2007.

13. Eric A. Hanushek and Dennis D. Kimko, "Schooling, Labor-Force Quality, and the Growth of Nations," *American Economic Review* 90, no. 5 (2000): 1184–1208.

14. Serge Coulombe and Jean-François Tremblay, "Literacy and Growth," *Topics in Macroeconomics* 6, no. 2 (2006): article 4.

15. Hanushek and Wößmann, "The Role of Cognitive Skills in Economic Development."

16. McKinsey & Company, "The Economic Impact of the Achievement Gap in America's Schools," McKinsey & Company Social Sector Office, April 2009.

17. Clive R. Belfield and Henry M. Levin, eds., *The Price We Pay: Economic and Social Consequences of Inadequate Education* (Washington, DC: Brookings Institution, 2007).

18. Eric Hanushek and Ludger Wößmann, "The High Cost of Low Educational Performance: The Long-Run Economic Impact of Improving PISA Outcomes," Organization for Economic Co-operation and Development, 2010.

19. Eric Hanushek and others, "Education and Economic Growth: It's Not Just Going to School, but Learning Something While There That Matters," *Education Next* 8, no. 2 (2008): 62–70.

CHAPTER 6: LOW STANDARDS HARM THOSE WE THINK ARE HELPED

1. OECD, *PISA 2006: Science Competencies for Tomorrow's World* (Paris: OECD, 2007), table 5.21b.

2. Katherine Baird, "Class in the Classroom: The Relationship Between School Resources and Math Performance among Low Socioeconomic Status Students in 19 Rich Countries," *Education Economics* (2011): 1–26.

3. Robert Haveman and Kathryn Wilson, "Economic Inequality in College Access, Matriculation, and Graduation" (paper presented at Maxwell Policy Research Symposium on Economic Inequality and Higher Education: Access, Persistence and Success, Syracuse, NY, September 23–24, 2005).

4. Robert Haveman and Timothy Smeeding, "The Role of Higher Education in Social Mobility," *Future of Children* 16, no. 2 (2006): 125–50.

5. David Leonhardt, "Is College Overrated? (Cont.)," *Economix*, New York Times blog, http://economix.blogs.nytimes.com/2010/05/18/is-college-overrated-cont.

6. Bridget Terry Long and Michal Kurlaender, "Do Community Colleges Provide a Viable Pathway to a Baccalaureate Degree?" *Educational Evaluation and Policy Analysis* 31, no. 1 (2009): 30–53.

7. Ross Wiener and Eli Pristoop, "How States Shortchange the Districts That Most Need Help," Education Trust, 2006.

8. Education Trust, "California's Hidden Teacher Spending Gap," 2005.

9. Daria Hall and Natasha Ushomirsky, "Close the Hidden Funding Gaps in Our Schools," Education Trust, March 2010.

10. Education Trust, *Core Problems: Out-of-Field Teaching Persists in Key Academic Courses and High-Poverty Schools*, November 2008.

11. Maureen Hallinan, "Ability Grouping and Student Learning," *Brookings Papers on Educational Policy*, no. 6 (2003): 95–140.

12. Kevin G. Welner, *Legal Rights, Local Wrongs: When Community Control Collides with Educational Equity* (Albany: State University of New York Press, 2001).

13. National Center for Education Statistics, "America's High School Graduates: Results of the 2009 NAEP High School Transcript Study," U.S. Department of Education, NCES 2011-462, April 2011.

14. National Center for Education Statistics, "Eighth Grade Algebra: Findings from the Eighth Grade Round of the Early Childhood Longitudinal Study, Kindergarten Class of 1998–99," U.S. Department of Education, NCES 2010-016, October 2010.

15. National Center for Education Statistics, *The Condition of Education 2007* (NCES 2007-064) (Washington, DC: U.S. Government Printing Office, 2007), table

SA-7; Jennifer Laird, Martha Alt, and Joanna Wu, "STEM Coursetaking among High School Graduates 1990–2005," MPR Research Brief, December 2009.

16. B. Dalton and others, "Advanced Mathematics and Science Coursetaking in the Spring High School Classes of 1982, 1992, 2004," U.S. Department of Education, National Center for Education Statistics, NCES 2007-312, August 2007.

17. National Center for Education Statistics, *Condition of Education 2007*, table 3.

18. Thomas B. Hoffer and others, "Social Background Differences in High School Mathematics and Science Coursetaking and Achievement," U.S. Department of Education, National Center for Education Statistics, NCES 95-206, August 1995.

19. Karen Levesque and others, "Vocational Education in the United States: Toward the Year 2000," U.S. Department of Education, National Center for Education Statistics, NCES 2000-029, February 2000.

20. Adam Gamoran and Eileen C. Hannigan, "Algebra for Everyone? Benefits of College-Preparatory Mathematics for Students with Diverse Abilities in Early Secondary School," *Educational Evaluation and Policy Analysis* 22, no. 3 (2000): 241–54; Jia Wang and Pete Goldschmidt, "Importance of Middle School Mathematics on High School Students' Mathematics Achievement," *Journal of Educational Research* 97, no. 1 (2003): 3–19.

21. Robert H. Meyer, "The Effects of Math and Math-Related Courses in High School," in *Earning and Learning: How Schools Matter*, eds. Susan E. Mayer and Paul E. Peterson (Washington, DC: Brookings Institution, 1999).

22. Xin Ma, "Early Acceleration of Students in Mathematics: Does It Promote Growth and Stability of Growth in Achievement across Mathematical Areas?" *Contemporary Educational Psychology* 30 (2005): 439–60.

23. Welner, *Legal Rights, Local Wrongs*, figure 4.9.

24. Wang and Goldschmidt, "Importance of Middle School Mathematics."

25. Valerie Lee, Julia Smith, and Robert Croninger, "How High School Organization Influences the Equitable Distribution of Learning in Mathematics and Science," *Sociology of Education* 70 (1997): 128–50.

26. Eric Maurin and Sandra McNally, "Educational Effects of Widening Access to the Academic Track: A Natural Experiment," Institute for the Study of Labor, Discussion Paper 2596, 2007.

27. Tuomas Pekkarinen, Roope Uusitalo, and Sari P. Kerr, "School Tracking and Intergenerational Income Mobility: Evidence from the Finnish Comprehensive School Reform," *Journal of Public Economics* 93 (2009): 965–73.

28. Ofer Malamud and Cristian Pop-Eleches, "School Tracking and Access to Higher Education among Disadvantaged Groups," National Bureau of Economic Research Working Paper 16914, 2011.

29. Welner, *Legal Rights, Local Wrongs*, 11.

30. Ibid., 10.

31. James E. Rosenbaum, *Beyond College for All: Career Paths for the Forgotten Half* (New York: Russell Sage, 2001), 74.

32. Barbara Schneider and David Stevenson, *The Ambitious Generation* (New Haven, CT: Yale University Press, 1999).

33. Tom Mortenson, "The Growing Importance of Inherited Educational Opportunities," National Scholarship Providers Association, October 25, 2006.

CHAPTER 7: THE TYRANNY OF TOO MANY VOICES, OR "TOO MANY COOKS SPOIL THE BROTH"

1. Robert M. Costrell, "A Simple Model of Educational Standards," *American Economic Review* 84, no. 4 (1994): 956–77.

2. Julian R. Betts and Robert M. Costrell, "Incentives and Equity under Standards-Based Reform," *Brookings Papers on Education Policy*, no. 4 (2001): 9–74.

3. Ludwig Wößmann, "Schooling Resources, Educational Institutions, and Student Performance. The International Evidence," *Oxford Bulletin of Economics and Statistics* 65, no. 2 (2003): 117–70.

4. Ludger Wößmann and others, *School Accountability, Autonomy and Choice around the World* (Cheltenham, UK: Edward Elgar, 2009).

5. Brian Bolduc, "Don't Know Much about History," *Wall Street Journal*, June 18, 2011.

6. David Cohen, "Governance and Instruction: The Promise of Decentralization and Choice," in *Choice and Control in American Education*, ed. William H. Clune and John F. Witte (London: Falmer Press, 1990), 2:346.

7. Martin West, "Overcoming the Political Barriers to Change," in *Stretching the School Dollar*, ed. Frederick Hess and Eric Osberg (Cambridge, MA: Harvard University Press, 2010), 276.

8. Michelle Davis, "Governance Challenges to Innovators within the System" (paper presented at the Rethinking Educational Governance in the 21st Century Conference, Fordham Institute, Washington, DC, December 1, 2011).

9. William H. Schmidt, Hsing C. Wang, and Curtis C. McKnight, "Curriculum Coherence: An Examination of US Mathematics and Science Content Standards from an International Perspective," *Journal of Curriculum Studies* 37, no. 5 (2005): 530.

10. Mark Schneider, "Math in American High Schools: The Delusion of Rigor," *Education Outlook*, October 2009, no. 10.

11. John W. Meyer, W. Richard Scott, and Terrence E. Deal, "Institutional and Technical Sources of Organizational Structure Explaining the Structure of Educational Organizations," in *Organizational Environments: Ritual and Rationality*, ed. John W. Meyer and W. Richard Scott (Beverly Hills: Sage, 1983), 191.

12. Quoted in Charles Payne, *So Much Reform, So Little Change* (Cambridge, MA: Harvard University Press, 2008), 33.

13. John Chubb and Terry Moe, *Politics, Markets, and America's Schools* (Washington, DC: Brookings Institution, 1990), 40.

14. Stephanie Saul, "Charter Schools Tied to Turkey Grow in Texas," *New York Times*, June 6, 2011.

15. Melissa Junge and Sheara Krvaric, "Federal Compliance Works against Education Policy Goals," *Education Outlook*, July 2011, no. 6.

16. Jay Greene and Greg Forster, "Effects of Funding Incentives on Special Education Enrollment," *Civic Report*, no. 32 (December 2002); Marguerite Roza, "The Machinery That Drives Education-Spending Decisions Inhibits Better Uses of Resources" (paper presented at the Rethinking Educational Governance in the 21st Century Conference, Fordham Institute, Washington, DC, December 10, 2011).

17. Payne, *So Much Reform, So Little Change*.

18. Schmidt, Wang, and McKnight, "Curriculum Coherence," 555.

CHAPTER 8: EXIT, VOICE, AND THE
"SOMETHING FOR EVERYONE" CURRICULUM

1. Eric Zorn, "Behind the Musings: The Annotated High Schools Column," *Change of Subject*, Chicago Tribune blog, http://blogs.chicagotribune.com/news_columnists_ezorn/2010/03/behind-the-musings-the-annotated-high-schools-column.html.

2. Garey Ramey and Valerie A. Ramey, "The Rug Rat Race," National Bureau of Economic Research Working Paper 15284, April 2010.

3. Andrew Hacker, "Can We Make America Smarter?" *New York Review of Books*, April 30, 2009, 37–40.

4. Albert O. Hirschman, *Exit, Voice, and Loyalty: Responses to Decline in Firms, Organizations, and States* (Cambridge, MA: Harvard University Press, 1970), 30.

5. Ibid., 44.

6. Ibid., 44–45.

7. Ibid., 45–46.

8. Ibid., 47.

9. Ibid., 43.

10. B. Dalton and others, "Advanced Mathematics and Science Course Taking in the Spring High School Classes of 1982, 1992, 2004," U.S. Department of Education, National Center for Education Statistics, NCES 2007-312, August 2007, figure 27.

11. OECD, *PISA 2006: Science Competencies for Tomorrow's World* (Paris: OECD, 2007), table 5.12a.

12. T. Snyder and S. Dillow, *Digest of Education Statistics, 2009*, U.S. Department of Education, National Center for Educational Statistics, NCES 2010-013, April 2010, table 54.

13. Kristen Klopfenstein, "Advanced Placement: Do Minorities Have Equal Opportunity?" *Economics of Education Review* 23, no. 2 (2004): 115–31.

14. Leland S. Cogan, William H. Schmidt, and David E. Wiley, "Who Takes What Math and in Which Track? Using TIMSS to Characterize U.S. Students' Eighth-Grade Mathematics Learning Opportunities," *Educational Evaluation and Policy Analysis* 23, no. 4 (2001): 323–41.

15. National Center for Educational Statistics, "The Nation's Report Card: Long-Term Trend 2008," NCES 2009-479, April 2009.

16. OECD, *PISA 2009 Results: What Students Know and Can Do*, Vol. 1 (Paris: OECD, 2010), table 1.3.4.

17. OECD, *PISA 2006: Science Competencies for Tomorrow's World* (Paris: OECD, 2007), table 5.12a.

18. Arthur Powell, Eleanor Farrar, and David Cohen, *The Shopping Mall High School: Winners and Losers in the Educational Marketplace* (Boston: Houghton Mifflin, 1985), 5.

19. James Vaznis, "They're Fighting to Stay on Top at Latin," *Boston Globe*, March 6, 2010.

20. Kevin G. Welner, *Legal Rights, Local Wrongs: When Community Control Collides with Educational Equity* (Albany: State University of New York Press, 2001), 8.

21. Zorn, "Behind the Musings."

CHAPTER 9: SOFT AMERICA MEETS HARD AMERICA: THE PERCEIVED HIGH COSTS AND LOW BENEFITS OF HIGH EXPECTATIONS

1. Herschel I. Grossman and Minseong Kim, "Educational Policy: Egalitarian or Elitist?" *Economics & Politics* 15, no. 3 (2003): 225–46.

2. Javier C. Hernandez, "Amid Complaints of Students Sliding By, New York Attempts Regulation," *New York Times*, July 13, 2009; Andrew Trotter, "Online Options for 'Credit Recovery' Widen," *Education Week*, May 22, 2008.

3. Trotter, "Online Options for 'Credit Recovery' Widen."

4. Hernandez, "Amid Complaints of Students Sliding By."

5. T. Snyder, S. Dillow, and C. Hoffman, *Digest of Education Statistics, 2008*, U.S. Department of Education, National Center for Education Statistics, NCES 2009-020, March 2009, table 110.

6. College Board, "Education Pays 2010," College Board Advocacy and Policy Center, 2010, figure 1.6.

7. OECD, *Education at a Glance: 2011* (Paris: OECD, 2011), table A8.2a.

8. Kalpana Pai, "The Impact of Educational Attainment on Labor Market Outcomes," Luxembourg Income Study Working Paper 475, March 2008.

9. Alberto Alesina, Edward Glaeser, and Bruce Sacerdote, "Why Doesn't the United States Have a European-Style Welfare State?" Harvard Institute of Economic Research Discussion Paper 1933, November 2001, table 2.5.

10. Ibid., table 2.2.

11. Timothy M. Smeeding, "Public Policy, Economic Inequality, and Poverty: The United States in Comparative Perspective," *Social Science Quarterly* 86, no. 1 (2005): 955–83.

12. Grossman and Kim, "Educational Policy: Egalitarian or Elitist?"

13. Mariann Lemke and others, "Characteristics of US 15-Year-Old Low Achievers in an International Context: Findings from PISA 2000," U.S. Department of Education, National Center for Education Statistics, NCES 2006-010, October 2005, table B-22.

CHAPTER 10: GETTING FROM HERE TO THERE

1. Richard Arum and Josipa Roksa, *Academically Adrift: Limited Learning on College Campuses* (Chicago: University of Chicago Press, 2011).

2. Damon Clark, "The Performance and Competitive Effects of School Autonomy," *Journal of Political Economy* 117, no. 4 (2009): 745–83.

3. Mona Mourshed, Chinezi Chijioke, and Michael Barber, "How the World's Most Improved School Systems Keep Getting Better," McKinsey & Company, November 2010.

4. Thomas Fuchs and Ludwig Wößmann, "What Accounts for International Differences in Student Performance? A Re-examination Using PISA Data," *Empirical Economics* 32, no. 2 (2007): 433–64; Ludwig Wößmann, "Schooling Resources, Educational Institutions, and Student Performance: The International Evidence," *Oxford Bulletin of Economics and Statistics* 65, no. 2 (2003): 117–70.

5. Ronald F. Ferguson and others, "How High Schools Become Exemplary: Ways That Leadership Raises Achievement and Narrows Gaps by Improving Instruction in 15 Public High Schools" (report for the 2009 Annual Conference of the Achievement Gap Initiative at Harvard University, Cambridge, MA, June 2009).

6. Charles Glenn, "Common Problems, Different Solutions," *Peabody Journal of Education* 82, no. 2 (2007): 530–48.

7. Elaine Allensworth and others, "College Preparatory Curriculum for All: Academic Consequences of Requiring Algebra and English I for Ninth Graders in Chicago," *Education Evaluation and Policy Analysis* 31, no. 4 (2009): 367–91.

8. Russ Whitehurst, "Don't Forget Curriculum," *Brown Center Letters on Education*, no. 3 (October 2009).

9. John Chubb and Terry Moe, *Politics, Markets, and America's Schools* (Washington, DC: Brookings Institution, 1990).

10. J. Stigler and J. Hiebert, *The Teaching Gap: Best Ideas for the World's Teachers for Improving Education in the Classroom* (New York: Free Press, 1999), chapter 7.

11. Commission on Effective Teachers and Teaching, "Transforming Teaching: Connecting Professional Responsibility with Students Learning," report to the NEA, December 8, 2011.

12. Andreas Schliecher, "The Importance of World Class Schools for Economic Success," *Testimony*, March 10, 2010.

13. UNICEF, "Child Poverty in Perspective: An Overview of Child Well-Being in Rich Countries," Innocenti Research Center Report Card 7, 2007.

14. Richard Rothstein, Tamara Wilder, and Whitney Allgood, "Providing Comprehensive Educational Opportunity to Low Income Students: How Much Does It Cost?," Campaign for Educational Equity, Teachers College, Columbia University, October 2011.

15. Donna Gordon Blankinship, "State Tracks Kids from Kindergarten to College," *Tacoma News Tribune*, November 20, 2011.

16. OECD, "The Impact of the 1999 Education Reform in Poland," OECD Education Working Paper 49, June 2011.

17. OECD, *Education at a Glance 2011: OECD Indicators* (Paris: OECD, 2011), 33.

18. Stephen Lamb, "Alternative Pathways to High School Graduation: An International Comparison," California Dropout Research Project Report 7, January 2008, 28.

19. Ibid., 29.

EPILOGUE

1. Robert Haveman and Timothy Smeeding, "The Role of Higher Education in Social Mobility," *Future of Children* 16, no. 2 (2006): 125–50.

Bibliography

Achieve, Inc. *American Diploma Project: Algebra II, End of Course Exam: 2008 Annual Report*, August 2008.

———. *Do Graduation Tests Measure Up? A Closer Look at State High School Exit Exams*, 2004.

———. *State College- and Career-Ready High School Graduation Requirements*, July 2010. http://www.achieve.org/files/CCRDiplomaTable-Feb-2011.pdf.

ACT, Inc. *ACT Profile Report, National, Graduating Class 2009*, 2009. http://www .act.org/ newsroom/data/2009/pdf/National2009.pdf.

———. "A First Look at the Common Core and College and Career Readiness," 2010.

———. "Rigor at Risk: Reaffirming Quality in High School Curriculum," 2007. http://www.act.org/ research/policymakers/pdf/rigor_summary.pdf.

Adams, Caralee. "Community Colleges Rethink 'Open Door' Admissions as Remedial Costs Rise." *College Bound*. Education Week blog.

———. "Data Driving College Preparation." *Education Week*, November 15, 2011.

Adelman, Clifford. "The Toolbox Revisited: Paths to Degree Completion from High School Through College." U.S. Department of Education, February 2006.

Aho, Erkki, Kari Pitkänen, and Pasi Sahlberg. "Policy Development and Reform Principles of Basic and Secondary Education in Finland Since 1968." World Bank Education Working Paper 2, May 2006.

Alesina, Alberto, Edward Glaeser, and Bruce Sacerdote. "Why Doesn't the United States Have a European-Style Welfare State?" Harvard Institute of Economic Research Discussion Paper 1933, November 2001.

Allensworth, Elaine and others. "College Preparatory Curriculum for All: Academic Consequences of Requiring Algebra and English I for Ninth Graders in Chicago." *Education Evaluation and Policy Analysis* 31, no. 4 (2009): 367–91.

Arum, Richard, and Josipa Roksa. *Academically Adrift: Limited Learning on College Campuses*. Chicago: University of Chicago Press, 2011.

Asia Society. *Math and Science Education in a Global Age: What the U.S. Can Learn from China*. New York: Asia Society, 2006.

Associated Press. "In Colorado, 1 in 3 New College Students Need Remedial Classes." *Community College Week*, January 25, 2009.

———. "More Than Half of UA Freshmen Require Remedial Work." *Tacoma News Tribune*, September 18, 2010.

Baer, Justin D., Stéphane Baldi, and Andrea L. Cook. "The Literacy of America's College Students." American Institute for Research, January 2006.

Bailey, Thomas. "Rethinking Developmental Education in Community College." Community College Research Center Brief 40, February 2009.

Baird, Katherine. "Class in the Classroom: The Relationship Between School Resources and Math Performance among Low Socioeconomic Status Students in 19 Rich Countries." *Education Economics* (2011): 1–26.

Baker, David, and others. "Instructional Time and National Achievement." *Prospect* 34, no. 3 (2004): 311–34.

Bandeira de Mello, Victor, Charles Blankenship, and Don McLaughlin. "Mapping State Proficiency Standards onto NAEP Scales: 2005–2007." U.S. Department of Education, National Center for Education Statistics, NCES 2010-456, October 2009.

Barone, Michael. *Hard America, Soft America: Competition vs. Coddling and the Battle for the Nation's Future*. New York: Crown Forum, 2004.

Belfield, Clive R., and Henry M. Levin, eds. *The Price We Pay: Economic and Social Consequences of Inadequate Education*. Washington, DC: Brookings Institution, 2007.

Betts, Julian R., and Robert M. Costrell. "Incentives and Equity under Standards-Based Reform." *Brookings Papers on Education Policy*, no. 4 (2001): 9–74.

Bishop, John H. "Nerd Harassment and Grade Inflation: Are College Admissions Policies Partly Responsible?" Cornell University, Center for Advanced Human Resource Studies, School of Industrial and Labor Relations, 1999.

———. "Signaling, Incentives, and School Organization in France, the Netherlands, Britain, and the United States." In *Improving America's Schools: The Role of Incentives*, edited by Eric A. Hanushek and Dale W. Jorgenson. Washington, DC: National Academy Press, 1996.

Blackburn, McKinley L., and David Neumark. "Omitted-Ability Bias and the Increase in the Return to Schooling," *Journal of Labor Economics* 11, no. 3 (1993): 521–44.

Blankinship, Donna Gordon. "State Tracks Kids from Kindergarten to College." *Tacoma News Tribune*, November 20, 2011.

Blau, Francine D., and Lawrence M. Kahn. "Do Cognitive Test Scores Explain Higher US Wage Inequality?" CESifo Working Paper 1139, 2004.

Bolduc, Brian. "Don't Know Much about History." *Wall Street Journal*, June 18, 2011.

Carmichael, Sheila B., and others. *The State of State Standards—and the Common Core—in 2010*. Thomas B. Fordham Institute, July 2010.

Cavanagh, Sean. "Many State Tests Said to Be Poor Indicators of College Readiness." *Education Week*, October 29, 2003.

Center for Research in Mathematics and Science Education. *Breaking the Cycle: An International Comparison of U.S. Mathematics Teacher Preparation*, 2010.

Chapman, Chris, and others. "Trends in High School Dropout and Completion Rates in the United States: 1972–2009." U.S. Department of Education, National Center for Education Statistics, NCES 2012-006, October 2011.

Chetty, Raj, John Friedman, and Johan Rockoff. "The Long-Term Impacts of Teachers: Teacher Value-Added and Student Outcomes in Adulthood." Executive

Summary of National Bureau of Economic Research Working Paper 17699, December 2011.

Chubb, John, and Terry Moe. *Politics, Markets, and America's Schools.* Washington, DC: Brookings Institution, 1990.

Clark, Damon. "The Performance and Competitive Effects of School Autonomy." *Journal of Political Economy* 117, no. 4 (2009): 745–78.

Cogan, Leland S., William H. Schmidt, and David E. Wiley. "Who Takes What Math and in Which Track? Using TIMSS to Characterize U.S. Students' Eighth-Grade Mathematics Learning Opportunities." *Educational Evaluation and Policy Analysis* 23, no. 4 (2001): 323–41.

Cohen, David. "Governance and Instruction: The Promise of Decentralization and Choice." In *Choice and Control in American Education,* Volume 2, edited by William H. Clune and John F. Witte. London: Falmer Press, 1990.

College Board. "Education Pays 2010." College Board Advocacy and Policy Center, 2010.

Commission on Effective Teachers and Teaching. "Transforming Teaching: Connecting Professional Responsibility with Student Learning." Report to the NEA, December 8, 2011.

Costrell, Robert M. "A Simple Model of Educational Standards." *American Economic Review* 84, no. 4 (1994): 956–77.

Coulombe, Serge, and Jean-François Tremblay. "Literacy and Growth." *Topics in Macroeconomics* 6, no. 2 (2006): article 4.

Cowen, Tyler. "Why Is Income Inequality in America So Pronounced? Consider Education." *New York Times,* May 17, 2007.

Cronin, John, and others. "The Proficiency Illusion." Thomas B. Fordham Institute, October 2007.

Dalton, B., and others. "Advanced Mathematics and Science Coursetaking in the Spring High School Classes of 1982, 1992, 2004." U.S. Department of Education, National Center for Education Statistics, NCES 2007-312, August 2007.

Darling-Hammond, Linda. *The Flat World and Education.* New York: Teachers College Press, 2010.

Davis, Michelle. "Governance Challenges to Innovators within the System."
    Paper presented at the Rethinking Educational Governance in the 21st Century
    Conference, Fordham Institute, Washington, DC, December 1, 2011.

Devroye, Dan, and Richard B. Freeman. "Does Inequality in Skills Explain Inequality
    in Earnings across Advanced Countries?" Centre for Economic Performance
    Discussion Paper 552, 2002.

Economist. "The Underworked American," June 13, 2009.

Education Trust. "California's Hidden Teacher Spending Gap," 2005.

———. *Core Problems: Out-of-Field Teaching Persists in Key Academic Courses and
    High-Poverty Schools,* November 2008.

———. "Shut Out of the Military: Today's High School Education Doesn't Mean
    You're Ready for Today's Army," December 2010.

Ferguson, Ronald F., and others. "How High Schools Become Exemplary: Ways
    That Leadership Raises Achievement and Narrows Gaps by Improving Instruction
    in 15 Public High Schools." Report for the 2009 Annual Conference of the
    Achievement Gap Initiative at Harvard University, Cambridge, MA, June 2009.
    http://www.agi.harvard.edu/ events/2009Conference/2009AGIConferenceRep
    ort6-30-2010web.pdf.

Figlio, David N., and Maurice E. Lucas. "Do High Grading Standards Affect Student
    Performance?" *Journal of Public Economics* 88 (2004): 1815–34.

Finn, Chester E., Jr., Michael J. Petrilli, and Gregg Vanourek. "The State of State
    Standards." *Fordham Report* 2, no. 5 (1998).

Fuchs, Thomas, and Ludwig Wößmann. "What Accounts for International
    Differences in Student Performance? A Re-examination Using PISA Data."
    Empirical Economics 32, no. 2 (2007): 433–64.

Fodero, Lisa. "CUNY Adjusts amid Tide of Remedial Students." *New York Times,*
    March 3, 2011.

Gamoran, Adam, and Eileen C. Hannigan. "Algebra for Everyone? Benefits of
    College-Preparatory Mathematics for Students with Diverse Abilities in Early
    Secondary School." *Educational Evaluation and Policy Analysis* 22, no 3 (2000):
    241–54.

Ginsburg, Alan, and others. "What the United States Can Learn from Singapore's World-Class Mathematics System: An Exploratory Study." American Institutes for Research, 2005.

Glenn, Charles. "Common Problems, Different Solutions." *Peabody Journal of Education* 82, no. 2 (2007): 530–48.

Greenberger, Ellen, and others. "Self-Entitled College Students: Contributions of Personality, Parenting, and Motivational Factors." *Journal of Youth Adolescence* 37 (2008): 1193–1204.

Greene, Jay, and Greg Forster. "Effects of Funding Incentives on Special Education Enrollment." Manhattan Institute for Policy Research Civic Report 32, 2002.

Greene, Jay P., and Marcus A. Winters. "Public High School Graduation and College-Readiness Rates: 1991–2002." Education Working Paper 8, 2005.

Grossman, Herschel I., and Minseong Kim. "Educational Policy: Egalitarian or Elitist?" *Economics & Politics* 15, no. 3 (2003): 225–46.

Hacker, Andrew. "Can We Make America Smarter?" *New York Review of Books*, April 30, 2009, 37–40.

Hall, Daria, and Natasha Ushomirsky. "Close the Hidden Funding Gaps in Our Schools." Education Trust, March 2010.

Hallinan, Maureen T. "Ability Grouping and Student Learning." *Brookings Papers on Educational Policy*, no. 6 (2003): 95–140

Hanushek, Eric A., and Dennis D. Kimko. "Schooling, Labor-Force Quality, and the Growth of Nations." *American Economic Review* 90, no. 5 (2000): 1184–1208.

Hanushek, Eric A., and others. "Education and Economic Growth: It's Not Just Going to School, but Learning Something While There That Matters." *Education Next* 8, no. 2 (2008): 62–70.

Hanushek, Eric. A., and Ludger Wößmann. "The High Cost of Low Educational Performance: The Long-Run Economic Impact of Improving PISA Outcomes." Organisation for Economic Co-operation and Development, 2010. http://www.oecd.org/dataoecd/ 11/28/44417824.pdf.

———. "The Role of Cognitive Skills in Economic Development." *Journal of Economic Literature* 46, no. 3 (2008): 607–68.

Hart Research. *2011 National Survey of School Counselors: Counseling at a Crossroads.* College Board Advocacy & Policy Center, November 2011.

———. *One Year Out: Survey among the High School Class of 2010.* College Board, 2011.

Hashway, Robert. *Assessment and Evaluation of Developmental Learning.* Westport: Praeger, 1998.

Haveman, Robert, and Timothy Smeeding. "The Role of Higher Education in Social Mobility." *Future of Children* 16, no. 2 (2006): 125–50.

Haveman, Robert, and Kathryn Wilson. "Economic Inequality in College Access, Matriculation, and Graduation." Paper presented at Maxwell Policy Research Symposium on the Economic Inequality and Higher Education: Access, Persistence and Success Conference, Syracuse, NY, September 23–24, 2005.

Heitin, Liana. "Study Challenges 'Idiosyncratic' High School Reading Selections." *Teacher Magazine,* October 28, 2010.

Hernandez, Javier C. "Amid Complaints of Students Sliding By, New York Attempts Regulation." *New York Times,* July 13, 2009.

Hiebert, James, and others. "Teaching Mathematics in Seven Countries: Results from the TIMSS 1999 Video Study." U.S. Department of Education, National Center for Education Statistics, NCES 2003-013, March 2003.

Higher Education Coordinating Board. *2008 Strategic Master Plan for Higher Education in Washington,* December 2007.

Hirschman, Albert O. *Exit, Voice, and Loyalty: Responses to Decline in Firms, Organizations, and States.* Cambridge, MA: Harvard University Press, 1970.

Hoffer, Thomas B., and others. "Social Background Differences in High School Mathematics and Science Coursetaking and Achievement." U.S. Department of Education, National Center for Education Statistics, NCES 95-206, August 1995.

John Locke Foundation. "Survey of End-of-Course Test Questions." *Spotlight* 393 (2010).

Johns, Emily. "Minnesota Must Pass Math Test Goes by Wayside." *Minneapolis Star Tribune,* May 30, 2009.

Junge, Melissa, and Sheara Krvaric. "The Compliance Culture in Education." *Rick Hess Straight Up.* Education Week blog. http://blogs.edweek.org/edweek/rick_hess_straight_up/2011/10/the_compliance_culture_in_education.html.

Kliebard, Herbert. *The Struggle for the American Curriculum: 1893–1958.* New York: Routledge Farmer, 2004.

Klopfenstein, Kristen. "Advanced Placement: Do Minorities Have Equal Opportunity?" *Economics of Education Review* 23, no. 2 (2004): 115–31.

Kuh, George D. "What Student Engagement Data Tell Us about College Readiness." *AAC&U Peer Review* 9, no. 1 (2007): 4–8.

Laird, Jennifer, Martha Alt, and Joanna Wu. "STEM Coursetaking among High School Graduates 1990–2005." MPR Research Brief, December 2009.

Lamb, Stephen. "Alternative Pathways to High School Graduation: An International Comparison." California Dropout Research Project Report 7, January 2008.

Lederman, Doug. "Graduated but Not Literate." *Inside Higher Ed*, December 16, 2005. http://www.insidehighered.com/news/2005/12/16/literacy.

Lee, Valerie, Julia Smith, and Robert Croninger. "How High School Organization Influences the Equitable Distribution of Learning in Mathematics and Science." *Sociology of Education* 70 (1997): 128–50.

Lemke, Mariann, and others. "Characteristics of US 15-Year-Old Low Achievers in an International Context: Findings from PISA 2000." U.S. Department of Education, National Center for Education Statistics, NCES 2006-010, October 2005.

Leonhardt, David. "Is College Overrated? (Cont.)" *Economix.* New York Times blog. http://economix.blogs.nytimes.com/2010/05/18/is-college-overrated-cont.

Lerner, Lawrence S., and others, "The State of State Science Standards." Thomas B. Fordham Institute, January 2012.

Levesque, Karen, and others. "Vocational Education in the United States: Toward the Year 2000." U.S. Department of Education, National Center for Education Statistics, NCES 2000-029, February 2000.

Levin, Henry M., and Juan Carlos Calcagno. "Remediation in the Community College: An Evaluator's Perspective." Community College Research Center Working Paper 9, May 2007.

Long, Bridget T., and Michal Kurlaender. "Do Community Colleges Provide a Viable Pathway to a Baccalaureate Degree?" *Educational Evaluation and Policy Analysis* 31, no. 1 (2009): 30–53.

Ma, Xin. "Early Acceleration of Students in Mathematics: Does It Promote Growth and Stability of Growth in Achievement across Mathematical Areas?" *Contemporary Educational Psychology* 30 (2005): 439–60.

Magan, Christopher. "Ohio Universities to Drop Most Remedial Classes." *Education Week*, October 11, 2011.

Malamud, Ofer, and Cristian Pop-Eleches. "School Tracking and Access to Higher Education among Disadvantaged Groups." National Bureau of Economic Research Working Paper 16914, 2011.

Mangels, Jennifer A., and others. "Why Do Beliefs about Intelligence Influence Learning Success? A Social Cognitive Neuroscience Model." *SCAN* 1, no. 2 (2006): 75–86.

Maurin, Eric, and Sandra McNally. "Educational Effects of Widening Access to the Academic Track: A Natural Experiment." Institute for the Study of Labor, Discussion Paper 2596, 2007.

McKinsey & Company. "The Economic Impact of the Achievement Gap in America's Schools." McKinsey & Company Social Sector Office, April 2009.

Medina, Jennifer. "Schools Are Given a Grade on How Graduates Do." *New York Times*, August 9, 2010.

Meyer, John W., W. Richard Scott, and Terrence E. Deal. "Institutional and Technical Sources of Organizational Structure Explaining the Structure of Educational Organizations." In *Organizational Environments: Ritual and Rationality*, edited by John W. Meyer and W. Richard Scott. Beverly Hills: Sage, 1983.

Meyer, Robert H. "The Effects of Math and Math-Related Courses in High School." In *Earning and Learning: How Schools Matter*, edited by Susan E. Mayer and Paul E. Peterson. Washington, DC: Brookings Institution, 1999.

Miller, Kara. "My Lazy American Students." *Boston Globe*, December 21, 2009.

Mortenson, Tom. "The Growing Importance of Inherited Educational Opportunities." National Scholarship Providers Association, October 25, 2006.

Mourshed, Mona, Chinezi Chijioke, and Michael Barber. "How the World's Most Improved School Systems Keep Getting Better." McKinsey & Company, November 2010.

Mueller, Claudia M., and Carol S. Dweck. "Praise for Intelligence Can Undermine Children's Motivation and Performance." *Journal of Personality and Social Psychology* 75, no. 1 (1998): 33–52.

Mullis, Ina, and others. *TIMSS 2007 International Math Report.* TIMSS and PIRLS International Student Center, 2008.

Murnane, Richard J., and others. "Do Different Dimensions of Male High School Students' Skills Predict Labor Market Success a Decade Later? Evidence from the NLSY." *Economics of Education Review* 20, no. 4 (2001): 311–20.

———. "How Important Are the Cognitive Skills of Teenagers in Predicting Subsequent Earnings?" *Journal of Policy Analysis and Management* 19, no. 4 (2000): 547–68.

Murnane, Richard J., John B. Willett, and Frank Levy. "The Growing Importance of Cognitive Skills in Wage Determination." *Review of Economics and Statistics* 77, no. 2 (1995): 251–66.

Murray, Vicki E. "The High Price of Failure in California: How Inadequate Education Costs Schools, Students, and Society." Pacific Research Institute, July 2008.

National Center for Education Statistics. "America's High School Graduates: Results of the 2009 NAEP High School Transcript Study." U.S. Department of Education, NCES 2011-462, April 2011.

———. "Average Performance of U.S. Students Relative to International Peers on the Most Recent International Assessments in Reading, Mathematics, and Science: Results from PIRLS 2006, TIMSS 2007, and PISA 2009." http://nces.ed.gov/surveys/international/reports/2011-mrs.asp#reading.

———. *The Condition of Education 2007.* U.S. Department of Education, NCES 2007-064. Washington, DC: U.S. Government Printing Office, 2007.

———. "Eighth-Grade Algebra: Findings from the Eighth-Grade Round of the Early Childhood Longitudinal Study, Kindergarten Class of 1998–99." U.S. Department of Education, NCES 2010-016, October 2010.

———. "Issue Brief: Characteristics of GED Recipients in High School: 2002–2006." U.S. Department of Education, NCES 2012-025, November 2011.

———. "NAEP 2008 Trends in Academic Progress." U.S. Department of Education, NCES 2009-479, April 2009.

Newmann, Fred M., Gudelia Lopez, and Anthony S. Bryk. "The Quality of
    Intellectual Work in Chicago Schools: A Baseline Report." Consortium on
    Chicago School Research, October 1998.

Nickell, Stephen J. "Poverty and Worklessness in Britain." *Economic Journal* 114, no.
    494 (2004): C1–C25.

OECD. *Education at a Glance 2011: OECD Indicators.* Paris: OECD, 2011.

———. "The Impact of the 1999 Education Reform in Poland." OECD Education
    Working Paper 49, June 2011.

———. *PISA 2006: Science Competencies for Tomorrow's World.* Paris: OECD, 2007.

———. *PISA 2009 Results: What Students Know and Can Do.* Vol. 1. Paris: OECD, 2010.

Pai, Kalpana. "The Impact of Educational Attainment on Labor Market Outcomes."
    Luxembourg Income Study Working Paper 475, March 2008.

Payne, Charles. *So Much Reform, So Little Change.* Cambridge, MA: Harvard
    University Press, 2008.

Pearson Foundation. "Second Annual Pearson Foundation Community College
    Student Survey," 2011. http://www.pearsonfoundation.org/downloads/ PF_CC_
    Survey_2011_Summary.pdf.

Pekkarinen, Tuomas, Roope Uusitalo, and Sari P. Kerr. "School Tracking and
    Intergenerational Income Mobility: Evidence from the Finnish Comprehensive
    School Reform." *Journal of Public Economics* 93 (2009): 965–73.

Perin, Dolores. "Community Colleges Protect Both Access and Standards? The
    Problem of Remediation." *Teachers College Record* 108, no. 3 (2006): 339–73.

Peterson, Paul E., and Frederick Hess. "Few States Set World-Class Standards."
    Education Next 8, no. 3 (2008): 70–73.

Phillips, Anna M., and Robert Gebeloff. "In Data, 'A' Schools Leave Many Not
    Ready for CUNY." *New York Times,* June 21, 2011.

Phillips, Brad, and Bruce Vandal. "Standards: A Critical Need for K-16
    Collaboration." *Education Week,* November 1, 2011.

Phillips, Gary W. "Expressing International Educational Achievement in Terms
    of US Performance Standards: Linking NAEP Achievement Levels to TIMSS."
    American Institutes for Research, April 2007.

———. "International Benchmarking: State Education Performance Standards." American Institutes for Research, October 2010.

Powell, Arthur G. *Lessons from Privilege.* Cambridge, MA: Harvard University Press, 1996.

Powell, Arthur G., Eleanor Farrar, and David K. Cohen. *The Shopping Mall High School: Winners and Losers in the Educational Marketplace.* Boston: Houghton Mifflin, 1985.

Radford, Alexandria Walton, and others. "Persistence and Attainment of 2003–04 Beginning Postsecondary Students: After 6 Years." U.S. Department of Education, National Center for Education Statistics, NCES 2011-151, December 2011.

Ramey, Garey, and Valerie A. Ramey. "The Rug Rat Race." National Bureau of Economic Research Working Paper 15284, April 2010.

Ravitch, Diane. *The Language Police.* New York: Random House, 2003.

———. *The Troubled Crusade: American Education, 1945–1980.* New York: Basic Books, 1983.

Romano, Lois. "Literacy of College Graduates Is on Decline." *Washington Post,* December 35, 2005.

Roosevelt, Max. "Student Expectations Seen as Causing Grade Disputes." *New York Times,* February 18, 2009.

Rosenbaum, James E. *Beyond College for All: Career Paths for the Forgotten Half.* New York: Russell Sage, 2001.

Rothstein, Richard. *Class and Schools.* Washington, DC: Economic Policy Institute, 2004.

Rothstein, Richard, Tamara Wilder, and Whitney Allgood. "Providing Comprehensive Educational Opportunity to Low Income Students: How Much Does It Cost?" Campaign for Educational Equity, October 2011. http://www. tc.columbia.edu/i/a/document/18662_2rothstein.pdf.

Rouse, Cecilia E. "Consequences for the Labor Market." In *In the Price We Pay: Economic and Social Consequences of Inadequate Education,* edited by Clive Belfield and Henry M. Levin, 99–124. Washington, DC: Brookings Institution, 2007.

———. "The Labor Market Consequences of an Inadequate Education." Paper presented at the Symposium on the Social Costs of Inadequate Education, Teachers College, Columbia University, New York, NY, October 24–25, 2005.

Roza, Marguerite. "The Machinery That Drives Education-Spending Decisions Inhibits Better Uses of Resources." Paper presented at the Rethinking Education Governance for the 21st Century Conference, Fordham Institute, Washington, DC, December 10, 2011.

Saul, Stephanie. "Charter Schools Tied to Turkey Grow in Texas." *New York Times*, June 6, 2011.

Schleicher, Andreas. "The Importance of World Class Schools for Economic Success." *Testimony*, March 20, 2010.

Schleicher, Andreas, and Vivien Stewart. "Learning from World-Class Schools." *Educational Leadership* 66, no. 2 (2008): 44–51.

Schmidt, William H. "What's Missing from Math Standards? Focus, Rigor and Coherence." *American Educator* (Spring 2008): 22–24.

Schmidt, William H., and others. "The Preparation Gap: Teacher Education for Middle School Mathematics in Six Countries." Center for Research in Mathematics and Science Education, Michigan State University, 2007.

Schmidt, William H., and Richard S. Prawat. "What Does the Third International Mathematics and Science Study Tell Us about Where to Draw the Line in the Top-Down Versus Bottom-Up Debate?" *Educational Evaluation and Policy Analysis* 21, no. 1 (1999): 85–91.

Schmidt, William H., Hsing C. Wang, and Curtis C. McKnight. "Curriculum Coherence: An Examination of US Mathematics and Science Content Standards from an International Perspective." *Journal of Curriculum Studies* 37, no. 5 (2005): 525–59.

Schneider, Barbara, and David Stevenson. *The Ambitious Generation*. New Haven, CT: Yale University Press, 1999.

Schneider, Mark. "Math in American High Schools: The Delusion of Rigor." *Education Outlook*, no. 10 (October 2009).

Schneider, Mark, and Lu Yin. "The High Cost of Low Graduation Rates." American Institute for Research, August 2011.

Smeeding, Timothy M. "Public Policy, Economic Inequality, and Poverty: The United States in Comparative Perspective." *Social Science Quarterly* 86, no. 1 (2005): 955–83.

Smith, BetsAnn. "Quantity Matters: Annual Instructional Time in an Urban School System." *Educational Administration Quarterly* 36, no. 5 (2000): 652–82.

Snyder, T., and S. Dillow. *Digest of Education Statistics, 2009.* U.S. Department of Education, National Center for Educational Statistics, NCES 2010-013, April 2010.

Snyder, T., S. Dillow, and C. Hoffman. *Digest of Education Statistics, 2008.* U.S. Department of Education, National Center for Education Statistics, NCES 2009-020, March 2009.

Sparks, Sarah D. "Case in Point: Setting the Bar for Algebra." *Inside School Research.* Education Week blog. http://blogs.edweek.org/edweek/inside-school-research/2010/10/setting_the_bar_for_algebra_ii.html.

Stigler, J., and J. Hiebert. *The Teaching Gap: Best Ideas for the World's Teachers for Improving Education in the Classroom.* New York: Free Press, 1999.

Stigler, James W., and others. *The TIMSS Videotape Classroom Study: Methods and Findings from an Exploratory Research Project on Eighth-Grade Mathematics Instruction in Germany, Japan, and the United States.* U.S. Department of Education, National Center for Education Statistics, NCES 1999-074, April 1999.

Stinebrickner, Ralph, and Todd R. Stinebrickner. "The Causal Effect of Studying on Academic Performance." *BE Journal of Economic Analysis & Policy* 8, no. 1 (2008): article 14.

———. "Learning about Academic Ability and the College Drop-out Decision." National Bureau of Economic Research Working Paper 14810, November 2009.

Strong American Schools. "Diploma to Nowhere." Delta Project on Postsecondary Education Costs, Productivity, and Accountability, 2009. http://www.deltacostproject.org/resources/pdf/DiplomaToNowhere.pdf.

Teacher. "Ohio Students Face Stricter Math Standards," January 5, 2010.

Toch, Thomas. *In the Name of Excellence.* New York: Oxford University Press, 1991.

Trotter, Andrew. "Online Options for 'Credit Recovery' Widen." *Education Week,* May 22, 2008. http://www.edweek.org/ew/articles/2008/05/21/38credit_ep.h27.html.

UNICEF. "Child Poverty in Perspective: An Overview of Child Well-Being in Rich Countries." Innocenti Research Center Report Card 7, 2007. http://www.unicef-irc.org/publications/pdf/rc7_eng.pdf.

Urbina, Ian. "As School Exit Tests Prove Tough, States Ease Standards." *New York Times,* January 12, 2010.

Valverde, Gilbert A., and William H. Schmidt. "Greater Expectations: Learning from Other Countries in the Quest for World-Class Standards in US School Mathematics and Science." *Journal of Curriculum Studies* 32, no. 5 (2000): 651–87.

Vaznis, James. "They're Fighting to Stay on Top at Latin." *Boston Globe*, March 6, 2010.

Venezia, Andrea, Kathy Reeves Bracco, and Thad Nodine. "One-Shot Deal? Students' Perceptions of Assessment and Course Placement in California's Community Colleges." WestEd, 2010.

Venezia, Andrea, and Michael W. Kirst. "Inequitable Opportunities: How Current Education Systems and Policies Undermine the Chances for Student Persistence and Success in College." *Educational Policy* 19, no. 2 (2005): 283–307.

Wang, Jia, and Pete Goldschmidt. "Importance of Middle School Mathematics on High School Students' Mathematics Achievement." *Journal of Educational Research* 97, no. 1 (2003): 3–19.

Washington State Department of Health. "School Achievement and Climate." Washington State Department of Health Adolescent Needs Assessment, January 2010. http://www.doh.wa.gov/cfh/assessment/docs/assessreport/schoolach10.pdf.

Welner, Kevin G. *Legal Rights, Local Wrongs: When Community Control Collides with Educational Equity*. Albany: State University of New York Press, 2001.

West, Martin. "Overcoming the Political Barriers to Change." In *Stretching the School Dollar*, edited by Frederick Hess and Eric Osberg. Cambridge, MA: Harvard University Press, 2010.

Whitehurst, Russ. "Don't Forget Curriculum." *Brown Center Letters on Education*, no. 3 (October 2009).

Wiener, Ross, and Eli Pristoop. "How States Shortchange the Districts That Most Need Help." Education Trust, 2006.

Wößmann, Ludger. "Schooling Resources, Educational Institutions, and Student Performance: The International Evidence." *Oxford Bulletin of Economics and Statistics* 65, no. 2 (2003): 117–70.

Wößmann, Ludger, and others. *School Accountability, Autonomy and Choice around the World*. Cheltenham, UK: Edward Elgar, 2009.

Zorn, Eric. "Behind the Musings: The Annotated High Schools Column." *Change of Subject*. Chicago Tribune blog. http://blogs.chicagotribune.com/news_columnists_ezorn/2010/03/behind-the-musings-the-annotated-high-schools-column.html.

Index

About the Author

Katherine Baird is associate professor of economics in the Politics, Philosophy, and Economics program at the University of Washington, Tacoma. She received her PhD in economics from the University of Massachusetts, Amherst, and also holds an MS in agricultural economics from Michigan State University and a BA in economics from the University of California, Berkeley. In 2008 she was a Fulbright scholar in economics at the Universidad del País Vasco in Bilbao, Spain.

Prior to beginning her career as an academic, Katie spent five years working in the field of agriculture and agricultural policy in Africa; during three of these she lived in a small rice-growing village in Mauritania's Senegal Valley. She also spent two years working in Washington, DC, for the U.S. Department of Commerce, the U.S. Department of State, and a private firm providing consulting services to federal agencies.

In addition to teaching, Katie also writes a regular column on public economics for Washington State's second-largest newspaper, Tacoma's *The News Tribune*. She and her husband live in Tacoma with their two sons and black lab.